Film and Genocide

Film and Genocide

Edited by

KRISTI M. WILSON

and

TOMÁS F. CROWDER-TARABORRELLI

The University of Wisconsin Press

Publication of this volume has been made possible, in part, through support from the **Anonymous Fund** of the College of Letters and Science at the University of Wisconsin–Madison.

The University of Wisconsin Press
1930 Monroe Street, 3rd Floor
Madison, Wisconsin 53711-2059
uwpress.wisc.edu

3 Henrietta Street
London WC2E 8LU, England
eurospanbookstore.com

Library of Congress Cataloging-in-Publication Data

Film and genocide / edited by Kristi M. Wilson and
Tomás F. Crowder-Taraborrelli.
        p.   cm.
Includes bibliographical references and index.
ISBN 978-0-299-28564-7 (pbk.: alk. paper)
ISBN 978-0-299-28563-0 (e-book)
  1. Holocaust, Jewish (1939–1945), in motion pictures.
    2. Genocide—In motion pictures.
  3. Motion picture producers and directors—Interviews.
  I. Wilson, Kristi M.   II. Crowder-Taraborrelli, Tomás F.
     PN1995.9.H53F55   2012
       791.43´658405318—dc23
            2011017751

Contents

Preface

In fact, at the end of the day I believe that people do want to know when there is some major tragedy going on, when there is some unacceptable situation happening in this world. And they want something to be done about it. That's what I believe.

JAMES NACHTWEY, in *War Photographer*

In recognizing our ability to identify with characters, whether Jewish, German, Kapo, or Communist, we move one step closer to guarding against that which permitted the Holocaust to develop—indifference. Perhaps the beam cast by film projectors can pierce the continuing willed blindness.

ANNETTE INSDORF, *Indelible Shadows*

The idea for this collection began in Buenos Aires as we were researching documentary films about genocide in Latin America during the cold war (referred to as Operation Condor) at the 2007 Second International Meeting for the Analysis of the Social Practices of Genocide.[1] During the week-long conference, we toured the infamous ESMA (The Naval Mechanics School) detention center with Daniel Feierstein, Director of the Center for Genocide Studies at the Universidad Nacional de Tres Febrero, Argentina, and heard presentations on topics such as post-genocide Bosnia, the Armenian diaspora in Mexico and public commemoration of the Armenian genocide, the figure of the disappeared person in Argentine cinema and poetry, and resistance to genocidal practices, among others. We noticed, in particular, that leading academics frequently referred to the Holocaust in the hopes of determining patterns in more contemporary, state-sponsored atrocities. The group of scholars, comprised primarily of historians and sociologists, also made passing references to well-known films, such as *Schindler's List* (1993) and *Hotel Rwanda* (2004), and suggested that these films spoke to the phenomenon of genocide in a way that a book could not.

In fact, genocide studies has, from its inception, been largely interdisciplinary, incorporating philosophy, literature, theater, and psychology, to name a few approaches. Pioneering genocide scholar Israel W. Charny claimed that the principles of interdisciplinary and ecumenical thinking were central to his work from the outset: "We included psychiatrists and psychologists, educators from the primary level to the collegiate, a rabbi who was also a philosopher and a fine novelist, and a director of theater. . . . The theater director and I, in turn, worked on a project of how to present in the media information about human rights abuses in ways which could help audiences to maintain their involvement rather than turn off their attention with a sense of helplessness."[2] As Levon Chorbajian and George Shirinian point out, Charny's approach to understanding genocide is not only interdisciplinary but also unusually broad and inclusive, leaving it open to criticism on the grounds that it lacks theoretical rigor. As Chorbajian points out, however, "it is important to recognize our current state of theorizing about genocide as the product of a recent, incomplete and evolving process as well as a contested one."[3] Robert Gellately and Ben Kiernan indicate a rise in the study of the Holocaust in the last two decades, as well as a parallel increase in the study of a variety of mass murder and human rights abuse cases.[4]

In several recent cross-cultural, comparatist books on genocide, such as Alexander Laban Hinton's and Kevin Lewis O'Neill's edited collection *Genocide: Truth, Memory, and Representation*; Adam Jones's *Genocide: A Comprehensive Introduction* and *Evoking Genocide*; and Robert Skloot's *The Theatre of Genocide: Four Plays about Mass Murder in Rwanda, Bosnia, Cambodia, and Armenia*, representation plays a fundamental role. Formally incorporating film and photography into genocide studies is a natural next step in the evolution of the field. While we recognize the dangers of oversimplification and trivialization, we have opted for a generally inclusive approach with respect to definitions because we feel that it best represents the type of dialogue and debate that already exists in many films about genocide and in theoretical discussions thereof.

A series of difficult questions arose when we first began research for this project: Can film and the power of the image say something about the unspeakable horrors of genocide that literature cannot? How do we determine what is an effective genocide film? Should a film about genocide attempt to determine the factors that led to the atrocities or focus on an individual's plight as a window into the lives of other victims? Can films reach wider audiences faster and appeal to their core emotions so that they will act? Or should film be considered just supplementary material to other sources of knowledge, such as photographs, history books, poems, or victims' testimony?

Ilan Avisar echoes the thoughts of a sector of film scholars who put their faith in the power of the cinematic image to penetrate the protective consciousness of the spectator, awakening moral outrage and disarming passivity through the physical experience of viewing a film: "Theoretically cinema has an advantage over literature in the quest for realism. Compared with words, the photographic image is a better means of objective representation and has a stronger immediate and sensuous impact on the viewer."[5] Others suggest further, that filmic representations of the Holocaust may impact how we study questions of ethics, evil, and genocide in this century.[6]

The authors in this collection address the way in which several films confront the problems of memory and identity in the twentieth and twenty-first centuries, in landscapes marked by genocide and its resultant forms of trauma. These chapters explore the often controversial construction and arrangement of memory, touching on such topics as the relationship between memories passed down by family members, the adaptation of survivors' tales in literary and film genres, the extraordinary ability of film to mimic the process of working through trauma and its subsequent demands on spectators, and the confrontation between memory and physical remains.

Many people have supported this project over the years as we worked between Buenos Aires and California. We would like to thank our contributors especially for their dedication and commitment to the collection. Carlos Castresana, Spanish court magistrate, prosecutor, and the coauthor of the formal complaint against Augusto Pinochet, along with Luis Moreno-Ocampo, chief prosecutor of the International Criminal Court, encouraged our fledgling forays into the field of genocide studies and crimes against humanity at the conference we organized on international criminal law at Stanford University in 2007. We owe a great deal of thanks to the Introduction to the Humanities (IHUM) Program at Stanford University. Professor Russell Berman and IHUM Director Ellen Woods lent us research support and an academic forum for debate and the exchange of ideas. We are also indebted to Soka University of America for a research leave and, in particular, to Professors Jay Heffron and William L. Ascher for awarding us a Pacific Basin Research Fund Grant to work on summer research for this anthology. We would also like to thank filmmakers Greg Barker and Nick Hughes, and Wojciech Plosa, Director of the Auschwitz-Birkenau Archives, all of whom provided photos for this book. Our research assistants, January Coleman-Jones and Jake Nevrla, helped us immensely with the manuscript preparation. Angela Leong helped us with images. Matthew Goldstein provided a fresh pair of eyes whenever needed, and our colleagues Laura Ruberto and Ryan Caldwell provided ongoing encouragement. We would not have been able to complete this book without the love and support of Sandra and Richard Wilson, and Dean and Melissa Primicias. Finally, thanks to Luke, Ian, and Félix for keeping our spirits high.

NOTES

1. In the fall of 2007, drawing on legal principles established during the Nuremberg Trials, the Argentine Supreme Court made an unprecedented decision to do away with a set of amnesty laws called the *Punto Final*. These laws provided court-protected immunity to military officers and civilian leaders for crimes against humanity committed during the "Dirty War," a period between 1976 and 1983, in which an estimated 30,000 people were tortured and disappeared in an international collective genocide referred to as Operation Condor (or Plan Condor). Operation Condor's success at fighting what was perceived to be the threat of international terrorism depended on the close cooperation of the military governments of Chile, Paraguay, Brazil, Argentina, Uruguay, and Bolivia. See Dinges, *The Condor Years*.

2. Totten and Jacobs, *Pioneers of Genocide Studies*, 433–34.

3. Chorbajian and Shirinian, *Studies in Comparative Genocide*, xx.

4. Gellately and Kiernan, *The Specter of Genocide*.

5. Avisar, *Screening the Holocaust*, 4.

6. See Picart and Frank, *Frames of Evil*.

Film and Genocide

Introduction

Defining Genocide: "Reckoning with Evil"

The term *genocide* was coined by Polish Jewish lawyer Raphael Lemkin in 1933 after years of exhaustive study of mass killings in the ancient and medieval contexts in Europe and the Americas. At a law conference in Madrid, Lemkin attempted to frame his concept of genocide in relation to Hitler's ascent in Germany and the Armenian case of atrocities. Lemkin argued that if it happened once in Armenia, it could happen again in modern Europe.[1] While he was unsuccessful at convincing other jurists that an international law was needed to ensure that heads of state could not be protected by their own laws when they authorized mass killings, the struggle for a definition of genocide began and is still waged today. In his groundbreaking 1981 book, *Genocide: Its Political Use in the Twentieth Century*, Leo Kuper keeps alive Lemkin's struggle to define genocide broadly. He suggests that we should understand the presence of genocide in all periods of history and take into account the variety and complexity of factors that have prompted such atrocities, in spite of its relatively modern, somewhat narrow, and politically contentious definition at the Genocide Convention of 1948:

> The strength of political factors and the inextricable interweaving of political considerations in so many genocides against racial, ethnic and religious groups, demonstrate the impossibility of separating the racial, ethnic and religious from the political, as seemingly required by the Genocide Convention with its exclusion of political groups from its scope. Can one really interpret the exterminating massacres of Hutu in Burundi in purely ethnic, non-political terms, thereby placing it within the terms of the Genocide Convention; or for that matter, can one interpret it in purely political non-ethnic terms, falling outside the purview of the Convention? The absurdity of this artificial separation between the political and other factors was, of course, foreseen by some of the representatives in the debates on the framing of the Convention.[2]

In keeping with Kuper's concerns about the efficacy of the Genocide Convention's definition of genocide, as recently as January 2009, in an Argentine editorial, Daniel Feierstein called for a reconceptualization of the Genocide Convention. In "Genocide, a Wrongly Typified Crime" ("Genocidio, delito mal tipificado"), Feierstein suggests that the legal path taken by the concepts of crimes against humanity and genocide as a way of understanding and prosecuting international instances of annihilation has been confused and inefficient. For example, for many judges and lawyers, almost no crime qualifies as genocide but many situations qualify as crimes against humanity. Alternately, he suggests that by the time the international community determines whether a situation constitutes a genocide, many deaths have occurred. He argues that we should return to Lemkin's original idea about genocide as "the systematic annihilation whose objective is to destroy the national identity of the oppressed through the use of terror."[3]

Lemkin's early efforts to have genocide taken seriously were full of loneliness and constant struggle. Before arriving to the United States to teach international law at Duke University in 1941, Lemkin lived the life of a refugee. After the German invasion of Poland, he tried to convince his family to depart with him. Lemkin's arsenal of knowledge about history and what Hitler was capable of was not enough to accomplish the difficult task: "I read in the eyes of all of them one plea: do not talk of our leaving this warm home, our beds, our stores of food, the security of our customs. We will have to suffer, but we will survive somehow. . . . What did I have to offer them? A nomadic life, a refugee's lot, poverty. So the question resolved itself: I would continue as soon as possible to Lithuania—alone. . . . I felt I would never see them again. It was like going to their funerals while they were still alive. The best of me was dying with the full cruelty of consciousness."[4]

Today, the question of how to recognize and convince others of the dangers of genocide before they occur has become a central tenant among scholars, filmmakers, and activist groups. Unfortunately, as Samantha Power suggests in *"A Problem from Hell": America and the Age of Genocide*, despite explicit coverage in the media, even today American politicians and the public are "extremely slow to muster the imagination needed to reckon with evil."[5] Powers suggests that American politicians are unable and unwilling to imagine that the unimaginable might be taking place. Such acts of imagination threaten the sense that we have moved beyond the type of violence that occurred during the Holocaust. She suggests that in the realm of domestic politics, efforts to stop genocide are futile. Greg Barker, director of *Ghosts of Rwanda* (2004), echoes Power's skepticism about policy and suggests that the battle to stop genocide is further compromised by the fact that the topic might not be popular with mainstream audiences: "I don't like just policy-driven films, I try to make something that works as a piece of film, that draws people in, conveys fundamental human emotions and dilemmas. . . . I'm not really thinking about an audience as I go about doing it. Because if you ask them, people don't particularly want to see films about genocide."[6]

Genocide films seem to straddle a very fine line between depicting the lack of power to stop these kinds of events and small glimmers of hope (in most cases characterized by the heroic behavior of a small number of individuals). A common trait in most popular films about genocide is a reliance on a hero character and his or her corresponding journey (see for example, *Hotel Rwanda*, *Schindler's List*, and *Life Is Beautiful*). As some of the chapters in this collection argue, films in this narrative style have often been criticized for being insensitive and for not realistically representing the social conditions of oppression. In "Genres of 'Yet An Other Genocide': Cinematic Representations of Rwanda," Madelaine Hron suggests that narrative structure poses the greatest problem for fictionalized representations of genocide. In particular, she argues that genocide points to the failure of the very bildungsroman model (with its emphasis on community building, positive resolution, and progress) associated with many fictional films about genocide. Nick Hughes, director of *100 Days*, addresses the same contradiction in his interview for this collection: "There is nothing good about genocide. Some filmmakers look for something that can end on a note of hope, a note of progression, a note of humanity. In the real story of the genocide, there is no hope."[7]

Many film critics and scholars remain puzzled by the confluence of entertainment and films about genocide. In 1989 Elie Wiesel called on Hollywood to stop producing movies about the Holocaust on ethical grounds: "No one can now retell Auschwitz after Auschwitz."[8] Alan Mintz suggests that the Holocaust in particular only succeeds as a central narrative trope in film because it has been systematically "softened for the public palate" and, thus, allowed to "move to the center of public awareness."[9] Interviews with film directors Nick Hughes, Irek Dobrowolski, and Greg Barker demonstrate how difficult it is to balance gripping storytelling and explicit images of atrocities while avoiding gratuitous titillation or "softening" of the subject.

Several of our contributors echo Andreas Huyssen's concern that, in spite of a vast array of material dedicated to its preservation, Holocaust memory is in danger of being diluted: "By the end of the 1990s, one must indeed raise the question of to what extent we can now speak of a globalization of Holocaust discourse. Of course, the recurrence of genocidal politics in Rwanda, Bosnia and Kosovo in the allegedly post-historical 1990s has kept the Holocaust memory discourse alive, contaminating it and extending it past its original reference point."[10] Indeed, iconic images from the Holocaust appear as common traits in many films about genocide. Tony Hughes D'aeth critiques what he sees as a "gravitational dependence on the Nazi Holocaust as a foundational traumatic event" in two Australian narratives about Aboriginal children: the report *Bringing Them Home* (Human Rights and Equal Opportunity Commission, 1997) and the film *Rabbit-Proof Fence* (Noyce, 2002).[11] Hughes D'aeth cites the presence of barbed wire fences, shaved heads, and settlement scenes that resonate with concentration camp images as indicative of the use of such iconic images. However, Irek Dobrowolski uses iconic images from the Holocaust in his 2005 film, *The Portraitist*, in order to rupture such a dependency. He manipulates photos taken by Josef Mengele's concentration camp photographer Wilhelm Brasse with computer animation in order to bring the victims closer to viewers—to "make those very well-known icons come alive"—through a manipulation of time and space.[12] As Stephen Cooper points out in his chapter for this volume, Dobrowolski was aware that he risked alienating audiences by manipulating and altering such well-known visual images of the Holocaust.

In working on her own screenplay about the Holocaust in 1979, Annette Insdorf struggled with similar concerns and reflected on the fine line between repelling audiences and encouraging empathy in them.[13] David Walsh echoes Insdorf's concerns about an artist's responsibility and restraint when dealing with misery and atrocities: "Life at present is difficult, and art's job is not to remove itself from that, but also not to lose itself in the painfulness and drown the spectator in misery—that can be another form of evasion."[14] He adds that there is great danger in overwhelming spectators to the point of inaction. Filmmakers should strive to keep audiences engaged and primed for action and social change. Although it might be problematic to call genocide films a genre, they do seem to reflect a common preoccupation with questions of what to show, how to show it, and how much is too much to show.

Film and World War II

The important role that film and photography played in documenting atrocities, serving as evidence, and even aiding in aerial warfare during World War II cannot be overstated. By the end of the nineteenth century, photography had already become synonymous with authenticity.[15] During World War I and II, film and photography were used to document battles and for propaganda purposes. Although visual images are now central to the narrative of warfare, scholars continue to debate the efficacy of photography and film to represent reality and document atrocities. Film historian Erik Barnouw discusses at some length the formal and technical innovations derived from the deployment of film crews during

World War II to satisfy an urgent national demand to bring home images of soldiers fighting on the battlefronts. The battlefronts soon became film locations for newsreel crews. As an example, Barnouw cites the German invasion of Norway, in which more than 300 cameramen were mobilized to document the fighting. In another instance, the attack on the Polish city of Gydnia had to be delayed "so that cameramen could take positions ahead of the assault troops, so as to document the full impact."[16]

American camera operators and filmmakers, such as George Stevens, John Huston, Frank Capra, Samuel Fuller, and Billy Wilder (whose mother, stepfather, and grandmother all died in Auschwitz), were asked by the U.S. government to film the horrific conditions at the end of the war. Military photographic units were allowed into the camps even before medical units. Barbie Zelizer argues that the extraordinary feature of the liberation of the concentration camps was that allied cameramen were able to document one of the greatest crimes in the history of humanity. Film crews were given the unprecedented task of framing the victims, their captors, the camps, and the neighborhoods around them. Albeit morally questionable, some cameramen viewed the camps as if they were working on the set of a horror film. Zelizer focuses on a particular detail of this unparalleled responsibility: the fact that there did not seem to exist "standards" to depict the world of the camps: "Although atrocity stories had been around as long as war itself, never before had the press come face to face with such extensive evidence of mass brutality and such an ability to document it. Covering the scenes of horror in the camps required overcoming both assumptions about earlier atrocity stories and inadequate standards that existed for depicting violence in word and image."[17]

Janina Struk cites at least one British soldier who witnessed events and later questioned the documentary power of atrocity photographs: "They are infinitely less terrible than the reality we saw because you can photograph results of suffering, but never suffering itself."[18] Enlisted men, who were encouraged to film and take photos of what they saw without supervision, shot much of the archival footage from the camps. Fuller, who on returning to America would become a prominent independent film director, shot a twenty-two-minute film of the liberation of Falkenau, in Czechoslovakia. He said that one of the reasons he had decided to enlist was his desire to become a documentary filmmaker: "I had a helluva opportunity to cover the biggest crime story of the century . . . and nothing was going to stop me from being an eyewitness."[19] Such images might appear to be closer to the truth or more authentic, but as Fuller's case demonstrates, certain sequences in these amateur films were edited, and scenes were orchestrated for the camera. In one instance, Fuller and some fellow soldiers ordered local Germans, under the threat of death, to carry out a burial and funeral procession for those who had perished in the camp.[20] The orchestration and filming of the funeral reveals the untold and perhaps unexplored complexities about genocide and its representation.

The postwar footage, shot mostly by American and Russian film crews, was carefully guarded and became key witness material in the Nuremberg Trials. In the words of Sir Hartley Shawcross, chief prosecutor for Great Britain, the main goal of the trials was "to provide an authoritative and impartial record to which future historians might turn for truth and future politicians for warning."[21] Film played a large part in this body of truth. Before the trials at Nuremberg, film had never been used in a court as evidence of atrocities. The prosecution used film as evidence on the grounds that it was necessary in order to offer proof of the unprecedented horror of the crimes.[22]

At Nuremberg, the American prosecuting team presented as evidence two 1945 films, *The Nazi Plan* and *Nazi Concentration Camps*, prepared by Hollywood director George Stevens. According to Lawrence Douglas, the prosecution claimed that it needed to use film in order to establish proof of the nature of the crimes under investigation.[23] Stevens and others attested to the truthfulness of the images in affidavits that were projected as part of the screening at Nuremberg, and *Nazi Concentration Camps* was later part of the Eichmann trials.[24] Stevens would later direct such classics as *Shane* (1953), *Giant* (1956), and the 1959 dramatic adaptation of *The Diary of Anne Frank*. Screenwriter Budd Schulberg collaborated with Stevens on *The Nazi Plan*. He was put in charge of photographic evidence for the Nuremberg Trials and collaborated with Stevens in selecting footage from captured German newsreels and propaganda films. *The Nazi Plan*, a four-hour film, incorporated footage from Leni Riefenstahl's film *The Triumph of the Will* and depicted the history of the Nazi Party. According to Ann Tusa and John Tusa, "The defendants adored every moment of it. . . . When they got back to the prison several of the defendants were in tears—of pride and nostalgia."[25]

Nazi Concentration Camps, by contrast, depicts gruesome images of surviving prisoners, victims of medical experiments, gas chambers, and open mass graves. The most devastating film evidence presented against the accused, however, was a forty-five-minute film shot by the Russians: "It showed the warehouse at Majdanek where 800,000 pairs of shoes had been neatly stacked, the piles of skulls, broken bodies, mutilated corpses. There were sequences where naked women were driven to mass graves; they lay down and were shot; the guards smile for the camera. The great bone crushers going to work on 150,000 corpses in Blagorschine Forest. The women bending over corpses stiffened by cold, trying to identify their husbands and children, patting the dead shoulders. The film surpassed in horror anything yet shown, anything envisaged from the evidence that had been heard."[26] This

Russian film reinforced for the incredulous the extent of the brutality of the crimes committed by the Nazis. During the screening, a spotlight was left on the defendants' box for security reasons, which produced a unique viewing situation. Courtroom spectators were torn between watching the footage and watching the reactions of the accused. For the prosecution, the presentation of these films was an important part of the evidence but also a potential problem. One concern was that "such evidence was so repellent, so difficult for the mind to take in, that the Americans should have been extremely selective. Instead, by inundating the court with it, they blunted the sensitivity of all their listeners, saturated them with horror until they could absorb no more."[27]

In 1945, however, British and U.S. audiences expressed a keen interest in seeing the footage from the camps, despite the fact that some theater owners expressed concern that the public was not ready.[28] The *Film Daily* reported record-breaking audiences for public screenings in the United States of concentration camp films that year. Daniel Anker's 2004 documentary *Imaginary Witness: Hollywood and the Holocaust* features a photo of a large crowd standing under a movie theater marquee that reads: "Official Army Signal Corps Films . . . Nazi Atrocities . . . Held Over! Maidanek 'Nazi Death Factory' See SS Guards Executed." According to Lawrence Baron, "The dead in the newsreels formed an anonymous mass, and the survivors appeared more like fleeting ghosts than living human beings. Understanding how demeaning and enervating the conditions in the camps and ghettos were required a leap of imagination that few Americans were willing to make."[29] The footage that screened in 1945 was eventually confiscated by the U.S. government and not seen again for several years. Tony Kushner argues that the very nature of the atrocity photographs and films in 1945 assisted in the process of their quick disappearance from public memory. Although the images had "made an impression," the atrocity materials, he wrote, "were such that many wished to put them out of mind as quickly as possible."[30]

According to Robert Melson, another downfall of the use of atrocity materials at Nuremberg was that the prosecution's reliance on film as evidence, rather than eyewitness testimony, had the "regrettable consequences of marginalizing Jewish victims, depriving the court of contact with those who could have challenged the conflation of political repression and genocide."[31] Documentary filmmakers, such as Claude Lanzmann, Lourdes Portillo and Susana Blaustein Muñoz, Patricio Guzmán, Rithy Panh, and others, have registered the importance of individual testimony in telling stories about genocide and in the prosecution of crimes against humanity. Guzmán's film *The Pinochet Case* (2001) serves as an excellent example of the role of testimony as a complement to the legal proceedings needed to bring *genocidaires* to trial.

Film scholars and critics seem to agree that there exists a small but respected cadre of films a filmmaker can consult when evaluating the complex strategies of narrating genocide. When asked to comment on representing the Holocaust, film critic David Walsh suggested a short list of influential films that includes: Alain Resnais's *Night and Fog* (1955), Ján Kadár's *The Shop on Mainstreet* (1965), Andrei Tarkovsky's *Ivan's Childhood* (1962), Orson Welles's *The Stranger* (1946), Fritz Lang's *Hangmen Also Die!* (1943), and others.[32] Resnais's *Night and Fog* remains to this day most critically acclaimed film about the Holocaust and one of the most commonly used films to teach the topic.[33] Joshua Hirsch suggests that the power of this film lies in its revolutionary use of modernist film techniques (primarily montage) to blur the boundaries between the past and the present as a way of demonstrating how historical consciousness is defined by a relationship between the two: "Like this montage form of historical consciousness, trauma is defined neither by the past event nor by the present vicissitudes of memory but by the relations between the two, the event's overwhelming of narrative memory, and memory's struggles to belatedly master the event. In addition, posttraumatic memory is characterized by montage-like relations of intrusiveness and remoteness, of vision and blindness, of remembering and forgetting."[34]

Night and Fog can also be understood according to Janet Walker's notion of "trauma cinema," a concept she applies comparatively to select films about the Holocaust and incest that embody a non-Hollywood, nonrealist mode of expression: "By *trauma cinema* I mean a group of films that deal with a world-shattering event or events, whether public or personal. Furthermore, I define trauma films and videos as those that deal with traumatic events in a nonrealist mode characterized by disturbance and fragmentation of the films' narrative and stylistic regimes."[35] While *Night and Fog* is celebrated for its innovative and avant-garde form of representing the traumatic events of the Holocaust, it has also been criticized for downplaying "the centrality of Jews as victims of Nazi genocide."[36]

Georgiana Banita argues that Atom Egoyan's film *Ararat*, like Resnais's *Night and Fog*, uses modernist film techniques to problematize the concept of seamless, fluid, historical memory in favor of what she calls *ethical memory*. This form of memory about the Armenian genocide, as historical consciousness, is further complicated by the Turkish government's denial of the event: "Memory appears both as the irruption of the past into the present and the bleeding of the present into the past."[37] In a similar vein, Kristi M. Wilson's contribution to this anthology addresses the concept of technological distancing in Errol Morris's documentary *The Fog of War: Eleven Lessons from the Life of Robert S. McNamara*. Wilson focuses on Morris's use of computer animation, archival footage, and the probing questioning of former secretary of defense McNamara to rupture the official U.S. history of the nuclear and firebomb attacks of Japanese cities with horrific, repressed memories from the past.

W. G. Sebald and others argue that we have only recently begun to address the horrors of air war. During World War II, film and photography allowed aerial bombing specialists to analyze targets and possible impacts on civilian populations. According to Jonathan Glover, such technological developments facilitated a psychological distancing process by which it became morally easy to annihilate large amounts of people from the air.[38] Erik Markusen and David Kopf refer to this type of mass killing as "technical distancing," while Kuper extends this notion to the context of firebombings and nuclear bombings and argues that it constitutes "white collar technological genocide."[39]

This volume as whole reflects a broad scholarly interest in understanding the legacy of genocide that continues to haunt contemporary life and popular culture. We have opted for a generally inclusive and comparative approach where particular definitions of genocide are concerned because we feel that it best represents the type of dialogue and debate already at play in many films and theoretical discussions about the topic. We see fruitful connections among many of the chapters that we hope will help advance the field of genocide studies.

Part I: Atrocities, Spectatorship, and Memory

In "Film and Atrocity: The Holocaust as Spectacle," Sophia Wood considers such films as *Schindler's List*, *Night and Fog*, *Shoah*, and *Life Is Beautiful* to explore the complex role of film in shaping awareness and memory of the Holocaust. Wood argues that the use of visual records of the Holocaust presents complex ethical concerns for those who believe that victims are further objectified through the "spectatorial stance" of the perpetrators. She suggests that even films of the liberation of concentration and extermination camps present certain ethical problems. While such footage positions the audience as "witnesses" to atrocity and bearers of memory, and is thus of great importance as evidence, the images also position the audience as spectators, voyeurs, and consumers of atrocity.

Jennifer L. Barker's chapter, "Documenting the Holocaust in Orson Welles's *The Stranger*," examines Welles's history as an antifascist writer and activist and the culmination of antifascist discourse in one of his least popular films. *The Stranger* (1946), starring Welles as a Nazi in hiding, Loretta Young as his young American wife, and Edward G. Robinson as the Nazi-hunting detective, raises the specter of a resurgence of Nazism in the United States. *The Stranger* was the first Hollywood film to incorporate documentary footage (as a film-within-a-film sequence) of the Holocaust, and, as such, follows closely on the tails of U.S. government documentary war films produced by John Huston, Frank Capra, Anthony Veiller, and others. Barker argues that *The Stranger* corresponds to Welles's interest in pedagogy, new theories about "visual education," and his concerns about social justice and participatory spectatorship.

Michael J. Lazzara takes on the argument that numbers, or "genocidal proportions," are accurate means of defining genocide in the Latin American political context. His chapter, "Remembering Revolution after Ruin and Genocide: Recent Chilean Documentary Films and the Writing of History," suggests that the collective Chilean memory of the Popular Unity period and Salvador Allende's "peaceful road to socialism" is deeply intertwined with the trauma, nostalgia, melancholy, and subjective crises that ensued from the genocidal practices of the military dictatorships. In particular, Lazzara focuses on the contentious spaces in the post-dictatorial documentary films whenever they try to communicate "truths" about the history of dictatorship from a contemporary moment associated with exile, defeat, and "the sanitizing language of consensus."

Georgiana Banita's chapter, "'The Power to Imagine': Genocide, Exile, and Ethical Memory in Atom Egoyan's *Ararat*," explores the vast variety of perspectives and multimediated positions that influence memory of the underrepresented Armenian genocide of 1915 in the first film to elaborate on the genocide in great detail. Banita's chapter tracks Egoyan's involvement in Armenian nationalist activities as an international relations student at the University of Toronto and his early character studies of Armenians in previous films, such as *Open House* (1982), *Next of Kin* (1984), and *Family Viewing* (1987), as ongoing efforts to answer the question: "How does an artist speak the unspeakable?"

Part II: Coloniality and Postcoloniality

Paul R. Bartrop's chapter, "Massacre and the Movies: *Soldier Blue* and the Sand Creek Massacre of 1864," considers the impact of the revisionist Western *Soldier Blue* in the context of late 1960s and early 1970s antiwar films inspired by the Vietnam War. Bartrop compares the events of the 1864 massacre of Cheyenne Indians by the U.S. government and Colorado volunteers at Sand Creek, Colorado, to their depiction in Ralph Nelson's 1970 film *Soldier Blue*. Drawing from Kuper's concept of the "genocidal massacre," Bartrop discusses the pedagogical possibilities for films such as *Soldier Blue* to articulate the affinity between colonialism and genocide where Native American communities are concerned. Bartrop extends this affinity to the context of the My Lai massacre during the Vietnam War and argues that *Soldier Blue* "held a mirror to U.S. society" and demonstrated that the events of the My Lai massacre were part of a U.S. tradition all too familiar to the few remaining descendants of Native Americans.

Donna-Lee Frieze's chapter, "The Other in Genocide: Responsibility and Benevolence in *Rabbit-Proof Fence*," explores connections between Emmanuel Levinas's philosophical theory of responsibility and the twentieth-century phenomenon of the removal of mixed-race children from Aboriginal communities in Australia with the intention to destroy the group. Frieze explores ways in which the film is in dialogue with Levinas's concepts of the ontological and ethical Other, and ways in which it prompts viewers to reexamine the apparent benevolence of an ultimately genocidal law.

Madelaine Hron's chapter, "Genres of 'Yet An Other Genocide': Cinematic Representations of Rwanda" presents a comprehensive look at films about the Rwandan genocide produced, for the most part, after the ten-year commemoration of the events. Hron argues that although films about Rwanda incorporate a variety of conventions from narrative genres, including Holocaust films, colonial ethnographies, romance stories, and Christian redemption myths, they ultimately constitute their own genre that can be broken into three basic categories: "retrospective accounts" (films like *Hotel Rwanda* [2004], *Shooting Dogs/Beyond the Gates* [2005], *Sunday in Kigali* [2006], and others), "post-genocide documentaries" (*In Rwanda We Say . . . The Family That Does Not Speak Dies* [2004], *Rwanda: Living Forgiveness* [2003], *Rwanda: A Killer's Homecoming* [2004]), and what she calls "interpenetrative" films (*Sometimes in April* [2005] and *Shake Hands with the Devil: The Journey of Romeo Dallaire* [2004]). Hron illustrates important distinctions between the Holocaust and the Rwandan genocide that make the overlapping of the film genres complicated.

Part III: Visual Documentation and Genocide

Kristi M. Wilson's chapter, "The Specter of Genocide in Errol Morris's *The Fog of War*," considers the way in which Errol Morris explores the grey zone between the concepts of mass killing and genocide in his Oscar-winning 2003 documentary. Morris's interview with McNamara and his use of archival footage from the fire and atomic bombings of Japanese cities reopen questions about the historical and literary treatment of what W. G. Sebald has termed "the horrors of air war" and what Kuper has called an undeniable case of "white-collar" genocide.

Marsha Orgeron's chapter, "GIs Documenting Genocide: Amateur Films of World War II Concentration Camps," explores the unofficial filmic records of the liberation of the concentration camps taken by active-duty U.S. soldiers. Though the subject of amateur films has been largely ignored by scholars, Orgeron suggests that there is a specific historical value to such material as unofficial and, thus, un-politically motivated and unmanipulated for audience consumption. The value in these films lies in each amateur filmmaker's relationship to the truth of what he saw at the time of the liberation of the concentration camps in Europe.

Out of all the chapters in this collection, Stephen Cooper's personal reflection on his week-long visit to the Open Society Archives in Budapest, a collection of approximately 23,000 feet of records about a variety of genocides, and his subsequent analysis of Irek Dobrowolski's documentary, *The Portraitist*, best exemplify the complicated position of the witness or spectator to genocide and the important role of film as evidence, then and now. Cooper's chapter, "Through the Open Society Archives to *The Portraitist*: Film's Impulse toward Death and Witness," is divided into two halves in which he grapples with notions of the practical and theoretical where photography and genocide are concerned. *The Portraitist* documents the complex story of Wilhelm Brasse, a Catholic professional photographer who was captured by the Nazis in Poland and forced to work in the death industry of the Third Reich under Joseph Mengele. Brasse took countless small portraits of prisoners before their deaths and some of the most iconic images of the Holocaust. Cooper's chapter brings together complex notions of subject, object, and producer where archival material is concerned.

Part IV: Interviews

Long before there was a popular interest in genocide, on a break between films, Greg Barker went with a friend to Rwanda to learn about the events that had occurred there. As it turned out, he found UN and NGO workers who felt forgotten by the rest of the world were ready to tell their stories to anyone who would listen. Thus in 1997 a very personal exploration began that would occupy Barker's mind for the next few years. In Richard O'Connell's interview with Barker, the director of *Ghosts of Rwanda* (2004), Barker takes us from the somewhat accidental beginning of his film as a series of recovered testimonies to the revelation of a more complex, high-level political story, inspired in part by the research in Samantha Power's work from 2000 in *The Atlantic*. Barker unveils his strategy for gaining the trust and, eventually, the perspectives of political players like Madeline Albright and Kofi Annan, Tony Lake, and General Dallaire. He also addresses the difficult issue of working with horribly grotesque and disturbing footage.

In an interview with Nick Hughes, *100 Days* director and BBC journalist, Piotr A. Cieplak asks critical questions of a film considered to be paradigmatic of the West's interest in the Rwandan genocide. Hughes, on assignment for the BBC when the Rwandan genocide broke out, is credited for obtaining the only film footage of the killings. This interview offers a fascinating window into a director's perspective as he negotiates aesthetic concerns while creating a film about a topic as bleak as genocide. Rather than resorting to a formulaic importation of white, European sympathetic characters designed to give the film an optimistic edge and, consequently, a box office boost, Hughes kept the focus of *100 Days* on victims' tales.

Stephen Cooper's interview with Irek Dobrowolski, director of *The Portraitist* (2005), provides an added window into one documentary filmmaker's struggle to tell the difficult tale of a Nazi prisoner, Wilhelm Brasse, who survived due to a particular skill he provided in the concentration camps. Dobrowolski's idea to tell Brasse's story was initially rejected by a Polish television station with no explanation and by the BBC on the grounds that such a story, about a person who was part of the Holocaust machinery, was immoral. In this interview, Dobrowolski talks about the personal relationship he cultivated with Brasse over a period of years and the confidence he gained from his subject, which allowed him to tell an insider's tale of an eyewitness to the horrors of Auschwitz. Dobrowolski's interview is particularly useful for Holocaust scholars and film scholars alike, as it combines a meditation on themes related to genocide and atrocity with a discussion of the physical experience of bringing archival photographs and material evidence into filmmaking.

Although, according to many, we live with an imperfect universal application of the Genocide Convention, filmmakers are in a unique position to push the limits of this application. The medium of film has the ability to conjure up images that call to mind the dimensions of atrocities committed (including genocide). Thus, film operates well as a vehicle for mourning and remembrance. The chapters in this collection address filmic representation and documentation of genocides motivated by such factors as colonialism and decolonization, religious and ethnic difference, totalitarianism, political groups, and ideologies. They navigate a troubled body of inquiries about form, content, and ethics where representing the unrepresentable is concerned. While a first collection on this topic might risk losing some strength because of its wide historical breadth, we feel that the collection clearly demonstrates some of the main concerns of filmmakers and film scholars with respect to the power of film to document, remember, and aid in the prosecution of genocidal crimes.

Notes

1. Power, *"A Problem from Hell,"* 19.
2. Kuper, *Genocide*, 93.
3. Feierstein, "Genocidio, delito mal tipificado."
4. Totten and Jacobs, *Pioneers of Genocide Studies*, 375–76.
5. Power, *"A Problem from Hell,"* xvii.
6. Barker, interviewed for this volume, 210.
7. Hughes, interviewed for this volume, 221.
8. Wiesel, "Art and the Holocaust." *The Nation* film critic Stuart Klawans called for a similar moratorium in a piece called "Lest We Remember: Saying 'Never Again' to Holocaust Movies": "By continually replaying, reframing and reinventing the past, these movies are starting to cloud the very history they came to commemorate." *Tablet*, December 5, 2008.
9. Mintz, *Popular Culture and the Shaping of Holocaust Memory in America*, 141, quoted by Sophia Wood in this volume, 31. As Wood suggests in her chapter, the affirmative ending of *Schindler's List* is a case in point.
10. Huyssen, "Present Pasts," 23.
11. Hughes D'aeth, "Which Rabbit-Proof Fence?"
12. Dobrowolski, interviewed for this volume, 232.
13. "How do you show people being butchered? How much emotion is too much?" Insdorf, *Indelible Shadows*, xiii.
14. Walsh, "Vancouver International Film Festival, 2008—Part 1."
15. Zelizer, *Remembering to Forget*, 9.
16. Barnouw, *Documentary*, 139, 151.
17. Zelizer, *Remembering to Forget*, 30.
18. Struk, *Photographing the Holocaust*, 132.
19. Orgeron, "Liberating Images?" 39. See also chapter 6, "Liberations," in Struk, *Photographing the Holocaust*.
20. Orgeron, "Liberating Images?" 39.
21. Tusa and Tusa, *The Nuremberg Trial*, 177.
22. Douglas, "Film as Witness," 451.
23. Ibid., 453.
24. Ibid., 453, 470. George C. Stevens and E. R. Kellog (director of film effects) certified, "The images of these excerpts from the original negative have not been retouched, distorted or otherwise altered in any respect." Ibid., 453.
25. Tusa and Tusa, *The Nuremberg Trial*, 169.
26. Ibid., 198.
27. Ibid., 168.
28. Struk, *Photographing the Holocaust*, 127.
29. Baron, *Projecting the Holocaust into the Present*, 34.
30. Struk, *Photographing the Holocaust*, 149.

31. Melson, *Revolution and Genocide*, 137.
32. David Walsh, personal interview, February 5, 2009.
33. See Hirsch, *Afterimage*, 41; and Shandler, "Films of the Holocaust," 228.
34. Hirsch, *Afterimage*, 41.
35. Walker, *Trauma Cinema*, 19.
36. Charny, *Encyclopedia of Genocide*, 228.
37. Banita, this volume, 91.
38. Glover, *Humanity*, chaps. 10 and 11.
39. Markusen and Kopf, *The Holocaust and Strategic Bombing*, chaps. 2, 5, and 10; Kuper, *Genocide*, 102.

Part I

Atrocities, Spectatorship, and Memory

1 Film and Atrocity

The Holocaust as Spectacle

SOPHIA WOOD

> The gaze is first personal and then social. If a crime is solved that
> is fine, but the initial impulse for the gaze is personal desire. This
> desire must be controlled, or suppressed and re-coded in acceptable
> social terms. The modernist gaze is, accordingly, shrouded in noble
> terms, but underneath it is prurient and self-serving.
>
> NORMAN DENZIN, *The Cinematic Society*

In Norman Denzin's illuminating appraisal of "cinematic" society, and the gaze of the "voyeur" that has permeated modern and postmodern modes of spectatorship, one can find a critique of "looking" that can be extended to the filmic representation of atrocity and public memory of the Holocaust. This chapter will interrogate the centrality and ubiquity of visual records of the Holocaust, first as evidence, and then as "aids" to memory.

From a starting point of acknowledgment that such material, utilized as evidence, defends against both Holocaust denial and the more understandable desire of society to believe that "such things cannot be possible"; this chapter will address the dehumanizing, ethically troubling aspects of Nazi-era atrocity photography and film, as well as liberation photography and film. This chapter will also trace a chronology of visual engagement and spectatorial fascination with the Holocaust, arguing that the revelation of atrocity and liberation images during and immediately after World War II marked the beginning of the Holocaust's evolution into a "spectacle."

Hotel Rwanda, 2004. Directed by Terry George.

The tension between attraction and repulsion that emerged in that period has arguably informed subsequent visual representations of the Holocaust in public memory and popular culture. The popularity of films such as *Schindler's List*, *Hotel Rwanda*, and *Life Is Beautiful* demonstrates a continuing (if not growing) desire to "gaze" at the Holocaust. This chapter will question our motivation for looking and will evaluate our potential for ever really "seeing" or comprehending the Holocaust as it impacted millions of individuals. In also exploring the approaches of documentary films about the Holocaust (*Shoah*, *Night and Fog*), this chapter ultimately pivots around difficult issues of consumption, voyeurism, authenticity, and "decency." Perhaps the "prurient" gaze outlined by Denzin has indeed been "re-coded" and made "socially acceptable" when directed at Holocaust images in the name of "memory" and "witnessing." While the starting contention is that early interest in the Holocaust related mainly to actual images of atrocity, this chapter will attempt to demonstrate that the genre of popular Holocaust film (and the subsequent complex interplay between film and genocide) emerged out of this initial appetite.

Images of Atrocity and Liberation:
The Holocaust Gaze

The visual images of the Holocaust that make up public memory of that event are many and varied. From clandestine glimpses of persecution and extermination snatched by bystanders and underground members, and the grinning, shameless, and triumphant images captured by the Nazis and their collaborators to record their "mastery," to the newsreels and photojournalism of liberation taken as twofold evidence: here is evidence of the unthinkable crimes committed and also literal, juridical evidence collated for the anticipated war crimes trials. These images have become embedded within, and integral to, the ways in which we remember the Holocaust. As Susan Sontag has reflected, such evidence ensures that the event continues to live on in our memories: "After the event has ended, the picture will still exist, conferring on the event a kind of immortality (and importance) it would never otherwise have enjoyed. While real people are out there killing themselves or other real people, the photographer stays behind his or her camera, creating a tiny element of another world: the image-world that bids to outlast us all."[1]

Thus certain images have become "icons" of Holocaust memory, endlessly recycled and reproduced in television programs, documentaries, and popular films, displayed at Holocaust museums and at the former killing sites themselves. The terrible mortality of millions, the torment, degradation, and industrialized decimation of a people, has been immortalized in images of abjection and humiliation. When one thinks of the Holocaust, it is likely that certain iconic scenes spring to mind, be they photographic or filmic: starving children and dead bodies covered in newspaper on the pavements of the ghettos; blank-faced men and naked women, some pregnant and some carrying babies, waiting by the edges of pits for their turn to be shot; the chaos of liberation; mounds of naked corpses, walking skeletons, the starving survivors barely distinguishable from the dead; the revelation of gas chambers, crematoria, and mass graves; the realization of the almost inconceivable estimated death toll.

With reference to such "staples" of Holocaust visualization, a film shot by the U.S. military photographers attached to the U.S. War Department, titled *Nazi Concentration Camps*, provides an interesting example of the camera's gaze (and of the spectatorial stance adopted by the public) at liberation. At one hour long and comprised of 6,000 feet of film selected out of 80,000 feet of liberation images (from both infamous and little-known camps), the film offers both familiar and unfamiliar images of what the liberators encountered when they reached the death camps. The film provided evidence for the Nuremberg Trials of war criminals and opened with a certificate and sworn affidavit signed by E. R. Kellog, Director of Photographic Effects, attesting to the film's authenticity. Beyond those scenes that crowd popular memory and that have informed the public imagination in the intervening decades, the film contains more obscure images, images that are still capable of "shocking." Of the familiar, iconic images, the footage of the liberation of Ohrdruf, Nordhausen, Buchenwald, and Belsen camps yields a significant number of them.

The film of Ohrdruf, liberated by the U.S. 4th Armored Division, features the charred bodies of victims on a wooden pyre being surveyed by incredulous, horrified

U.S. servicemen. The commentary that accompanies this segment of the film explains that General Eisenhower had instructed those filming to be "unflinching" and not cover up any of the horror, stating, "I want you to see for yourselves and be the spokesmen for the United States." A photographic still of the pyre and the stunned soldiers now forms the beginning of the United States Holocaust Memorial Museum in Washington. This particular scene could be said to mark the beginning of the much discussed "Americanization" of the Holocaust, or at least of the development of a very particularized, American view of the Holocaust, whereby the event is positioned as the complete opposite of everything the United States stands for. This is a theme that will be addressed further in my discussion of *Schindler's List*.

Even more extreme than the smoking remains of Ohrdruf, the liberation sequences from Buchenwald include some of the most ghoulish footage of all of the liberation imagery. Twelve thousand stunned Weimar citizens are frog-marched into the camp by liberators to behold the terrible sights therein. The camera records the horror and fascination of the crowd being shown lampshades made out of the skin of inmates, the flayed skin of victims retained by their murderers because of their interesting tattoos, ink drawings—often obscene, as the commentary informs us—idly etched by Nazis on notepads of human "paper"; seemingly the most fascinating of all—the two shrunken heads of Buchenwald—a veritable genocidal freak show offered up to the emerging "Holocaust gaze," one characterized by repulsion but also by curiosity. The display of "relics" might be said to be the start of the public engagement with Holocaust artifacts. Holocaust "memory" is always a more popular endeavor when there are "sights" (as well as sites) to be seen. The contemporary trend of Holocaust tourism, and visitation to Holocaust museums removed from the European context of destruction, can be explained at least partly in terms of the "lure" of artifacts: the shoes, hair, even prosthetic limbs of the victims, now stacked in display cases for the benign, sorrowful, or prurient gaze of the onlookers.

But it is Belsen that offers some of the most unsettling footage in terms of its dehumanization of the individual victims of the Holocaust. The film of bodies, strewn everywhere around the camp and being bulldozed into pits, the voiceover that speaks of the camp "clean-up" operation—all of these memorialize the victims almost as human litter, as so much potentially contagious mess to be removed. As John Dixey, one of the British medical students involved in the relief work at Belsen, admitted: "If it had been several hundred bodies one might have been really desperate and affected by it, mentally or psychologically at any rate. But no, it was on such a huge scale, it was rather like trying to count the stars. There were thousands and thousands of dead bodies and you couldn't really relate to them as people, you couldn't really consider them to be your aunt or your mother or your brother or your father because there were just too many and they were being bulldozed into graves."[2] Such images can teach us little about the individual, human experience of the Holocaust victim. Such extremity compels and yet at the same time distances. For all of the evidential or educational "necessity" of such images, this chapter argues that the testimony of those who survived the Holocaust can reanimate this "human waste," can articulate the manifold suffering of those nameless bodies, can reinvest them with their humanity and dignity in a way that film, whether factual or artistic, never can.

In the footage taken at Mauthausen, one follows the gaze of the camera as it regards the open-mouthed, naked bodies of the victims, covered with flies. One is reminded of some artistic representation of hell: gaping mouths are frozen in eternal torment and pain. Here Lilie Chouliaraki's work on the "spectatorship of suffering" is enormously useful. Though speaking of starving Argentinean children, what Chouliaraki observes can be extended to the bodies of the Holocaust dead. For all the simulated "closeness" achieved by the interrogative gaze of the camera, "zooming in on these children's emaciated body parts 'fetishizes' their fragile bodies and maintains a radical distance between them and the spectators."[3] Chouliaraki continues, stating that "the visualization of suffering does not always humanize the suffering. Visualization may cast the suffering in the aesthetic register and, thereby, actually dehumanize them." Such is the artistic distance created by the fetishistic gaze of the camera that even genocide is reduced to a "tableau vivant."[4]

As reflected earlier, such archival material can still "shock" on occasions, with footage that has not quite been subsumed into (and somehow "softened" within) the repository of public memory. Film of the liberation of the concentration camp of Leipzig includes footage of the bodies of recently murdered inmates who had been confined to barracks and then set on fire by the fleeing Nazis shortly before liberation. Having fled the burning barracks, alight, these individuals had been shot and lay where they fell. One sees the deathly tableau envisaged by Chouliaraki, almost aesthetic in its display of "unfamiliar" Holocaust corpses: not lying naked, prone, stacked on top of one another, but crawling along the ground and clinging to the electrified fences, giving the impression of suspended animation. The camera pans the perimeter fence where Russian women, recently freed from slave labor under the Nazis, gaze into the camps—a benign and sorrowful gaze of solidarity and pity. Perhaps what Jorge Semprun envisaged when he spoke of the "fraternal" gaze that fellow comrades leveled at the scenes of destruction that so horrified (and yet attracted) the uninitiated—those who had not experienced the Holocaust as victims—applies here: "Looking at these wasted bodies, with their protruding bones, their sunken chests, these bodies piled twelve feet high in the crematorium courtyard, I'm thinking that these were my comrades. I'm thinking that one has to have experienced their death, as we have, in order to look at them with that pure, fraternal expression."[5]

Equally, the film taken of the liberation of the former asylum-cum–killing institution at Hadamar exhibits horrors that few beyond Holocaust "experts" are familiar with. The camera follows the process of an open-air autopsy of victims exhumed from the mass graves, some 20,000 bodies, while the commentary informs the viewer that when the 10,000th victim had been dispatched by morphine injection at the hands of the Nazi doctors, a celebration party was held. Once again, the evidential capacity of such filmic material aside, do not such victims, such bodies, endure what Alvin Rosenfeld has termed a "double dying"—murdered, buried, exhumed, and subjected to the scrutiny of pathologists, all before the hungry gaze of the camera? Such hunger, such a desire to "look" at the Holocaust, has undoubtedly informed the emergence of fictional narratives of the Holocaust that seek to reimagine and re-create that particular horror.

Hollywood and the Holocaust

When one thinks of the genre of popular film, exemplified by the output of Hollywood, perhaps one's overriding expectation of such products relates to the likelihood of our being entertained, stimulated, and distracted from the "everyday" by them. Thus when popular films tackle a subject of the magnitude of the Holocaust, uncomfortable questions of voyeurism arise. Alan Mintz has stated, "We have an urgent need to imagine the Holocaust, while at the same time we have a poverty of images. . . . We have only some grainy footage shot by the Nazis with which to feed our visual memories."[6] This surely raises the question, why do we need a "visual memory" of the Holocaust?

Might it be that we have "consumed" the original, genuine images so fully that we need new images, images that are not grainy, or (obviously) "ethically troubling," images that we can gaze at with impunity? As Sontag has observed: "To consume means to burn, to use up—and, therefore, to need to be replenished. As we make images and consume them, we need still more images; and still more."[7] In a later reflection on atrocity, Sontag asserts: "It seems that the appetite for pictures showing bodies in pain is as keen, almost, as the desire for ones that show bodies naked."[8] Far from being somehow humanizing, it could be argued that being immersed in images of suffering can increase our appetite for them, while undermining our sensitivity. Sontag reflects that seeing too much can have a negative effect: "It can also corrupt them. Once one has seen such images, one has started down the road of seeing more—and more. Images transfix. Images anaesthetize. . . . The shock of photographed atrocities wears off with repeated viewings."[9] The increasing engagement with Holocaust films is evidence of just such a transfixed and anaesthetized public gaze. Popular films, the "best" example of which follows next, domesticate and universalize extremity; they bring atrocity, in a fetishized guise, into the realm of the everyday.

Schindler's List is arguably the most well-known Holocaust film of all time. It is also a paradigmatic example of a big, Hollywood movie. Yet how well suited is the Hollywood film to the memory and the transmission of the facts of the Holocaust? From the outset one might expect a certain trivialization or a focus on emotion rather than realism. One need only think of the ubiquity of the "happy ending" to the format of the Hollywood film to appreciate how uncomfortable this union of trauma and candied entertainment could potentially be. Hollywood is about dreams rather than nightmares. The Hollywood film needs to be reassuring, has to be all things to all people. As Geoffrey Nowell-Smith asserts: "Hollywood is the biggest fabricator of fantasy, and that is its enormous and unchallenged strength. It is a strength which arises partly from the system, from a market orientation which—initially for domestic consumption but increasingly for export as well—requires films to provide satisfaction across the board."[10] A major concern here relates to the fact that the true horror of the Holocaust will never find its way into a popular film, primarily because a mainstream audience does not want to deal with such things. Bound up with this is the idea that, as the Holocaust is ultimately sanitized in popular film, Hollywood Holocaust films will always be defined by what is concealed rather than by what is shown. Ilan Avisar asserts that certain things will always be left out of the popular film on the Holocaust, or shown in a softened guise, "stark realities of extreme horrors, piercing pain, and unendurable dark realizations bereft of hope and of life are accommodated to popular taste."[11]

To secure an audience, popular Holocaust films must be ultimately life-affirming. Consumers of Hollywood films, in particular, do not want to confront the full trauma of the Holocaust or the sense of rupture that surely follows from it. In this tendency of Hollywood to gloss over the actualities of the Holocaust, Avisar detects a cynical decision to avoid the truth at all costs: "What we actually have in most American Holocaust films is a deliberate refusal to leap into unfaith."[12] Judith Doneson asserts, however, that we have to be more realistic about what we expect from such films and accept the impossibility of visually reconstructing the Holocaust adequately: "It is inevitable that the Holocaust as interpreted in American film is different from the realities of Auschwitz."[13] Doneson situates the problems surrounding *Schindler's List* within the wider controversy over the blurring of boundaries between the spheres of history (the factual) and of entertainment (the invented). Doneson asserts, "*Schindler's List* did advance the concern among

27

historians that history is becoming the charge of the media. During the past thirty years in particular, history as entertainment has become the trend."[14]

This trend was much in evidence in 1994, when *Schindler's List* was released to near-universal acclaim and went on to win seven Academy Awards, as well as enjoying massive box office success. The film represented the first major mainstream visual interpretation of the Holocaust. While earlier films (such as *Sophie's Choice*) had used the Holocaust as a backdrop, *Schindler's List* represented the first significant attempt to tell and show the Holocaust from the ghettos to the gas chambers. While being every inch the classic Hollywood film, *Schindler's List* had an "arty," European feel and eclipsed earlier films such as *Judgment at Nuremberg*. Yet after the initial praise, at a public and popular level, criticisms began to emerge. It soon became apparent that the film had polarized popular and critical opinion. Critics argued that the film offered a "soft" version of the Holocaust, while proponents of the film insisted that its reach was doing more for memory than any other form of Holocaust commemoration of recent decades. The visual style of the film has also been commended; Miriam Hansen has asserted that *Schindler's List* is "a more sophisticated, elliptical, and self-conscious film than its critics acknowledge."[15]

Brian Cheyette goes further to defend Spielberg's decision to make a film about the Holocaust and to provide a visual memory of the event. Seemingly supporting the idea of Holocaust films as "documents," Cheyette acknowledges the fact that the director has "struggled to turn into images that which was thought to be unrepresentable."[16] Cheyette praises not just the intention behind the film but also Spielberg's success in creating the definitive popular film on the Holocaust: "That it is, unquestionably, the best film on this subject within its particular set of conventions is the measure of Spielberg's outstanding achievement."[17]

Yet a compelling criticism made of *Schindler's List* relates to its emotivism, the way that audience identification with the plight of the Jews is achieved by appealing to people's feelings. Frank Manchel, however, has argued that this approach is not without its positive aspects when one is trying to forge a lasting memory of the Holocaust: "Stirring emotions is one powerful way to get millions of uninvolved and uninterested audiences into examining a complex issue."[18] With reference to the infamous gas chamber/shower scene that will be discussed more fully later, Omer Bartov defends Spielberg against the charge that the director overstepped the line of decency, implying instead that he was really guilty of drawing back from the ultimate reality of the gas chamber—the fact that those who entered it did not reemerge. Bartov asserts, "To be sure, no film can recreate an inhuman reality. We cannot blame *Schindler's List* for not showing people actually being gassed, but only for showing them *not* being gassed."[19] Janina Struk has argued, however, that regardless of the fact that these showers were simply showers, Spielberg has intruded into territory that should not be entered into through film. Struk states, "Spielberg pushed the reality angle further when he filmed a group of naked women with shaven heads packed tightly in what we, the audience, believe to be a gas-chamber. Even the Nazis, as far as we know, drew the line at filming in the gas-chambers."[20]

Yet who among the audience would want to see such literal representation of industrialized mass murder? We are not shown the Holocaust in its awful totality, and this is surely because we would (hopefully) turn away from such explicit re-created images if they were offered to us. Mintz asserts that with this in mind, we should adopt a less critical approach to Spielberg's film and accept that a greater degree of barbarism would have undermined its reach and educational function: "If *Schindler's List* had reached out to shake up its audience through atrocity and sensationalism, it would have taught nothing and left little impact, in addition to not having won the enormous viewership it did."[21]

Doneson shares this view, that certain things go unsaid or "unshown," not simply because of the impossibility of representation but also because of our un-willingness to confront such scenes. Thus, by and large, we are only given that which we can deal with, since "all tragedies have within them moments that go unwritten in order to spare us, to allow us to continue living. This is especially true of Auschwitz—few of us could tolerate the ultimate reality of the Holocaust."[22] One of the most sustained criticisms of *Schindler's List* then is that it creates a false and sentimentalized picture of the Holocaust. Ordinarily, when one thinks of the Holocaust, one is struck by the loss, destruction, and rupture caused by the event. *Schindler's List* is part of a contemporary climate whereby a new emphasis is placed on survival, heroism, and redemption in relation to the Holocaust. The film is therefore as much about survival and goodness as it is about evil and death; more attention is paid to the salvation of the few than to the abandonment and murder of the many.

Through the figure of Oskar Schindler, we are encouraged to believe that the human potential for good withstood even the trials of the Nazi era. It is a film about survival, but not the somber, mutilated survival we read of in the testimony of Elie Wiesel or Charlotte Delbo. This is Holocaust survival Hollywood-style. The Jews of *Schindler's List* are saved through a conscious act of will, of *goodness*. They are not liberated starved and filthy, stricken by grief and desolation. They are plucked from cattle trucks, rescued from the very barracks of Auschwitz itself and taken to Schindler's haven/factory. Families remain intact, marriage services are performed, and even the Sabbath is observed. We may see deaths in the ghetto and the camp, yet we know that the "Schindler Jews" will survive. At the end of the film, we see the survivors and their descendants in Israel and we are comforted by the sense of continuity and renewal. We are not encouraged to think of the majority of the Jews who died in the Holocaust or about the family lines that stopped forever at Auschwitz, Treblinka, Majdanek, and other such places. Bartov has argued that by concentrating on the exception rather than the rule, *Schindler's List* is not making us confront the ultimate realities of the Holocaust: "the fact that in the real Holocaust most of the Jews died, most of those sent to the showers were gassed. . . . The film distorts the reality of the Holocaust by leaving out that most common and typical feature of the event—namely mass industrial killing."[23]

If *Schindler's List* is an affirmation of life rather than death, one must then reflect on the question of how representative the film is and also meditate on the problems ensuing from it becoming a "master narrative" of the Holocaust. Gillian Rose recognized the problems inherent in forms of Holocaust representation that seek to comfort rather than inform. Rose criticized the emphasis placed on the Talmudic blessing, applied here to Schindler, that "whosoever saves a life saves the whole world." In a bizarre reversal of utilitarian ideals, we are encouraged to celebrate the survival of the few rather than the many. Rose asserted that the film was even more offensive than the book in this regard: "The ruthlessness of saving one or 1,000, and our exultant participating in that narrowly bounded victory, is *facetiously* contrasted with the Talmudic blessing. . . . The book makes clear the pitiless immorality of this in the context: the film depends on it as congratulation."[24]

It is this attempt to comfort us that is one of the most problematic aspects of the film. Horror is undoubtedly lessened or softened, the result being that one of the greatest outpourings of evil (however glacial and bureaucratic its ultimate distillation became) in the modern period is reduced to the status of a teary melodrama. Increasingly, it would appear that *Schindler's List* is not really a film about the Holocaust. As Michael Wildt asserts, "Spielberg did not depict the Holocaust as a whole: he made a film about Oskar Schindler and Amon Goeth."[25] An obvious question might be why Spielberg chose such an unrepresentative story with which to highlight the Holocaust in popular film. Indeed the film not only gives an inaccurate picture of the Holocaust as a whole, it even gives an inaccurate picture of this small part of the Holocaust.

The story of Oskar Schindler, through both the novel and the film, sees a morally ambiguous individual undertake a transformation into an almost Christlike figure. History is manipulated to ensure that complex or distracting side issues are ironed out so that our enjoyment of a sentimental epic is not hindered. Thus the last scenes with Schindler involve distortion and have been widely panned for their gross sentimentality. It is known that Schindler's last moments with "his" Jews were rather different than the film would have us believe. Frank Manchel asserts that Spielberg glossed over the fact that "Schindler was too scared about his fate to say anything, that the car was lined with money for a safe getaway, and that he fled not only with his wife but also with his mistress."[26]

Yet history has not only been tampered with in order to leave intact the integrity of the film's hero. Tim Cole asserts that much more important historical realities of the Holocaust have been "skirted" in order to leave our faith intact: "We have been spared the gas chambers and we are spared a final scene of mass shootings. We have—perhaps—been spared the Holocaust."[27] The historical inaccuracies of *Schindler's List* provide the best counterargument to the assertion that Holocaust films, simply by touching on the event in any way, are automatically "educational." The hype surrounding a film such as *Schindler's List* and the authenticity conferred on it because it is based on a "true story" encourage many to regard it as some kind of "document," a way to find out about the Holocaust. Given that entertainment and a sentimentalized view of history dominate in popular representations of past events, even in the case of the Holocaust, one must question the validity of the "education" argument. The lessons one might learn from the Holocaust of history relate to powerlessness and despair, yet the film actively refutes this. People "decide" to survive; Schindler decides to save. We may witness bursts of horror that add drama, but ultimately we are misled. Mintz recognizes the influence of Americaniza- tion in this growing tendency to look for positive stories of the Holocaust. He asserts, "The Hollywood imperative remains untouched: move viewers through cycles of dread and relief, give them a larger-than-life adventure to identify with, and in the end, of course, leave them a sense of uplift."[28]

The fact that the Holocaust has been softened for the public palate, according to Mintz, accounts for its contemporary dominance in popular culture. In many ways, it is almost as if there is a tacit agreement between cinema and society, allowing the Holocaust to "move to the center of public awareness on the condition that it has a message of affirmation to offer us."[29] This obviously further undermines the argument that we are being "educated" by such films. *Schindler's List* is seen by many as too facile, as reducing the Holocaust to one story that obscures the plight of the majority of victims. Bartov asserts that the necessity of ending the Hollywood film on a positive note is a major failing of American films on the Holocaust: "By ending the film with an emotional catharsis and a final humanization of his hero, Spielberg compels us to consider the compatibility of the conventions and con- straints of American cinema with the profound rupture of western civilization at the core of the Holocaust."[30]

Whatever the problems many scholars have with the educational "message" of Spielberg's film, the fact remains that the director went to great lengths to secure a very particular look for *Schindler's List*, one that would hopefully boost its "truth claims." Spielberg created a film that looked European and seemed a world away from the "glibness" of Hollywood. Spielberg shot in black and white, in Poland, using non-American actors. The film looked "historical" and had a documentary-like quality to it. As Struk asserts, it was as though Spielberg had literally re-created the past: "Still images of Jews having their sidelocks cut surrounded by amused Nazis, of Jews made to shovel snow and of Jews carrying their belongings through the streets during the deportation from the ghettos, were re-enacted with precision."[31]

Critics have argued that this "historical" look had as much to do with aesthetics, with Spielberg's desire to distance the film from the showy vulgarity normally associated with Hollywood, as with a determination to create an "authentic" mood and context. It is ironic that Spielberg has contributed greatly to the Americanization of the Holocaust by creating such a massively popular film, when he tried so consciously to make an "un-American" film. Yosefa Loshitzky maintains, "The most commercial director, associated with the 'classics' of American popular culture, 'Europeanized' his film on the Holocaust as though a "European Look" guaranteed critical respectability."[32] The fact that Spielberg integrated aspects of European film into *Schindler's List* has led to complaints that the film is really about artifice and manipulation. The black-and-white footage is seen by many as an attempt to lend authority and gravity to the film. Others argue that *Schindler's List* has "cheated" its way to the position of prime film on the Holocaust, by borrowing from European Holocaust films while ensuring success by omitting the full horror of the event. Hansen has argued that Spielberg reached the mainstream by climbing on the shoulders of other, more uncompromising, films and then presented his film as the *definitive* film on the Holocaust. Hansen states that the film "recycles images and tropes from other Holocaust films, especially European ones; but, as a classical narrative, it does so without quotation marks, pretending to be telling the story for the first time."[33]

Thus while at a popular level the film is seen as more "arty" than the average Hollywood film, at a critical level the film is still regarded as inferior. Beyond the style of the film and how it looks, as we have established, the way the plot deals with the Holocaust conforms entirely to the populist conventions of Hollywood. Bartov has spoken of the "positively repulsive kitsch" of the last scenes involving Schindler.[34] Mintz has asserted that the choice to pick such a life-affirming story of the Holocaust and to make a film out of it amounted to "artistic timidity," arguing that the integrity of the film (and consequently its cultural value) was undermined by the determination to keep the viewer happy at all costs.[35] He states that this sentimentalized approach to the Holocaust "amounts to a vulgarization of something profoundly tragic and to a betrayal of the millions of victims who were not saved."[36]

Mintz asserts that popular filmmakers who work on the Holocaust do not worry about the risk of vulgarizing the Holocaust and are keen to address the subject in their films because they see it as an "agent of moral seriousness." Mintz argues that the seriousness of the Holocaust "confers on the American popular mind the possibility of escape from vulgarity."[37] Thus filmmakers take the risk of trivializing or vulgarizing the Holocaust because they believe that the somber subject matter can elevate the genre of popular cinema. Of course, the very physical environment of the cinema is, in itself, a challenge to this newfound "seriousness" of approach. Clearly the way most people normally behave at the cinema (munching through popcorn and sweets) would seem inappropriate at a film such as *Schindler's List*. As Struk has asserted: "In the USA, the Jewish Federation Council of Los Angeles issued psychological guidelines, the Viewer's Guide To Schindler's List . . . which included the recommendation that consuming refreshments was not suitable."[38]

A further problem of morally simplistic, popular representations of the Holocaust à la *Schindler's List* relates to the need to universalize and sensationalize extreme experiences in order to make them fit with the average person's frame of reference. When the Holocaust is presented in a sentimentalized and trivialized way, we are encouraged to believe it is primarily a human (rather than a Jewish) tragedy, one we can all share. We are led to identify more with Schindler, the hero, than with the Jews who exist in the film only to be killed by Goeth or saved by Schindler.

The visual representation of Nazi atrocity is also a sensitive area. As viewers, we often regard the action from the perspective of the killers; in particular, when we see Goeth aiming his rifle at potential victims, we literally look down the barrel of the gun with him. Geoffrey Hartman asserts that this particular brand of voyeurism should make us feel uncomfortable: "To see things that sharply, and from a privileged position, is to see them with the eyes of those who had the power of life and death."[39] Yet it is in his portrayal of female Jews that Spielberg has courted the greatest controversy. The one scene that most people remember from *Schindler's List* is surely that which involves the "accidental" deportation of the female "Schindler Jews" to Auschwitz. We are shown the scene of distraught, naked women waiting for what turns out to be a shower. This is surely Holocaust voyeurism at its very worst, with suspense created by the fact that both the women and the audience expect gas to issue from the showerheads. Sarah Horowitz has denounced this scene as pornographic. She contends: "The audience is permitted to anticipate viewing the ultimate atrocity. . . . The anticipated enactment of genocide is thrilling because it is forbidden and at the same time permitted because it is artifice."[40]

A similar erotic fascination with the female victim of atrocity is at play in the scenes between the commandant of Plaszow, Amon Goeth, and his beleaguered Jewish maid Helen Hirsch. An uncomfortable sexual dynamic is set up in the unequal relationship between the all-powerful Goeth and the vulnerable object of his desire (and his violence), Hirsch. While this kind of situation is representative of the Holocaust experience of many women, Horowitz recognizes a different motivation in the decision to include it in the film. She argues that the scene with Goeth and the half-dressed Hirsch "titillates the viewer with the suggestion that Helen Hirsch, already marked for death, will be sexually violated as well before the genocide is completed."[41] *Schindler's List* has proved that Hollywood's Holocaust is bound by the straightjacket of convention and chronology. Assuming the audience knows nothing, the American Holocaust film must show all, preferably in a neat time line, from the ghettos to the concentration camps, from the liberated concentration camps to the (implied) salvic closure of Israel.

In view of this, one must question whether the less obvious, more abstract approach of some European Holocaust documentaries might provide an all-too-necessary alternative to Hollywood. One might also assert that a less literal approach to Holocaust representation offers us a different spectatorial role and perspective, encouraging us to reflect on the Holocaust rather than merely passively consuming images of it. As such, it is interesting to consider what Lisa Saltzman has written concerning Theodor Adorno, Hebraic ethics, and the Holocaust art of Anselm Kiefer. Saltzman has linked Adorno's famous postwar injunction against writing poetry after Auschwitz to the second commandment, which forbids the creation of graven images. She summarizes the connection thus: "Moses prevents the Jews from entering into a fetishistic relationship with the image. Adorno, writing against a spectatorial experience of pleasure and desire, again invokes a language of prohibition and taboo."[42] Saltzman asserts that Adorno, though talking about art rather than film and the Holocaust, advocates a spectatorship that is "deeply wary of fetishism." Saltzman also argues that only abstract representation can "circumvent the possibility of a libidinous engagement with the object."[43] When the "object" concerned is the Holocaust as it is depicted in film, this "libidinous engagement" seems particularly inappropriate. We have to face the question of how we watch Holocaust films, not just what is shown in a given film but also how we view it. While we may need more complex and respectful forms of representation, we also have to accept our responsibility as viewers.

In the art of Anselm Kiefer, Saltzman identifies the possibility of an ethical spectatorship of visual forms of Holocaust representation. Claude Lanzmann's 1985 documentary, *Shoah*, offers the more abstract form of representation, commended by Adorno, and also offers the viewer the opportunity to engage with the Holocaust in a manner that is neither libidinous nor fetishistic. Lanzmann's landmark Holocaust documentary is in many ways a unique achievement, entirely different from prior and subsequent Holocaust films. *Shoah* represents the very different approach of the European filmmaker to the representation of a European event, an approach that resulted in *Shoah* being the polar opposite of *Schindler's List*.

At nine-and-a-half hours long, *Shoah*'s duration alone puts it beyond the attention span of the mainstream audience, for who (without a particular interest in the Holocaust) would sit through such an epic production? Beyond the simple question of its length, *Shoah* was singular in how it looked at and represented the Holocaust. Lanzmann's determination to make a film about the past, which was in fact firmly rooted in the present, is evident in the total rejection of archival footage. Instead of the usual recycling of the ultimately dehumanizing liberation footage, or the ethically troubling reliance on the images of the ghettos or mass shootings taken by the Nazis themselves, Lanzmann created a new image of the Holocaust. Lanzmann's picture of the Holocaust is one inextricably linked to the testimony of the perpetrators, bystanders, and, most importantly, the victims. Consequently, though it is a visual representation, the film resonates with the *voices* of those interviewed. The Holocaust is *told* rather than *shown*.

Shoah is a film primarily comprised of interviews interspersed with contemporary shots of the locations particular to the Holocaust. The length of *Shoah* is also the result of the pauses and silences that inhabit and characterize the film, be it the pause of the victim unable to continue their testimony or the silence of languid shots of the Polish countryside. Through these silences, *Shoah* encourages us to reflect on the Holocaust, though such reflection obviously requires some prior knowledge of the event. While *Shoah* is crammed with all of the most horrible details of the Holocaust, a degree of knowledge (and interest) in the Holocaust is presumed in the viewer. This is not the "beginning-middle-and-end" Holocaust of *Schindler's List*.

The lack of archival footage, in contrast to the approach of a comparable documentary like *Night and Fog*, does indeed move us nearer to the "ethical spectatorship" envisaged by Saltzman. With none of the reconstructed violence and atrocity that have featured so prominently in the majority of Holocaust films, we are not encouraged to "consume" the Holocaust. As Gertrud Koch comments, "There are no images of the annihilation itself: its representability is never once suggested by using the existing documentary photographs that haunt every other film on this subject."[44] By breaking with the conventions of visual representation, Lanzmann's film has indeed transcended the realm of the purely visual. Because of the lengthy translation process, we are forced to concentrate more intently as we wait for the interviewee's response.

In *Shoah*, listening is as important as watching, as Nelly Furman argues: "Lanzmann's tour de force is to have turned cinematographic viewing into a listening experience, transforming spectators into listeners, who, in turn, become bearers of those testimonies."[45] One might assert that the very concept of listening in relation to Holocaust representation is much less controversial than watching. One cannot (as easily) hear too much about the Holocaust, but in terms of the visual, the threshold is lower; one can be shown too much. *Shoah* offers an alternative to the Holocaust voyeurism of recent decades, an opportunity to retreat from spectatorship and consumption.

Lanzmann's film also lacks the comforting elements that find their way into most popular films on the Holocaust. It is not an "easy" film, nor is it a life-affirming one. While films such as *Schindler's List* are characterized by a distinct and redemptive closure, *Shoah* is endlessly circular, insisting as it does on the permanence of the Holocaust and the indelible traces left on landscapes and victims alike. It is no coincidence that the final shot of *Shoah* is of a steam train and cattle trucks waiting in the Polish countryside. *Shoah* is not a film that seeks to present the Holocaust as something from the past, an event from history under which we can draw a line and then move on. The pace of the film is slow; the interviews and landscapes are often bleak and disturbing. No effort has been made to adapt the Holocaust to public taste. Andre Pierre Colombat quotes Marcel Ophuls (the maker of *The Sorrow and the Pity*) thus: "Lanzmann never winks at his spectators, and he does not try to seduce or please them."[46] However scrupulous Lanzmann was in his rejection of archival visual material to illustrate his narrative, the issue of "re-creation" has informed critical reflection on the film. Lanzmann was criticized for the way he elaborately staged interviews to make a greater impression on the audience but at questionable impact on the survivor. Thus Lanzmann took Simon Srebnik, survivor of Chelmno, back to Poland and filmed him rowing up the Narew River singing the songs he used to sing for the Nazis when he was a boy prisoner in leg irons. We also see Abraham Bomba, a survivor of Treblinka, who had been forced to cut women's hair before they were gassed, now retired but interviewed cutting hair in a Tel Aviv barber shop rented by Lanzmann for this very purpose.

Lanzmann was obviously trying to bring to life in the present the horror of the past. Yet it was precisely the trauma of the resurgence of these violent memories that made many of Lanzmann's interviewees break down. Indeed Andre Pierre Colombat suggests that Lanzmann's reliving approach is as controversial to some as the idea of re-creating the Holocaust as a "film set" is to others. Colombat asserts that these sequences raise "the problem of the moral position of a film director asking a survivor to 'relive' a chapter of the Holocaust that is part of his or her personal experience, even for the purpose of an historical film or a work of art."

Those who argue that *Shoah* is a carefully constructed vehicle for Claude Lanzmann's personal obsessions rather than an impartial documentary on the Holocaust often assert that Lanzmann's choice of victims was highly selective and designed for effect. These critics conclude that this amounts to both an exploitation of the victim and a deliberate manipulation of the audience. As Bartov asserts, "He seems to have sought witnesses strong enough to testify at some length and coherence, yet sufficiently 'weak' to finally break down in front of the camera."[47] However it is more likely that Lanzmann chose very "particular" witnesses for the unique perspectives they could offer on the Holocaust rather than for the pathos achieved by their emotional vulnerability. Simon Srebnik and Mordechai Podchlebnik were included as the only survivors of Chelmno. Abraham Bomba's testimony shed light on the final moments of the women who were murdered at Treblinka. Fillip Muller offered a very rare perspective as a survivor of the Sonderkommando of Auschwitz. Indeed the majority of the survivors interviewed by Lanzmann were from work details and, as such, were able to testify to one of the most horrific aspects of the Holocaust, the fact that the industrialized killing process required the forced assistance of its intended victims.

Lanzmann picked those who could tell the kind of stories that are generally deemed too unpalatable for the public, such as the testimony of Itzhak Dugin, who was forced to exhume, with bare hands, the bodies of the murdered Jews of Vilna in order to burn them and obliterate all traces of their life and death. In the first grave alone, there had been 24,000 bodies, and Dugin testified, "When the last mass grave was opened, I recognized my whole family."[48] This is precisely the kind of fact that would never intrude into a popular Holocaust film.

Night and Fog

If *Shoah* is a film about listening, telling, pauses, and silence, Alain Resnais's 1955 documentary, *Night and Fog*, had already offered a completely different approach to the transmission of the facts of the Holocaust. Unlike the prohibitively long *Shoah*, with its repudiation of archive footage (indeed of the "visual"), *Night and Fog* is just thirty minutes long and made use of historical footage and photographs. Directed by Resnais, with a text written by Jean Cayrol, a French Catholic survivor of Auschwitz, *Night and Fog* offers a brutal and short evocation of the Holocaust. Unlike *Shoah*, *Night and Fog* had a decidedly linear narrative, giving descriptions—backed up by black-and-white archival footage—of

Nuit et Brouillard (*Night and Fog*), 1960. Directed by Alain Resnais.

deportation, arrival at the camp, the misery and industrialized death therein, all interspersed with contemporary color footage.

To this day, *Night and Fog* is one of the most shocking visual representations of the Holocaust, and this is problematic, even beyond the desire this may induce in the viewer to turn away from the images on the screen. In wanting to create a vivid and truthful picture of the Holocaust, Resnais had to make use of certain questionable archival forms. To depict the pride and power of Germany, Resnais included footage from the Nazi filmmaker Leni Riefenstahl's *The Triumph of the Will*. Yet much more problematic is the inclusion of footage and photographs taken by the Nazis themselves to document their crimes. Thus we see smug-looking *Schutzstaffel* (SS) smiling at the camera as Jews are packed into cattle trucks, and photographs of naked Jewish women waiting to be shot by the *Einsatzgruppen* (mobile killing squads). Last, we have the liberation footage that documents the unimaginable scale and nature of the crime but that somehow fails to respect the dignity and humanity of the individual Holocaust victims. We thus see the severed heads of victims, wild-eyed skeletal survivors, and corpses everywhere: smoking on pyres, strewn across the camp ground, and being bull-dozed into pits.

Here we face the problem of the voyeuristic consumption of images of atrocity. We are also confronted by the question of whether it is ethical to remember the victims as the perpetrators presented them or as the horrified liberators encountered and beheld them. Indeed certain aspects of *Night and Fog* are almost "clichéd," if one can use such a banal word about such extreme subject matter. The images in *Night and Fog* tie in with what Barbie Zelizer has written regarding liberation photography. Zelizer stated: "The most frequent early objects of depiction were among those that later resurfaced as Holocaust iconography—skulls and corpses, barbed-wire fences separating survivors and victims from the outside world, camp courtyards, accoutrements of atrocity such as crematorium chimneys and furnaces."[49] Thus certain iconic images provide a visual reference point for us, and *Night and Fog* distils some of the worst of these images into a relatively short film. Yet in some ways, these images have become so familiar that we have become numb to their impact. The shocking, show-all approach of *Night and Fog* (though necessary at the time) has blunted our senses to the extent that we are no longer as affected by them as we once were. As Zelizer affirms, "As we stand at century's end and look back, the visual memories of the Holocaust set in place fifty-odd years ago seem oddly unsatisfying. The mounds of corpses, gaping pits of bodies, and figures angled like matchsticks across the camera's field of vision have paralyzed many of us to the point of critical inattention."[50]

While the voice-over is provided by a survivor, the "voice" of the survivor does not permeate the film as it does in *Shoah*. The victims of *Night and Fog* are anonymous, and this serves to universalize the Holocaust. While *Shoah* might be said to be too accusatory and partisan, *Night and Fog* tries to be too even-handed, to the detriment of the historical record. While the Jewishness of the victims is alluded to, by the Stars of David on the deportees, among other things, at no point is it acknowledged that the Jews were the primary victims (and primary targets) of the Holocaust. *Night and Fog* does not explore the role of anti-Semitism (its unique character and longevity); the Holocaust is presented simply as the natural consequence of totalitarianism. The sense that *anybody* could have been the victim and *anyone* the perpetrator permeates the film. For many, this universalistic strand to *Night and Fog* is the greatest weakness of the film. As Ilan Avisar argues, "The flaw of *Night and Fog* is not one of distortion or even of totally ignoring the Jewish suffering, but rather a failure to present the assault against the Jews as an essential pillar of the Nazi phenomenon."[51]

Indeed the main problem with a film like *Night and Fog* relates to the fact that the "visual" is prioritized above all else. Because we have so much faith in what we can see with "our own eyes," we take such images in unquestioningly, even though they may actually be giving us only a superficial insight. One could, however, assert that *Night and Fog* represents the middle ground between a film such as *Shoah* and a film such as *Schindler's List*. While aspects of voyeurism and universalism might make Resnais's film seem inferior to Lanzmann's, it is undoubtedly more accessible. To gain the full benefit of what is offered to the viewer in *Shoah*, one must have the patience and interest to watch all nine-and-a-half hours, and one must also possess some prior knowledge of the event—it is neither a shortcut to, nor the last word on, the Holocaust. *Schindler's List*, on the other hand, is dogged by the criticisms that necessarily arise when the Holocaust is re-created for dramatic effect. At over three hours long, *Schindler's List* also requires a degree of dedication on the part of the viewer. Indeed when one considers the inventions and upbeat, life-affirming distortions of a film like *Schindler's List*, *Night and Fog* seems a more appropriate form of representation, whatever its potential for voyeurism.

One can get a more realistic glimpse of the Holocaust in thirty minutes of *Night and Fog* than one gets in over three hours of Spielberg's film. Its stark brutality ensures that the Holocaust is not sentimentalized or domesticated. It may deal inadequately with the specificity of Jewish victimhood, but it makes clear that the Holocaust was about misery and death in many forms, all terrible and deliberate. While the film is short and relatively self-contained, it is still a world away from a popular film on the Holocaust. *Night and Fog* is driven by a moral imperative to remember, and this is not tainted by a need to entertain or engage the viewer. Consequently it is not an "easy" film to watch.

This brings us to the heart of the debate about Holocaust films and documentaries, namely whether they should be "enjoyable" to watch. While *Night and Fog* may not conform to the kind of visualization considered ethical in my earlier discussion of Saltzman and Lanzmann, Resnais's film does not encourage us to consume a "safe" image of atrocity as *Schindler's List* does. Nor is the film as self-indulgent as Lanzmann's project. As Ilan Avisar reflects, "Indeed, the power of this film is that despite the employment of rich and complex cinematic language, the message is enhanced while avoiding the effect of pleasing aesthetics or the special gratification of indulgence with profundities."[52] While *Shoah* and *Night and Fog* (as documentaries as well as European films) cannot be fairly compared to a film such as *Schindler's List*, the recent European Holocaust film *Life Is Beautiful* provides a more suitable comparison.

Life Is Beautiful:
Tragi-Comedy and the Holocaust

The massive success of *Schindler's List* undoubtedly paved the way for the reception of *Life Is Beautiful* (1998), which, with its more-or-less happy ending, might be deemed to be Europe's answer to *Schindler's List*. By tapping into the sudden interest in the Holocaust, and in some ways following the American format, Roberto Benigni, who cowrote, directed, and starred in the film, created one of the most successful foreign-language films of recent years. The film also won three Oscars at the 1998 Academy awards. Like all successful Holocaust films, *Life Is Beautiful* tells of the exception rather than the rule, making survival seem a more representative aspect of the Holocaust than death. Yet unlike other Holocaust films, Benigni's was awaited with particular trepidation because of its billing as a "Holocaust comedy." The initial reaction to this, even before the release of the film, was one of outrage at the mere idea of a juxtaposition of humor and atrocity. On watching *Life Is Beautiful*, however, those who knew anything about the Holocaust quickly realized that the film contained a good deal more humor than it did atrocity.

A tale of father and son, Guido (Benigni) and Giosue, it soon becomes clear that the chief problem with *Life Is Beautiful* relates not to the way the film brings the Holocaust into the sphere of kitsch comedy but instead to the perennial problem of misrepresentation. Many central aspects of the plot amount to a complete and utter distortion of reality. Beyond his near miraculous entrance into the camp at such a young age, Giosue's continued existence there depends on his remaining hidden in the barracks. Guido, fully aware of the reality of their situation, convinces his son that their "stay" at the camp is voluntary, that they can leave whenever they want, and that if Giosue manages to remain hidden, he will win a tank at the end of the "game." In the Holocaust world of *Life Is Beautiful*, there are no unfriendly elements aside from the Nazis, no Kapos ready to kill the child, no barrack-mates willing to denounce him for an extra ration of bread. The reality of children's experiences within the concentration camp, their selection on arrival or abuse within them, is too disturbing for us, and Benigni, to properly contemplate.

Ultimately this is a film with a happy ending. Giosue lives to be reunited with his mother, Dora, who has survived the women's camp. As the liberators enter the camp in a huge tank the inference is clear; Giosue has won the prize. Simply by surviving, he is a Holocaust "winner." Thus despite the death of Guido, the sacrificial/token victim, the message of the film is essentially life-affirming. The voice-over at the end of the film makes a mockery of the situation prisoners found themselves in. The voice of the adult Giosue asserts, "This is my story. This is the sacrifice my father made. This was his gift to me."[53] This implies a freedom of choice, of will, open to the victims of the Holocaust. It suggests that fathers, if they chose to, could protect their children even in the concentration camps. How much more accurate a depiction of the father-and-son experience of the Holocaust can be found in Elie Wiesel's *Night*? Indeed for the survivor, and for anyone who has read such testimony, the misrepresentation offered by *Life Is Beautiful* seems an outrage, as monstrous as the idea that the death of even a fictional victim such as Guido should be celebrated as a "sacrifice."

Conclusion

Having considered the continued engagement with the Holocaust in visual culture, it is clear that without some prior knowledge of the Holocaust, and a healthy cynicism regarding the "transformative potential" of images of atrocity, the actual and re-created scenes that make up our memory are at best gratuitous and at worst indecent. The public gaze leveled at the Holocaust should be continually, critically appraised. Even the academic, scholarly gaze of the historian needs to be examined carefully regarding motivation and spectatorial perspective. Struk, in her beautifully observed, scrupulously "ethical" meditation on Holocaust photography, has written of the experience of sifting through archival footage that is troubling beyond the immediate "shock value" of what it shows. Even for the purposes of "pure" historical memory, Struk communicated a strong sense of shame in examining a particular image of three naked Jewish men standing by a pit in Sniatyn, Ukraine, in 1943, awaiting execution. The men are surrounded by soldiers, and the snapshot conveys a sense of action paused; the victims are posed before the camera, so that the camera might record the last moments before their murder. In a way to which anybody who has spent time in an archive of Holocaust-era visual material can relate, Struk confessed: "I felt ashamed to be examining this barbaric scene, voyeuristic for witnessing their nakedness and vulnerability, and disturbed because the act of looking at this photograph put me in the position of the possible assassin."[54]

At odds with such appropriate shame, one must consider the perspective of those capturing such images of atrocity. The Germans and Ukrainians posing alongside the victims exhibit a sense of excitement at what they are participating in and watching. The excitement is heightened by their awareness that the camera is capturing the event for posterity. Struk likens their proud posturing with the poses "normal" people affect for their holiday snaps; yet their casual demeanor cannot disguise their self-consciousness at being involved in something "momentous." Without such awareness of the extremity of the acts being perpetrated, there would be no need to record them: "Photographing the enemy was equal to possessing or conquering it. Publically to humiliate, degrade, and possibly kill the "real" Jew was metaphorically to destroy the image of the mythical Jew. Taking photographs was an integral part of the humiliation process; in a sense it completed the violation."[55] With this in mind, perhaps we, as a society, supposedly concerned with the "memory" of such events, should reconsider the faith we place in visual images—be they authentic or artistic. The compelling horror of the early images of Holocaust atrocity that emerged during and immediately after World War II has clearly fueled an engagement with the Holocaust as a "spectacle." The Holocaust, in a softened, fetishized, corrupted form, has secured a place in our visual culture. The Holocaust is increasingly remembered through visual means (to the exclusion of written testimony, which can tell us so much more about the Holocaust experience). Yet such visual forms are often inadequate to the task of understanding or comprehending the Holocaust. Without a sense of what the Holocaust really was, how can genuine memory be achieved?

NOTES

1. Sontag, *On Photography*, 11.
2. *The Relief of Belsen*, 19–20.
3. Chouliaraki, *The Spectatorship of Suffering*, 87.
4. Ibid., 102, 103.
5. Semprun, *The Cattle Truck*, 75.
6. Mintz, *Popular Culture and the Shaping of Holocaust Memory in America*, 147.
7. Sontag, *On Photography*, 179.
8. Sontag, *Regarding the Pain of Others*, 36.
9. Sontag, *On Photography*, 20.
10. Nowell-Smith and Ricci, *Hollywood and Europe*, 12.
11. Avisar, *Screening the Holocaust*, 129.
12. Ibid., 131.
13. Doneson, *The Holocaust in American Film*, 231.
14. Ibid., 230.
15. Hansen, "Schindler's List Is Not *Shoah*," 205.
16. Cheyette, "The Holocaust in the Picture-House," 18.
17. Ibid., 19.
18. Manchel, "A Reel Witness," 96.
19. Bartov, *Murder in Our Midst*, 170.
20. Struk, *Photographing the Holocaust*, 183.
21. Mintz, *Popular Culture and the Shaping of Holocaust Memory in America*, 130.
22. Doneson, *The Holocaust in American Film*, 188.
23. Bartov, *Murder in Our Midst*, 168.
24. Rose, *Mourning Becomes the Law*, 45.
25. Wildt, "The Invented and the Real," 244.
26. Manchel, "A Reel Witness," 99.
27. Cole, *Selling the Holocaust*, 92.
28. Mintz, *Popular Culture and the Shaping of Holocaust Memory in America*, 141.
29. Ibid., 153.

30. Bartov, "Spielberg's Oskar," 168.

31. Struk, *Photographing the Holocaust*, 183.

32. Loshitzky, *Spielberg's Holocaust*, 5.

33. Hansen, "Schindler's List Is Not *Shoah*," 206.

34. Bartov, "Spielberg's Oskar," 44–45.

35. Mintz, *Popular Culture and the Shaping of Holocaust Memory in America*, 139.

36. Ibid., 139.

37. Ibid., 157.

38. Struk, *Photographing the Holocaust*, 182.

39. Hartman, "The Cinema Animal," 61–62.

40. Horowitz, "But Is It Good for the Jews?," 128.

41. Ibid., 127.

42. Saltzman, *Anselm Kiefer and Art after Auschwitz*, 20.

43. Ibid., 21.

44. Koch, "The Aesthetic Transformation of the Unimaginable," 21.

45. Furman, "Called to Witness," 69.

46. Colombat, *The Holocaust in French Film*, 306.

47. Bartov, *Murder in Our Midst*, 172–73.

48. Lanzmann, *Shoah*, 7.

49. Zelizer, *Remembering to Forget*, 97.

50. Ibid., 1.

51. Avisar, *Screening the Holocaust*, 16.

52. Ibid., 17.

53. Benigni and Cerami, *Life Is Beautiful: Screenplay*, 162.

54. Struk, *Photographing the Holocaust*, 3.

55. Ibid., 64.

2   Documenting the Holocaust in Orson Welles's *The Stranger*

JENNIFER L. BARKER

The Holocaust is a massive cataclysm that distorts everything around it. Physicists sometimes speak of gravitational masses as twistings and distortions of the even geometry of the surrounding physical space; the greater the mass, the larger the distortion. The Holocaust is a massive and continuing distortion of the human space.

ROBERT NOZICK, *The Examined Life*

The Stranger, directed by Orson Welles, is a 1946 film featuring Welles as Franz Kindler, an architect of the Holocaust who has erased his past and is hiding out in a small American town biding his time until the Nazis return to power. *The Stranger* has long been considered "the worst" and least "personal" of Welles's films, both by auteur critics and by Welles himself.[1] Much of the critical dismissal of the film is rooted in auteur theory and its advocacy of Welles and his originality and genius. *The Stranger*, Welles's most explicitly political, topical, and conventional film, as well as his biggest box office success, does not mesh well with the auteurist image of Welles as a creative and misunderstood genius.[2] The film was an anomaly, unwelcome proof that Welles could be "normal," that he "didn't glow in the dark" as he told Leslie Megahey in

45

1982.[3] Welles himself most clearly began voicing his dislike of the film in the 1950s, when auteur theory was being developed by *Cahiers du cinéma* critics and filmmakers such as André Bazin and François Truffaut. In fact, it was in a Bazin interview with Welles in the September 1958 issue of *Cahiers* that his dislike of *The Stranger* was phrased most clearly in terms of its lack of authorship, as "the one of my films of which I am least the author."[4] A number of critics have furthered the sense of unoriginality by emphasizing the film's resemblance to Alfred Hitchcock's *Shadow of a Doubt*.[5] Welles, ever the showman, was undoubtedly aware of his key position in theories of film authorship—*Citizen Kane* was a favorite example—and the film's rejection has been reinforced by decades of film critics who echo that "there is nothing" of Welles in the film.[6]

Dismissal of committed or didactic political works during the cold war was a common practice, and this has unfortunately contributed to a critical under-appreciation for an intriguing film, one that also clearly reflects Welles's contemporaneous interests in its themes and style. Its explicit focus on fascism and genocide closely mirrors Welles's extensive writing and lecturing on the subject in 1944 and 1945, and its pedagogical approach to the documentation of atrocity also represents ideas Welles discussed in interviews at the time. Stylistically, the film represents a particular kind of evolving antifascist style that was common in the 1930s and 1940s. *The Stranger* may not be Welles's most "Wellesian" film, but it is certainly a work that merits further analysis, especially as a cultural text that expresses fascination with and fears about fascism typical of Welles and many other Americans immediately following World War II. It also tackles the problem of representing the atrocity of the Holocaust, and those responsible for it, in a way that uniquely addresses American complacency during and after the war.

Filmed in the fall of 1945 and screened in the spring of 1946, *The Stranger* deals specifically with the problem of a renascent fascism and focuses on giving shape to its hidden manifestation in postwar America. Significantly, the film focuses not on the workings of mob justice and the legal system—although they play a part in the action—but rather on the innovative use of filmed documentation of the atrocity of the Holocaust as the ultimate enforcer of social justice. The Holocaust footage—screened for the first time in a Hollywood film—is included in the film as a private screening for Mary Longstreet, a woman who has ignorantly married an infamous Nazi official and refuses to believe in his guilt. *The Stranger*'s displacement of responsibility and culpability from the law to the individual is an important element of Welles's ideas about fascism and promotes his assertion that fascism can only be addressed at the level of the individual psyche. The problem of fascism is thus represented in the film primarily within the confines of a personal struggle between Kindler and Mary, or rather, Mary's unconscious, and tends to portray fascism as manageable and contained. Yet the key to resolving this personal struggle is the use of the Holocaust footage, which depicts the immensity of atrocity practiced in the public sphere, and which causes a traumatic reaction in Mary that intervenes in the working of her unconscious moral sensibility and, consequently, her conscious ethical choices. This film-within-a-film functions as a pedagogical tactic, a way of instructing Mary, and by extension, the audience, in a nonpassive form of spectatorship. In *The Stranger*, social justice relies, therefore, on a process of traumatic intervention and identification in the reception of a text that announces rather than elides the reality of atrocity. One of the greatest challenges of representing genocide involves incorporating and communicating the complex history of a multitude of individuals. Through its use of documentary footage, *The Stranger* manages to unite a limited focus on individual experience with the greater need for social justice within American borders.

The Stranger is a postwar psychological thriller set in Harper, Connecticut, a healthy American town firmly ensconced in traditions and the past.[7] The town represents an innocent and gullible community where Franz Kindler, an über-Nazi-in-hiding (Orson Welles) has disguised himself as Professor Charles Rankin and is trying to erase his identity. Part of this erasure involves marrying Mary Longstreet (Loretta Young), a "forthright" young woman who is the daughter of a U.S. Supreme Court Justice and who is conveniently oblivious to his brooding ways. Mr. Wilson (the hard-nosed Edward G. Robinson) is the dogged detective who is tracking Kindler; he's aided in this endeavor by Konrad Meinike (Konstantin Shayne), another Nazi, whom Wilson frees from prison on the chance that he will seek out Kindler. He does, but Kindler quickly kills Meinike in order to secure his own disappearance (made possible in the first place by the rather unlikely lack of any corroborating evidence about his identity in Germany, including a complete dearth of photographs). He's not quick enough, however, as Mary meets Meinike before he dies, and Wilson suspects a connection. Wilson enlists the aid of Mary's family, her subconscious, and traumatic film footage from concentration camps in order to flush Rankin out of his hidden identity. In the end, Mary's subconscious takes over, and she helps to kill her husband, who is ultimately impaled on an angel's sword in the machinery of the town's clock tower that he has been obsessively repairing over the course of the film.

The film was released by RKO as an International Picture and was produced by Sam Spiegel (billed as S. P. Eagle) with a screenplay by Anthony Veiller and the uncredited John Huston, from a story by Victor Trivas. It is variously reported that Welles asked to direct the film, or was asked to by Spiegel, on the condition that he shoot the script as-is and agree to cuts made by editor Ernest Nims, which he did. As he stated in an interview in 1965: "I never expected to have control over the editing of *The Stranger*."[8] In his 1958 interview with Bazin, Welles claimed: "John Huston did the script, without being in the credits; I did it to show I could be just as good a director of other people's stories as anyone else. . . . But I didn't write a word of the script. No, I'm wrong; I did write one or two scenes that I liked well enough, but they were cut; they took place in South America and had nothing to do with the story. No, that film had absolutely no interest for me."[9] Later he revised this estimation. By the time his conversation with Peter Bogdanovich was published in *This Is Orson Welles* (1992), he reaffirmed that John Huston "wrote most of the script—under the table, because he was in the army at the time and couldn't take credit."[10] But he also claimed: "I worked on all of it during general rewriting with Anthony Veiller and Spiegel—wrote all the stuff in the drugstore as well as the first two or three reels of the picture"—the scenes which were cut. When asked if he was responsible for the death scene at the end, he admitted, "I'm afraid so."[11]

Much criticism about the film has focused on what aspects of the script Welles worked on and whether the film could have been better, but the goal is rather to focus on what the screenplay and direction accomplish together. There are a number of possibilities as to who contributed to the screenplay, and the sympathies and techniques of all four authors—Huston, Veiller, Trivas, and Welles—can be clearly seen in the final product. Previous to *The Stranger*, John Huston had been working on documentary war films for the U.S. government, such as *Know Your Enemy: Japan* (1945), with Frank Capra, and *Let There Be Light* (1946), which he directed. *Know Your Enemy* employed a number of graphic scenes of war atrocities. The scenes depicting the physical and emotional trauma of war veterans in *Let There Be Light* were deemed so graphic and shocking by the government that it was not released until 1980. Anthony Veiller had also been working on war films with Frank Capra, including *The Nazis Strike* (1943), *Two Down and One to Go* (1945), and *War Comes to America* (1945). *War Comes to America* is a film detailing America's slow and reluctant involvement in World War II and subtly indicts Americans for safely being mere spectators of the war. In the 1930s, Trivas directed and wrote stories for a number of films, the most famous being *Niemandsland* (*No Man's Land*) in 1931. It was an antiwar film about World War I that featured sympathetic portraits of a Russian Jew and a black man. The Nazis banned and destroyed the film (although a copy was later found in the United States in the 1960s). Because of Nazi anti-Semitic policies, he fled first to Paris and then to the United States, where he wrote the story for *The Stranger*.

While the film's themes are clearly in line with those credited for writing the script, they are also ones Welles found immensely sympathetic at the time: the hidden manifestation of fascism in postwar America, the problem of genocide, and the psychological dimensions of power. Although Welles's approach to fascism in his films can best be described as complex and inconclusive, he was clearly a committed antifascist in terms of his politics in the 1940s. There is ample evidence from his 1944 speeches and 1945 *New York Post* columns (*The Orson Welles Almanac* and *Orson Welles Today*) that Welles considered fascism a modern evil. His notion of fascism was somewhat broad, however; in his 1944 one-man political show, "The Nature of the Enemy," he argued: "What is Fascism? . . . In essence it is nothing more than the original sin of civilization, the celebration of power for its own sake."[12] He also clearly understood fascism as a form of psychological insanity, a common perception in the 1940s—a belief visibly inscribed in *The Stranger* by his acting. In a speech in December 1944, he argued: "Whatever form it [fascism] takes, no matter how it may adapt itself to local conditions, to regional myths and prejudice, it will always be some form of nationalism gone crazy."[13] These ideas are clearly articulated in the film in Rankin's comments at the dinner table, delivered in the same cadences as Welles's political speeches. Welles also focused in his columns and speeches on American complacency during and after the war and ignorance about the presence of fascism. During a 1946 radio show, the *Orson Welles Commentaries*, he argued: "Forced to acknowledge Hitler's enmity, conservatives are loath to admit that even as he surrendered in Europe he succeeded in America." In response to this attitude, he suggests personal responsibility followed by action: "To live in freedom without fighting slavery is to profiteer."[14]

To this sense of individual responsibility he added the artist's indebtedness to his public. In a populist sentiment that disappears with his later dismissal of *The Stranger*, he noted: "My subject today is the question of moral indebtedness. . . . I believe I owe the very profit I make to the people I make it from. If this is radicalism, it comes automatically to most of us in show business as being generally agreed that any public man owes his position to the public."[15] Perhaps the most intriguing connection between his populist attitudes and the filming of *The Stranger* is his somewhat surprising ambition, at the time, to be a teacher. In an interview with Hedda Hopper in October 1944 (during filming), he reported: "My real interest in life . . . lies in education. I want to be a teacher. All this experience I've been piling up is equipping me for that future. I shall know how to dramatize the art of imparting knowledge. I shall have the equipment of the theater, the radio, motion pictures."[16] Noting that he wants to return to the Todd School and "give full rein to my ideas," he avows a special interest in "the new theories of visual education that are sweeping the old mossback college profs off their feet."[17] Indeed, he had been preparing educational films about democracy in 1944 with his Mercury Theatre staff. He hoped to coordinate a confluence of educators, entertainers, and politicians who would use visual media (movies and slide shows) to enlighten and instruct.[18] Although his educational plans never materialized—he told Barbara Leaming that his plans for "popular education" were rejected by all the big foundations—his interest in pedagogy is clearly present in *The Stranger*.[19]

The Stranger was more popular and less technically challenging than Welles's previous films, and in that respect it was able to reach (and potentially "teach") a wider audience. Its mixture of mystery and melodrama also provided a good format for the examination of American complacency and responsibility in the war, especially at the level of the individual. *The Stranger* begins by dramatically shifting responsibility for indicting Nazi war criminals from the collective legal realm (the Nuremberg Trials) to that of the individual. We are first introduced to Mr. Wilson as he tells the other members of the Allied War Crimes Commission: "What good are words? I'm sick of words! Hang the repercussions and the responsibility. If I fail *I'm* responsible." He is passionate, self-righteous, and melodramatic in his insistence that releasing one arch Nazi criminal is required and justified in order to find another: "You can threaten me with the bottom pits of hell and still I'll insist. This obscenity must be destroyed!" The movie thus announces itself as insistently antifascist, melodramatic, and individualistic from the beginning. It also closely mirrors the sentiments and contrasts of *War Comes to America*, the documentary Anthony Veiller worked on as a writer (along with Philip and Julius Epstein) in the spring of 1945. The narration of this documentary critiques the role of Americans as spectators who only understand the war in terms of newsreels and who were notably unsympathetic to the plight of suffering countries. It contrasts the lighthearted fun of teenagers in a small American town with footage of atrocities in Europe and Asia. As it documents growing awareness, it focuses on the sentiment of disbelief people experienced while watching *Confessions of a Nazi Spy*: "We sat in our movie theaters unbelieving. . . . Could these things really be?"[20] This same incredulity is the bedrock on which Kindler builds a home in Harper.

To drive home its point, the movie focuses on this idea of individual responsibility in an exaggerated manner. Although Wilson declares that he accepts full responsibility for the fates of Kindler and Meinike, he soon transfers this accountability to Mary Longstreet Rankin. Mary functions as a kind of scapegoat in the film, the person within which the town's (and America's) struggle for purification takes place. Mary's centrality to the process of justice is markedly implausible on the level of rational plot development, but it makes sense when viewed in light of her symbolic status as a typical American, one especially vulnerable to the lure of fascism because she is a woman, and therefore susceptible to emotional manipulation—according to popular theories of the time.[21] She is a manifestation of the fraught connection made between nation and individual woman as culpable for the ravages of war because she is "sleeping with the enemy."[22] In Mary's case, she enters into the union innocently, but she is nonetheless identified as a traitor who must pay for her mistake by becoming the *only* person "in all the world . . . who can identify Franz Kindler." She is somewhat exonerated by Wilson and her father, however, who argue that she will be blameless for betraying her husband: "if you've innocently married a criminal, then there's no marriage." Thus she must risk her life, but she does so with no public shame attached.

Despite this acknowledgment, Mary is the subject of much manipulation and blame in the film. Rankin and Wilson alternately vie for her attention and plan ways to traumatize her into silence or speech, respectively. Rankin wishes her to silence her conscience and Wilson wants her to awaken her subconscious. Rankin explains the impact of this choice: "In failing to speak, you become part of the crime." This seems to be a warning for the film's audience as well, an idea made even more bluntly in *War Comes to America* and in Welles's columns. Mary, who is the clearest stand-in for an audience in the film—she is even treated to a private screening—is made to learn this lesson the hard way. Instead of engaging her rationally or arresting Kindler for questioning (and from all appearances, Kindler seems ready to crack), Wilson hopes to arrive at justice through the use of an affective identification with victims of the Holocaust. Conveniently, and unbelievably, Wilson has no evidence to show Mary to help her see through Kindler's mask; instead he relies on psychological theories of traumatic confrontation and the insistence that Mary must deal with Kindler herself. In contrast to Kindler's hypnotic stares and emotional manipulation (he insists he killed Meinike because Mary's love made him "weak"), Wilson exposes her to physical danger and a hoped-for mental collapse.

In fact, both Rankin and Mary devolve into hysteria as the web of lies tightens around them. Mary's claustrophobia is embodied in her fight with a necklace that she finally rips from her throat, sending pearls flying everywhere. For Rankin, it is articulated in his obsession with fixing the town clock as he squirms in the quickly shrinking world of his ambition, having moved from a leading official in a conquering nation to a small town teacher. As his realm shrinks, however, he extends it psychologically inward and outward. It is as if "the German's dream world comes alive" and seeps into every corner of the town. A number of scenes are nightmarish in nature and style, and are clearly sourced as "Nazi" from the beginning of the film when Meinike is searching for Kindler. They feature a combination of expressionist lighting and unexpected camera angles, focusing on conveying the psychological elements crucial to the story—the hysteria and psychosis of Kindler's vision of the world.

A likely source for the heavily stylized acting and expressionist style in *The Stranger* is Sergei Eisenstein's *Ivan the Terrible*, which Welles wrote about enthusiastically in the May 29 "Orson Welles Today" column. In discussing the two 1944 biopics, *Wilson* and *Ivan the Terrible*, he describes what each does best (and worst), while overall favoring the Soviet style over Hollywood. Definite influences can be seen in *The Stranger*, especially in Kindler's dramatic gestures, popped eyes, and double takes, and in the use of shadows to map out the presence of power. Eisenstein himself was influenced by 1920s expressionism in his movie, and one can see the influence of expressionism (especially the horror genre) extensively in *The Stranger* as well. Rankin has the exaggerated facial expressions of a silent film star, and like Nosferatu and Dr. Caligari, he attempts to control the actions of an innocent person but is defeated in the end by his own weakness. In keeping with his aspirations to produce something like Eisenstein's effect, his villain is larger than life and unrealistic. It is an interesting approach, although it falls short in the film. Welles may be trying to convey the complex nature of Kindler's madness with the exaggerated gestures of expressionism, but Kindler comes across as confused and harried.

Welles's acting in *The Stranger* has been a source for much speculation and argument over the years. Critics have found Rankin/Kindler alternately sympathetic, not "even momentarily attractive," unbelievable but fun, "impossibly hammy," "one of the American cinema's few convincing portraits of a fascist," "operatic," and "just Mr. Welles, a young actor, doing a boyishly bad acting job in a role which is highly incredible."[23] Truffaut, one of his more sympathetic critics, wrote that Welles's acting is "distracted and melancholy" and "slightly hallucinated and quite unique."[24] This impression results because he generally ignores the other actors; his delivery is aimed at the space between actors and audience. As Truffaut notes: "He plays walking toward the camera but not on its axis, proceeding like a crab while looking the other way."[25] This style is theatrical, and Michael Anderegg has suggested it promotes a kind of "pedagogic tendency wedded to a Shakespearean approach to performance."[26] Citing Erving Goffman's theory of "disclosive compensation," he argues that Welles enacts his conflict about the character to show the audience that Kindler is evil and focus attention on American naïveté.[27]

While this argument seems theoretically sound, it isn't really borne out in the acting; the main thing Welles communicates is Kindler's distraction and caginess. At best, his role is stylized and melodramatic, and at worst, unintentionally funny. Welles said it best when describing *Ivan the Terrible*: "When the Russian method fails it is funny; it falls flat on its bottom, and we laugh."[28] Kindler does make us laugh a little, which unfortunately undermines his portrait of depravity. In the end, we never really understand how Kindler handled his astounding power in Germany or why or how he was drawn to genocide. As a man responsible for orchestrating mass murder, he seems surprisingly rattled when his plans are foiled. He continually says and does things that confirm his culpability, behaving like a man who can't quite believe the Third Reich was defeated and that he is, in fact, a married professor living in a small American town where the big cheese is gossipy Solomon Potter (Billy House), the town clerk. We see touches of the sadism he is famous for, but Welles's characterization ultimately undermines this, making it less real. He often comes across as more of a "baffled ogre" than a particular American nightmare about fascism.[29]

More successful is his contrast of expressionist and realist styles. When discussing *Ivan the Terrible* in his column, Welles made an important distinction: "When the American movie-maker becomes aware of a discrepancy between his film and the appearance of life, he corrects the difference in favor of 'realism.' This search for the direct and the literal produces some of our best effects. The Russians go out for the effect itself—and when they find what they're after—they manage moments of an exclamatory and resonant beauty on a level of eloquence to which our school cannot aspire."[30]

These different approaches are evident in *The Stranger*, and the film develops an interesting contrast between the two styles. Welles ended his column on Soviet versus Hollywood styles of filmmaking by asserting: "We have much to learn from each other."[31] This contrast is, in effect, the stylistic equivalent of the antifascist force that defeated German imperialism, liberated the concentration camps, and ended the war: the combined forces of the American and Soviet armies. As the aesthetic embodiment of the popular front, it seems appropriate for an exploration of *The Stranger*'s subject matter: how to convey the mind of a Nazi criminal, the reality of the Holocaust he is responsible for, and all within the context of a sleepy American town that knows almost nothing of these matters.

Welles approaches this challenge by establishing the two worlds as stylistically distinct, but then overlapping them as the film progresses. The town is depicted in a naturalist style, a "normal" everyday rational reality familiar to American audiences from their own experience and typical for Hollywood films. The expressionist style, on the other hand, defines a space that is briefly glimpsed in the scenes in Latin America—a film noir world of crime, espionage, and deception and a horror film world of monstrosity.[32] Over the course of the film, this expressionist style encroaches on and reframes the familiar landscape of the town as it comes into contact with the "strangers."

The world of the "strangers" is styled as emotive and irrational. It is conveyed visually, for example, by framing Meinike and Kindler with expressionist lighting and shadows, and obscuring Wilson with the smoke from his own pipe. The expressionist style is based on the distortion of reality and realistic elements, focusing on one thing with the exclusion of others for emotional effect, creating a visual structure for the film that is suitable for representing the distorting influence of the Holocaust. As a critic in *Hollywood Review* noted: "The camera, entrusted to the brilliance of Russell Metty, hunts, spies and records the significant details like the eye of a wise serpent. We're catapulted into the depths of the story with such force and precision that we find it startlingly real, in spite of its macabre and faintly grotesque qualities."[33] The looming shadows, odd camera angles, and exaggerated acting all conspire to emphasize the horror of a familiar world gone wrong.

This "otherness" is framed as a visual disturbance in another way as well. When Meinike goes to the photographer who knows where Kindler is, his face is captured in the lens of the camera and we are able to watch the two converse in the same space—shot and reaction shot in the same frame. Here the relation of Nazi power is exposed in its diminished space—evil revealed and contained within the lens of a camera. Mary is similarly framed. When we first see her, it is through a window; she is in a private domestic sphere that is wholly open to the rest of the world because she has nothing to hide. She is in the act of hanging curtains; however, she will soon frantically close them when she is keeping secrets about Rankin. Later in the film, when she makes up her mind to murder Rankin, her psychological conflict is framed in one shot; the darkness of her back—the deception she is putting behind her—contrasts with the image of her face brightly projected from inside a mirror.

The church clock, a central figure in the movie, also functions as an example of this dual nature.[34] It graphically and symbolically marks the contrast between a "Soviet" and "Hollywood" style. From the beginning, when we see the church featured on a picture postcard, the clock represents a kind of Hollywood version of American realism. It is the center of town and religious security, and in one shot, framed from inside the town store, it looks like an idyllic painting with Potter's signature as artist (his name is written on the window). Throughout the film, however, the clock tower opens to darker meanings and partakes of "moments of an exclamatory and resonant beauty" that have to do with the irrational under-belly of human psychology, murderous intent, and justice.[35] Inside it becomes a dark and empty pit, with a ladder precariously ascending as if from hell. The figures set in motion when Rankin fixes the clock enact heavenly justice: an angel, with simple features, chases a baroque devil with the changing hours, swords drawn in constant pursuit. They are roughly equivalent to the idea of Harper as a place of purity, and the strangers—Kindler, Meinike, and even Wilson—as dangerous and corrupting forces marked as monstrous by the use of shadows, smoke, and exaggerated features. Yet the point of bringing these opposing forces—and styles—together is to reveal the inherent strangeness of the vision of a "pure" American town, as well as reluctantly admitting the familiarity of the xenophobic Nazi vision of a purified racial unity.[36]

This transformation takes shape in a scene in which Mary is engulfed in Kindler's shadow stretching across the room. Waking up in alarm, she tells Rankin the dream as she smokes a cigarette, describing how Meinike's shadow is thrown across a deserted city square: "But when he moved away, Charles, the shadow stayed there behind him and spread out just like a carpet." Her tone here is perfect, capturing both fear and surprise. It is her first nightmare, she says, and she seems unable to interpret it. She does not understand, until late in the film, that the shadow is the prison of Kindler's psychosis, the distorted world he carries inside of him, which imprisons everyone around him. She also discovers later that this shadow includes the bodies of the Jewish dead turned into an anonymous mass by Meinike and his fellow Nazis. Mary can no longer assert: "In Harper there's nothing to be afraid of." Kindler is already transforming Mary into a person she cannot recognize; when he admits his crimes to her she accepts blame: "I'm already a part of it, because I'm a part of you." As Wilson's pursuit of Rankin begins to eliminate his chances of "passing" in the town, his tactics change from subtle manipulation to outright domination. He finally fixes the clock he has been working on laboriously and remarks: "The chimes have awakened Harper." While at first the townspeople are excited about the newly functioning clock, it soon becomes clear that it is slowly unhinging them; its insistent, regimented, and disruptive "voice" shatters the serenity of the townspeople in a literal manifestation of Kindler's plans.

What Kindler has done and plans to do is examined in detail in a scene that includes filmed documentation from the postliberation concentration camps. Allusions to the Holocaust are made verbally throughout *The Stranger*, but the real impact comes from the film footage, which visually documents the effects of genocide on the victims, the perpetrators, and the not-so-innocent bystanders. The reality portrayed by the Holocaust footage is inherently nightmarish and disturbing: humans have *become* distorted versions of themselves; humans have *distorted* versions of themselves. Although the material is inherently realistic and "unmediated," the reality is so beyond the norms of experience that psychologically it approaches expression that has more in common with surrealism. The radical distortion of humanity that was captured in documentary films and photographs during and after the war combined a detached scientific approach to the natural world with a surrealist focus on transforming received notions of perception, resulting in a documentary modernist style that also lent itself to the concerns of social justice.

In *The Stranger*, the inclusion of actual Holocaust footage is also situated in terms of the necessity of a responsible spectatorship. The movie not only stresses learning how to see—to witness—acts of atrocity, but it also advocates that action must follow. In addition, there is an insistence on the power of aesthetics as a communicative necessity and the process of traumatic identification and intervention in the reception of art. A similar narrative and stylistic technique had also been utilized in two films from 1936: Fritz Lang's *Fury* and Hitchcock's *Sabotage*. Both featured a film-within-a-film (a cartoon in *Sabotage* and documentary footage in *Fury*) in order to create a moment of pedagogical spectatorship in the pursuit of social justice. All three films insist on the emotional and aesthetic power of expressive images, but *The Stranger* does so overtly within a broader context of antifascism and global justice.

It is not certain who is responsible for including the footage of the concentration camps. According to Clinton Heylin, "scenes of concentration camp horrors" are mentioned in the script, which would point to Veiller or Huston, who were making war documentaries at the time.[37] Welles may also have been a source for the idea, or at least amenable to it, despite the fact that he later seemed ambivalent about the use of documentary footage or elements of the "real" in film. In conversation with Bogdanovich, his response to the assertion that "*The Stranger* was the first commercial film to use footage of Nazi concentration-camp atrocities" was conflicted: "Was it? I'm against that sort of thing in principle—exploiting real misery, agony, or death for purposes of entertainment. But in that case, I do think that, every time you can get the public to look at any footage of a concentration camp, under any excuse at all, it's a step forward. People just don't want to know that those things ever happened."[38] He further elaborates that during the filming of *Is Paris Burning?* he thought it was "intolerable" that a scene about "loading Jews into cattle cars in the station in Paris" was shot in the same station they had actually been shipped from during the war; he also found the use of German war veterans and survivors of concentration camps as extras morbid.[39] This aversion to the "real" is generally clear in his stylized approach to filmmaking and his penchant for melodrama and theatrical displays.

In 1945, however, he evidenced a different approach. In his May 7 *New York Post* column, "Orson Welles Today," he contrasted the excitement and luxury of a conference in San Francisco with the RKO Pathé newsreel footage of the liberated concentration camps:

> I think you'll be glad with me that it has been made so difficult to avoid those hideous sights. They are the proof of the nightmare. The heaped-up dead in evidence. The burdened ovens. The ingenious machinery for the pit of pain. The eyeball blinking in the open grave. The tawdry skeleton that turns out to be still alive, the survivor squatting among the cadavers, opening his toothless mouth,

naming the guilty without speech. . . . Patton and Bradley their eyes choked full of this . . . A huge black anger knocking heavy blows at the commander's hearth. You can feel the weight of it. It pushed the breath out of you so that you cannot shout or weep or vomit. You can only stare—. Then there are the Germans, the householders, the solid citizens. They are dressed like people. You recognize the costumes. . . . These creatures are less alive than the death they have been called to view and bury.[40]

The comparison Welles outlines here is clearly sketched in *The Stranger* as well. The film focuses on the necessity of insisting that people see, even if it means forcing them, a practice utilized in Germany after liberation. Welles notes: "In one camp there is a little house with something very terrible inside of it. The German people are made to enter and to look about them. Of course they can't be made to see." This image is screened for Mary in the movie. She is equally squeamish about the subject, and especially the bodies of the dead. But Welles's point is that she is the target audience: "If your stomach is weak you are the one they were after when they decided to show these films in the movie houses. It is figured that the people who don't like to see such things may not like to remember what they hear and read. Such things must be seen. Then it is hoped they will remember, always." As with the fruitful comparison between Hollywood and Soviet film styles, Welles asserts: "This summary of horror and the bright flashes of the Conference in San Francisco are well met on the same reel of celluloid. They have something to say to each other."[41]

It is clear that the visual power of the newsreels had struck him deeply and it is no surprise that clips from them would be included only a few months later in *The Stranger*. The juxtaposition of grim images of the war with the glamour of a blight-free environment filled with youth and health at the San Francisco conference becomes, in the film, the contrast between documentary footage of the Holocaust and a Hollywood version of a vigorous small town America. For Welles, the post-liberation film from the concentration camps marks the most important revelation of the war: that the death and decay witnessed in physical reality is the result of moral and spiritual decay, a cult of death that is obscured by the glamour that fascism projects. He writes: "No, you must not miss the newsreels. They make a point this week no man can miss: The war has strewn the world with corpses, none of them very nice to look at. The thought of death is never pretty but the newsreels testify to the fact of quite another sort of death, quite another level of decay. This is a putrefaction of the soul, a perfect spiritual garbage. For some years now we have been calling it Fascism. The stench is unendurable."[42] The inclusion of small bits of newsreel footage in the film cannot match the visual and emotional impact of the actual newsreels being shown all over the country; as Bosley Crowther noted in his review of the film, "The atom-bomb newsreels on the same bill are immeasurably more frightening."[43] But *The Stranger* is able to frame the viewing of such material in a specific and suggestive way; it gives the audience a model for how to view genocide and teaches through Mary's experience.

There are four concentration camp scenes included in the film; all were shot immediately following the war, and at least three of the four were from *Nazi Concentration Camps* (1945), directed by George Stevens. They were also being used as evidence during the Nuremberg Trials, which were taking place during filming of *The Stranger*. The juxtaposition between the documentation of real atrocity and the authenticity of a constructed Hollywood reality is oddly captured in the message broadcast at the beginning of the Nuremberg Trial footage: E. R. Kellogg, a Hollywood director of film effects and Navy Lieutenant, testifies that the Holocaust footage has not been retouched—Hollywood ironically verifies reality and marks it as legitimate.[44] Of the three clips included from the trials footage, two were taken from material filmed at Ohrdruf, wherein Patton and Eisenhower forced Nazis, who "deny knowledge" of the camps, to view their atrocities. The clips in *The Stranger* show labor bosses entering a wood shed where there is a lime pit filled with bodies, as well as the piles of dead bodies themselves. Another clip pictures a victim at Nordhausen, where the allied medical personnel were moving inmates for treatment in allied hospitals, although many were too malnourished to survive. The clip features a man being moved onto a stretcher who appears to be begging or praying as he looks at the camera. The other clip shown during the film offers up evidence of the mass destruction of humans that took place during the Holocaust: a view of a gas chamber.

What Mary fears most in *The Stranger* is dead bodies. The only body she knows about is Meinike's and she expects to see it: "Charles, will they make me look at the body? Because I couldn't do it." Mary, who has never seen a dead person, is instead subjected to a screening of documentary footage of concentration camp victims. She is the one witness for both sides of the war and the film snaps at her—asserting its evidence, its "documented reality" of a world of suffering Mary apparently knows nothing about. She is the ignorant American who is so incapable of reading someone's personality that she marries a Nazi. Wilson arranges the scene for a film audience of one—Mary is seated next to the film apparatus—but the screening (and perhaps the interrogation as well) is aimed at the larger audience of *The Stranger*. The use of the documentary footage asserts the power of history over the beauty of the image, modeling a way of representing suffering as a visual intervention rather than a voyeuristic pleasure (a practice Theodor Adorno had warned against).[45] Hardly fascinated, Mary watches unwillingly and with significant

The Stranger, 1946. Directed by Orson Welles.

consequences. Half the time, Mary's reactions are framed in the shot as she views the documentary footage from the Holocaust, and the other half we see what she sees—the screen, or Wilson, or sometimes Wilson standing in front of the screen. Wilson narrates what is happening in the footage—detailing the gruesome details, and we see the faint play of the newsreel reflected onto Mary's face as it is imprinted into her thoughts and emotions.

At the moment that she sees a mass grave of Jews at a concentration camp—unidentified bodies—Wilson says: "It's my job to bring escaped Nazis to justice. It's that job that brought me to Harper." Mary begins to make a connection and turns to Wilson, saying: "Well, surely you don't think . . . I've never so much as even seen a Nazi." He responds: "Well, you might without your realizing it. They look like other people, and act like other people, when it's to their benefit." She gazes again at the film, her face moving toward it in curiosity and shock, and the camera cuts from her shining face to Wilson's more shadowed one as he references the gas chamber on the screen: "A gas chamber, Mrs. Rankin. The candidates were first given hot showers so that their pores would be open and the gas would act that much more quickly." As she reacts in horror, he walks in front of her to stand in front of the screen: "And this is a lime pit, in which hundreds of men, women, and children were buried alive." While he stands in front of the screen, the bodies of the dead are projected onto his face, and Mary asks, "Why do you want me to look at these horrors?" Wilson moves toward the projector, blocking it, and then dramatically declares: "All this you're seeing, it's all the product of one mind. The mind of a man named . . . Franz Kindler." In order to drive home his point he jerks the projector toward Mary while saying Kindler's name and his face is bathed in light as she jumps back.

Wilson elaborates, telling Mary that Kindler was the most brilliant of the younger minds in the Nazi party, pinpointing him as directly responsible for the slaughter she is witnessing on the screen: "It was Kindler who conceived the theory of genocide." He continues with the almost bizarre assertion that Kindler had managed to remain publicly invisible: "Unlike Goebbels, Himmler, and the rest of them, Kindler had a passion for anonymity. The newspapers carried no picture of him. And just before he disappeared he destroyed every evidence that might link him with this past, down to the last fingerprint." Wilson then makes the connection Mary has been striving to avoid: "There's no clue to the identity of Franz Kindler, expect one little thing. He has a hobby that almost amounts to a mania: clocks." He pauses as they watch a man helped onto a stretcher on screen. Wilson then tells her about releasing Meinike, referring to him as "an obscenity on the face of the earth. The stench of burning flesh was in his clothes." Mary, still watching the film, looks desperate as Wilson intones his *coup de grâce*: "Now in all the world there is only one person who can identify Franz Kindler. That person is the one who knows, knows definitely, who Meinike came to Harper to see." With this remark, the film reel ends and suddenly snaps in Mary's ear: you you you. She leaps up, shouting: "My Charles is not a Nazi!" Despite Wilson's efforts, she refuses to admit that Meinike visited her, insisting: "You can't involve me in a lie. That's all it is, is a lie." Her denial is not directed at the Holocaust itself, per se, but certainly some of her anxiety in the scene is sourced in the overwhelming nature of what she has just seen. She has made an affective identification with what she has seen; it has become a part of her just as Rankin has, and the two cannot coexist in her self.

Mary leaves the house hysterically laughing and gasping, and her father, seeming to understand the source of her pain, insists that she need not feel the unity or loyalty that marriage brings with it if she has unknowingly married a criminal. But she continues to sob: "He's good. He's good." With this cry she is asserting her own lost innocence and moral purity as well. The struggle Mary has with her sub-conscious is not only in her acceptance of what Rankin/Kindler is and has done but also in her own responsibility for what happens to him. In his subsequent discussion with Adam Longstreet, Wilson asserts that even though he can disprove Rankin's identity, he needs to do more, to prove that he's Kindler. He insists that this can only happen through Mary's identification of Meinike, making Mary a symbolic scapegoat. He says to Adam: "He may kill her. You're shocked at my cold-bloodedness. . . . Naturally we'll try to prevent murder being done." The judge looks pained but agrees to continue pushing Mary toward a breakdown. At this moment, the clock begins chiming again after decades of silence: the fight is on. Angel and devil chase each other around the clock tower and Mary's conscious, conscience, and subconscious battle for supremacy over her will. Typically (as an American) unwilling to face the reality of the war, these images become "buried alive" in her unconscious, where they work to unmask the figure of the tyrant who is blocking them—Rankin.

Wilson has faith in Mary's "will to truth" as her greatest *ally*. He tells Adam: "We have one ally, her subconscious. It knows what the truth is and is struggling to be heard." In a sense, her subconscious is working to open her eyes and awaken her to social justice, just as America's future allies were before America entered the war. Newsreels and other documentary films functioned in the same way as the newsreel screened for Mary: they asserted a reality that demanded an engaged response, and that wore away at the widespread denial and ignorance about what was happening in concentration camps in Europe. The denial that existed in close proximity to the camps themselves is also invoked in the film. Harper townsfolk know nothing about Rankin's real identity, and though they have a sense of sinister events, they don't take them seriously. One woman jokes at Mary's dinner party:

"The murderer's a fiend, who'll turn out to be a highly respected member of the community. He's too intelligent to do away with residents of Harper. . . . They'd be missed, so he picks tramps and the like. There may well be ten . . . or a dozen . . . graves out there in the woods." The woods near Harper, as a site for secret murders, echoes the sinister operation of a concentration camp such as Buchenwald, located in the woods near Weimar, Germany. The townspeople of Weimar were either honestly or willfully ignorant of what was happening to the "non-residents" so close to them. Newsreel footage included in *The Stranger* documents the reactions of townspeople forced to visit the camps after liberation; their reactions enact the same horror, denial, and hysteria modeled by Mary in the film.

Rankin's greatest ally, on the other hand, is that same silence, denial, and ignorance—the will to believe that evil does not exist. He tells Mary, "We're quite safe if you say nothing." She dramatically replies, "They can torture me and I won't tell them anything!" But in fact they have already tortured her in a way, with exposure to the knowledge of genocide and her complicit support of the man who masterminded its implementation. She ultimately keeps her word to Rankin; she doesn't *say* anything to anybody about his guilt. But she does inadvertently ruin his attempt to murder her, alerting Wilson to his plan.[46] Not that she needs much help at this point. Rankin seems to be undergoing his own struggle with his subconscious: he writes up an incriminating list of what he's going to do and draws a swastika (backward) on the notepad by the phone in Potter's shop. This might merely be melodrama, but he also unnecessarily traps himself in the clock tower instead of leaving town when he knows the game is up. Kindler is not much of a villain by the end of the film, certainly not the kind of man who orchestrated the death of millions. When he comes home expecting Mary to be dead and sees her in the living room, his eyes practically pop out of his head. He is a defeated man at this point, mechanical like the clock. He also suddenly develops moral scruples, saying about Noah, "If he dies, his blood will be on your hands!" Their roles are reversed and Mary suddenly develops a backbone, snarling his name, "Franz Kindler!" while handing him a poker from the fireplace and ordering him: "When you kill me don't put your hands on me!"

The scene is cut short by the entrance of Wilson and Noah, and Kindler is forced to hole up in the clock tower, the last bastion for his Nazi dream world. It is here that justice, not tragedy, reigns. In a reversal of Nazi policy and a metaphorical allusion to the words on Buchenwald's gate—*Jedem das Seine* ("to each his own")—Kindler gets what he deserves. In the film, the brunt of the responsibility has been directed toward Mary, and so it is she who must lose her political innocence and face Kindler in the end. Her subconscious finally awakened, she says, "I came to kill you." Although Kindler insists it is she who will die, he is quickly outnumbered as Wilson appears and reports to him: "The citizens of Harper have come after you. The plain little ordinary people. . . . You can't fool them anymore. . . . There's no escape." Trapped in his clock tower, Kindler first pleads for clemency and then tries to escape. It is true that the townsfolk have massed under the clock, a populist image, but it is Mary who enacts the revenge; grabbing the gun, she shoots wildly, breaking the clock's mechanism and hitting Rankin in the arm. Detective Wilson, finally ready to take control, demands the gun and shoots, but there are no more bullets. It is Mary's "will to truth" that triumphs, just as Kindler's "will to power" has made him weak. Although injured by Mary, Rankin is ultimately killed by the machinery he set into motion; pierced by the sword of the clock's angel, he falls to his death.

Although it is the angel that triumphs on the clock, it is the melodramatic expressionist style that dominates the final scene. Welles's ending features a spectacular death: an evil man is skewered on the sword of an angel, then plunges to his death in front of a crowd of people. As he later admitted, the ending of the film is "Pure Dick Tracy. I had to fight for it. Everybody felt, 'Well, it's bad taste and Orson's going too far,' but I wanted a straight comic-strip finish."[47] This choice was perhaps based on his belief that a larger-than-life "socko finish" was missing from the war itself.[48] He wrote in his May 8 column: "Act three draws to its end and we, the spectators, sit watching and waiting to see the villain die before our appreciative eyes. But something's lacking. He's not exciting in the same high and spectacular style that marked his entrance. There's a touch of Wagner, maybe— but no dramatic lighting, no mighty mob scene. The showmanship employed in selling Fascism to a buyer's market is missing. In violation of all sound dramatic construction, the death scene is being played off-stage."[49] He felt that the end of the war required something that would resonate dramatically, creating catharsis: "In a sense this poor staging is responsible for the odd and almost empty feeling you may have had about the war's conclusion in the west. . . . We feel curiously cheated—not by the events themselves, but by the queer disorder of the sequence."[50] Welles did achieve a "socko finish" in *The Stranger*. Yet this dramatic approach didn't really tell the truth about fascism as the documentary footage did. A feeling of emptiness and lack of drama were more to the point. "The truth doesn't always obey the rules of melodrama," as Welles also noted.[51]

The end of the film brings the fight between good and evil to a close. It's "V-day in Harper," Wilson says. The clock has once again been stopped. The clock tower is the appropriate place for the action to climax in the film. It has functioned as a liminal demarcation zone, much as the clock tower at Buchenwald marked the transition between the world of small-town normality in Weimar—a town famous for its contribution to the philosophy of rationality—and a world of nightmarish reversal, a ghoulish distortion of rationality, measured out by the regular chiming of the clock. The Buchenwald clock was famously stopped at the time of the allied liberation, and it has remained stopped. The clock in *The Stranger* represents a reversal of this demarcation of the end of the war and the Holocaust; it begins to chime again when Wilson reveals Rankin's real identity to Mary and is silenced with Kindler's death. Less dramatically, Wilson deflates this serious note by refusing to climb down the ladder and loudly complaining about his injuries as he lights his pipe, a conquering hero with smoke curling devilishly around his head. His final words to Mary, who remains off camera—"Goodnight, Mary. Pleasant dreams"—are so abrupt they function as irony. Wilson's breezy enjoyment of his success is laughable. It is quite clear that Mary will *not* have pleasant dreams; the fascist menace has been destroyed in the person of Kindler, but within her mind its presence remains, as it does in the film in the form of the documentary footage, which insists on a continued vigilance.

Featuring a dialectic between the empirical and rational documentation of film and the surreal and irrational workings of the human psyche, *The Stranger* manifests the call to social justice within a single interlocking moment of film spectatorship within the movie. Not only does it dramatize the problem of American complicity with fascism, but it also instructs the audience on how to engage with the documentation of fascist atrocity. It does so by focusing on individual experience and responsibility, specifically in the character of Mary, an innocent individual caught within the machinations of a violent public sphere. Yet by focusing in so closely, it tends to make of renascent fascism something more manageable and contained—and exciting—than it really was; we see, after all, only snippets of the atrocities filmed so thoroughly after the war. One of the greatest challenges of representing a genocide, particularly the Holocaust, involves encompassing its complex impact of a multitude of individuals. *The Stranger* successfully posits a need for social justice within American borders and even a model for how to embrace responsibility; but it leaves us with the question of how to accurately represent, in film, the complex historical, political, and psychological matrix of a nation's relation to social justice and to the enormity of genocide.

NOTES

1. See, for example, Bazin, Bitsch, and Domarchi, "Interview with Orson Welles," 74. See also Bogdanovich, *The Cinema of Orson Welles*, 7.

2. *The Stranger* grossed $3.216 million over its filming costs of $1.034 million. See Thomson, *Rosebud*, 268.

3. Megahey, "Interview from *The Orson Welles Story*," 189.

4. Bazin, Bitsch, and Domarchi, "Interview with Orson Welles," 74.

5. Including Brady, *Orson Welles*, 380; Naremore, *The Magic World of Orson Welles*, 123–24; Truffaut, foreword to *Orson Welles: A Critical View*, 14; and Higham, *Orson Welles*, 226. Truffaut is probably the first to have pointed this out. Naremore goes so far as to suggest that uncredited screenwriter John Huston and producer Sam Spiegel lifted scenes straight out of the film, although he seems to be confusing the ending of *Shadow of a Doubt* (1943) (which takes place on a moving train) with *Vertigo* (1958) (atop a bell tower), which in fact echoes the ending of *The Stranger*, with the body falling from a clock tower.

6. Bazin, Bitsch, and Domarchi, "Interview with Orson Welles," 74.

7. The film actually has elements of different genres, including horror and film noir in addition to the thriller.

8. Cowie, *The Cinema of Orson Welles*, 85.

9. Bazin, Bitsch, and Domarchi, "Interview with Orson Welles," 74.

10. Bogdanovich and Rosenbaum, *This Is Orson Welles*, 187.

11. Ibid., 186, 189.

12. "Orson Welles Plans Anti-Fascism Tour," 7. Welles's "The Nature of the Enemy" speech toured five cities in January and February 1944 on a "platform of anti-Fascism."

13. Welles, "Survival of Fascism."

14. Welles, "To Be Born Free."

15. Ibid.

16. Hopper, "Orson Reveals Life Goal."

17. Ibid. Welles attended the Todd School in Illinois as a youth. He makes numerous subtle references to it in *The Stranger*.

18. Ibid.

19. Leaming, *Orson Welles*, 317.

20. *War Comes to America* (Capra and Litvak, 1945).

21. This theory of female psychological susceptibility was popular in the nineteenth century. See, for example, *La psychologie des foules* in Le Bon, *The Crowd*, 15–44.

22. This is a theme explored in a number of movies, including *Notorious* (1946), *Hiroshima, mon amour* (1959), and *Ryan's Daughter* (1970).

23. See Bogdanovich and Rosenbaum, *This Is Orson Welles*, 7; Anderegg, *Orson Welles, Shakespeare, and Popular Culture*, 148; Scheuer, "Cinematic Tricks Aid 'Stranger'"; McBride, *Orson Welles, Actor and Director*, 45–46; Higham, *Films of Orson Welles*, 108; Callow, *Orson Welles*, 2:270; and Crowther, "The Stranger," 18, respectively.

24. Truffaut, foreword to *Orson Welles*, 16. Of course, this element of his acting may also have been a result of the amphetamine injections he was receiving daily at the time to lose weight (Callow, *Orson Welles*, 2:269).

25. Truffaut, foreword to *Orson Welles*, 16.

26. Anderegg, *Orson Welles, Shakespeare, and Popular Culture*, 148.

27. Ibid.

28. Welles, "Orson Welles Today," *New York Post*, May 29, 1945, 12.

29. Callow, *Orson Welles*, 2:274.

30. Welles, "Orson Welles Today," May 29, 1945, 12.

31. Ibid.

32. Welles claimed he shot a much longer sequence that was cut by Nims; none of this footage is extant, although the script indicates it would have been a more thorough rendering of the morally depraved Nazi "dream world," including more dead bodies.

33. "The Stranger," *Hollywood Review*, May 21, 1946, 12.

34. The clock had been in the Los Angeles County Museum and Welles had it moved and reconstructed on the lot. Higham, *Films of Orson Welles*, 100.

35. Welles, "Orson Welles Today," May 29, 1945, 12.

36. There is an interesting potential for the critique of an invisible American fascism (racism) in the film, although it is not made explicit and is possibly coincidental: the first names of the key characters are all of Jewish origin: Adam, Noah, and Mary Longstreet, their servant Sara, and Solomon Potter. Their dog, Red, even has the name of a political outsider.

37. Heylin, *Despite the System*, 163.

38. Bogdanovich, *The Cinema of Orson Welles*, 189.

39. Ibid.

40. Welles, "Orson Welles Today," *New York Post*, May 7, 1945, 10.

41. Ibid.

42. Ibid.

43. Crowther, "The Stranger," 18.

44. Kellogg, "Testimony," 2:433.

45. Adorno writes: "The so-called artistic representation of the sheer physical pain of people beaten to the ground by rifle-butts contains, however remotely, the power to elicit enjoyment out of it. The moral of this art, not to forget for a single instant, slithers into the abyss of its opposite." Adorno, "Commitment," 189.

46. In this, Mary's greatest ally is Sara (Martha Wentworth), her servant, who actively intervenes to keep her safe at home. When Mary accuses her of fussing, Sara promptly falls to the floor and screams: "My heart! I can't breathe. The pain . . . No, Miss Mary, please don't leave me. Maybe I'm dying!" Her fake heart attack, as ridiculous (and funny) as it is, saves Mary. One wonders if a different investigator would also have taken a more sympathetic approach: Welles stated in a number of interviews that he wanted to cast Agnes Moorehead in the role of the investigator, and certainly this ingenuous casting could have changed the dynamics of the plot in interesting ways.

47. Bogdanovich, *The Cinema of Orson Welles*, 189–90.

48. Welles, "Orson Welles Today," *New York Post*, May 8, 1945, 10.

49. Ibid.

50. Ibid.

51. Ibid.

3 Remembering Revolution after Ruin and Genocide

Recent Chilean Documentary Films and the Writing of History

MICHAEL J. LAZZARA

Historizar es una forma de unir lo que fue con lo que es . . .

[Historcizing is a way of uniting what was with what is . . .]

PILAR CALVEIRO

Quotidian definitions of *genocide* tend to emphasize numbers or statistics as the primary methodology for determining whether genocide occurred in a given context. If the number of dead strikes us as large—so the logic goes—then the extermination of an ethnic, racial, religious, or political group amounts to genocide; if the number strikes us as small, then we ask whether a given tragedy has truly reached "genocidal proportions." This numbers argument, I would like to argue from the outset, is dangerous and inaccurate. In fact, it has been used repeatedly in post-Pinochet Chile to defend the extermination of leftist revolutionary opposition by pro-dictatorship factions that were first interested in instituting a neoliberal counterrevolution and later in upholding neoliberalism as immovable and unquestionable. How many times have we heard that over 30,000 people disappeared in Argentina, while in Chile it "only" took

3,000 murders to achieve the country's so-called economic miracle? It goes without saying that such utilitarian arguments do not hold sway. Not only are they flawed in their logic, but they are also morally and ethically reprehensible.

Let's be clear, then. What happened in Chile between 1973 and 1990 *was* genocide.[1] Scholars have well established that Augusto Pinochet and his henchmen sought to eliminate all political and ideological opposition in calculated and premeditated ways. This elimination took place in waves. In the first wave, which occurred between late 1973 and 1974, the regime focused on eliminating the Movimiento de Izquierda Revolucionaria (MIR), the most radical leftist group considered by Pinochet to be public enemy number one. In waves two and three, targeted repression focused on the Communist Party and the Socialist Party in 1975 and 1976, respectively. Beyond these killings, often euphemistically referred to as "forced disappearances," the 2004 *Valech Report* established that over 30,000 people were tortured as part of Pinochet's genocidal state policy. Additionally, tens of thousands went into voluntary or involuntary exile.

These are facts. But if we leave our definition of genocide there, we risk missing a key point: genocide is more than just mass killing. It includes moral debasement and attacks on art, cultural practices, politics, language, and identity. Its implementation is highly structured and bureaucratic. The media, technology, official rhetoric, institutions, and civil society: all of these entities are essential for implementing genocides of the type that occurred in Chile. In that sense, as Keith Watenpaugh has noted, "genocide is modern in both its intention and its function."[2] Perhaps one might say that it is the major theme of twentieth-century modernity: in the name of preserving economic and political power, governments exterminate sectors of the population deemed undesirable or detrimental to the healthy functioning of the body politic. The years of dictatorship and the years that followed in Chile have undeniably proven that the genocide of 1973 to 1990 had a traumatic, deep, and lasting impact on the social body.

At the same time, Chile's genocide must be seen as part of a larger history—a larger neoliberal backlash that occurred in Latin America from the 1960s through the 1990s, and that left about half a million people dead and countless others traumatized. This backlash, of course, is linked to broader histories of colonialism, economic and cultural imperialism, and particularly to cold war politics. The 1960s and 1970s were the years in which the utopian vision of a more just society, a society founded in socialist ideals, went head to head with traditional oligarchic power that sought to preserve its chokehold on society and to advance the interests of capitalist ideology. The political, economic, and personal fallout of that historical confrontation has been profound and has generated responses by artists, intellectuals, and common citizens still struggling to make sense of the past amid a torrent of competing, conflicting, and often whitewashed memory narratives. This is not the place to recap all that has been said about the complexities of narrative and memory in post-dictatorship Latin America.

Instead, I would like to focus on a very specific question: How is Chile's revolutionary past being remembered and represented in the present by documentary filmmakers whose lives have been marked by a history of genocide and displacement? My hypothesis is that the memory of Chile's (and by extension Latin America's) revolutionary moment is difficult to capture and assess fully in present cultural production precisely because our vision of that past—in this case the Popular Unity period and Salvador Allende's "peaceful road to socialism"—is inseparable from the trauma, nostalgia, melancholy, and subjective crises that ensued from the military dictatorships' genocidal practices. What the 1960s and 1970s mean today (or if they can still have meaning at all) comes across in these filmmakers' works as a kind of generational crisis par excellence with no easy answers. In many ways, both in terms of form and content, these documentary films point to subjectivities at a crossroads that are still working through the traumas associated with "defeat" and the "end" of the revolutionary moment. Many former militant filmmakers are now getting older and are making films that are clearly marked by a sense of generational disillusionment. Artists like Patricio Guzmán or Carmen Castillo wonder *on film* whether their past struggles to change society were too radical, or if they can still have relevance in a suffocating neoliberal context with which they cannot identify.

Yet despite the profundity of their crises and disillusionment, these films also channel a narrative desire that I find hopeful. The filmmakers want to believe that social or political change (that is, change inspired by past revolutionary politics and rooted in the rebellious histories of the 1960s and 1970s) can still occur—although it is most likely to occur, when it does, in ways that aren't grandiose or transcendental and that germinate slowly from the grassroots level. Put another way, these filmmakers see the *venceremos* (we will overcome) of Allende's time resonating with new generations who long to have their voices heard, in new social movements, or perhaps in the recent "left turn" that has taken root in many parts of Latin America.[3]

In the Southern Cone, documentary film has been a key medium through which the revolutionary moment has been revisited. While post-dictatorial films on the revolutionary era strive to communicate "truths" about that time, most of the films I have seen reveal a deeper "truth" about the narrative tensions that arise when trying to capture a historical moment from a present marked by exile, survival, trauma, defeat, and the sanitizing language of consensus. More than historical analyses, these films are about memory and subjectivity; they are about the difficulty of writing history from ruins. In this chapter, I will focus on three productions from the Chilean filmic "archive" on militancy: two recent "personal documentaries" (Patricio Guzmán's *Salvador Allende* and Carmen Castillo's *Calle Santa Fe*) and a "militant" film from the early 1970s (Miguel Littín's *Compañero presidente*), which began circulating again in Chile in 2008. I am interested in examining the differing *narrative impulses* at work in these films. My wager is that, taken together, they can open a reflection on how the past is being written *from* the present and *in* the present. That is, taken together they can show how Chilean filmmakers of the revolutionary generation and Chilean society as a whole are using film as a medium through which to *struggle* with the memory of the revolutionary past and to ask important questions about the repercussions that the past can have for politics in the present. What might Allende mean today, particularly in a neoliberal context in which militancy remains stigmatized as an "error" or a "failed" utopian project?

Patricio Guzmán's *Salvador Allende* (2004): Between Restorative and Reflective Nostalgia

In one of the most lucid books I have read about Latin America's revolutionary period, *Política y/o violencia: Una aproximación a la guerrilla de los años 70* (Politics and/or Violence: An Approach to the Guerrilla Movements of the 1970s), Pilar Calveiro, speaking about the Argentine context, critically responds to certain "heroic" narratives of militancy that tend to immortalize or romanticize the past as utopia or turn militants and their leaders into untouchable, sacred icons.[4] Such heroic narratives, she argues, "impede analysis" of the complex local and global factors that led to the rise of revolutions and to their subsequent extermination by military dictatorships. Mired in personal traumas and dramas, these narratives, in many cases, not only fail to historicize the rise of revolutionary movements, but they also strive to restore a reassuring narrative harmony or "closure" to the post-traumatic subject who seeks to make sense of the past. They are narratives that risk eclipsing our view of history's contradictions and that fail to give us a critical understanding of who the militants were (why they thought as they did, or what they did or didn't do to bring about the violence that ultimately destroyed them).[5] Calveiro notes that "when the memory of a past whose logic was eminently political is constructed as an individual, private memory, it recovers [the personal aspect of past experience] but betrays, at least in part, the political sense of what that moment was."[6] Mindful that no narrative construction ever exhausts the complexities of experience, one might ask, then: How can the revolutionary moment be narrated in ways that, on one hand, do not ignore its historical complexities, and on the other, do not discard as inconsequential the challenges of representing the past from a post-traumatic position? In other words, how can *historicity* and deep analysis be conjugated with the particular concerns of post-traumatic subjectivity and the potential productivity of revisiting that past for imagining dissent in the present?

In the last few years, debates around these issues have been taking place among Latin American and Latin Americanist intellectuals from both sides of the North/ South divide. Particularly noteworthy is a recent article by John Beverley in which he argues that certain prominent intellectuals (namely Beatriz Sarlo, David Stoll, Elizabeth Burgos, and others) emblematize a kind of "paradigm of disillusion with the armed struggle."[7] In the case of Sarlo, Beverley previously argued—probably exaggeratedly so—that she emblematizes a kind of "neoconservative turn" in Latin American literary and cultural criticism.[8]

As Beverley notes, a common narrative has come to characterize the revolutionary generation to which both he and the previously mentioned intellectuals belong— a generation that at one time supported armed struggle as a viable and necessary method of liberation for societies plagued by colonial and economic imperialism: "According to this narrative, the illusion of the revolutionary transformation of society that was the inspiration for armed struggle was our romantic adolescence, but also one prone to excess, error, irresponsibility, and moral anarchy. By contrast, our biological and biographical maturity, represented by our role and our responsibilities as parents and professionals, corresponds to the hegemony of neoliberalism in the eighties and nineties."[9] Beverley is uncomfortable with any cultural narrative that would write off the very real political struggles of the 1960s and 1970s—despite their utopian impulse—as a mere youthful adventure that should be viewed today as a failure or an error. Such narratives, in Beverley's opinion, reflect both a melancholy and a residual guilt in many former revolutionary thinkers that has not been worked through sufficiently.

Although Beverley's article reflects that he shares the same generational crisis as Sarlo and others who have disavowed armed struggle in their public discourse, he holds firm to the idea that even if one does not espouse taking up arms to change society today, one must recognize that relegating the armed struggles of the 1960s and 1970s to the dustbin of history fails to acknowledge that the "heritage of armed struggle" continues to have an enormous impact on the present.[10] This heritage can be seen today in social movements and leftist governments in many Latin American countries.[11] Therefore, rather than understanding neoliberalism as a finality—as the end of history—Beverley, advocating for a wider historical lens, chooses to see neoliberalism as a "blockage" to revolutionary change. He admonishes that revolutionary struggles can still emerge, even in neoliberal times, but notes that they will inevitably take new and unexpected forms. (In the case of Chile, one might mention the student protests of the *pingüinos* or the sustained struggles of the Mapuche nation, which at times has accepted violence as a necessary means to assert its rights to autonomy in the face of harsh and often violent state repression.) At stake, I think, is the question of restoring a sense of futurity to the present, which, in the opinion of Christopher Connery, was a crucial part of the structure of feeling of the 1960s that our neoliberal present has sought to quell.[12]

Patricio Guzmán's 2004 documentary, *Salvador Allende*, dramatizes the tensions that stem from the differential relationship between an effervescent revolutionary past and a present in ruins—a present shot through with nostalgia, doubt, pain, questions, and feelings of failure. Far removed from the aesthetic of his epic film, *La batalla de Chile* (The Battle of Chile, 1975–79), at more than thirty years' distance from the original experience, *history in the making* (unpredictable, full of irreconcilable viewpoints, twists, and turns) has given way to subjective reflection and an obsession with the unrecoverable.[13] The film's title, *Salvador Allende*, is deceptive insofar as it seems to announce a documentary that will lay out the intricacies of a biography or perhaps engage in a deep analysis of a political life and its relevance for a nation. Instead, what the viewer finds is a film about Guzmán himself, about how the artist's own life was marked by Allende such that it will remain forever entwined with the fallen president's revolutionary project and untimely death. On one hand, the film is a nostalgic vindication of Allende's spirit and legacy, but on the other hand—and perhaps even more important—it is a vehicle through which Guzmán nurses and works through his own traumas and shattered dreams.

Viewers will remember that *Chile: La memoria obstinada* (Chile: Obstinate Memory, 1997) opens with an image of the bombing of La Moneda, the same image with which *La batalla de Chile* begins. Readers will recall that on September 11, 1973, hawker hunter planes bombed Chile's presidential palace from the air, destroying the foremost symbol of Chile's democratic tradition and setting into motion a bloody military coup; democratically elected Socialist President Salvador Allende committed suicide inside the palace on that same fateful day. Curiously, in *Salvador Allende*, Guzmán returns—obsessively—to this original traumatic moment, the bombing of La Moneda, with one suggestive particularity: just as the bombing and the burning appear on screen, all sound ceases. The film goes completely silent, as the march of history is shattered. The symbolism is obvious: La Moneda in flames represents the ruin of politics as it was practiced until 1973, the ruin of democracy, of history, and of popular power. Consequently, the silent image of the catastrophe—which recurs several times in the latter half of Guzmán's film—functions as a palimpsest over which to elaborate sound, over which to elaborate a narrative that can work through a traumatized memory. In effect, the traumatic image par excellence—La Moneda in flames—becomes the moment

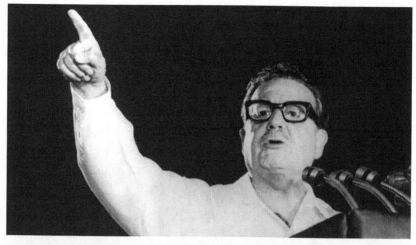

Salvador Allende, 2004. Directed by Patricio Guzmán.

with which every subsequent moment in Guzmán's life (and filmic trajectory) must dialogue.

Ruins, then, are the narrative motor that sets Guzmán's entire film in motion. The documentary's opening sequence reduces Allende to *remains*, to a series of objects left behind that metonymically refer us to a lost history and an absent body. A wallet, a presidential sash, an eyeglass case bearing the initials S. A. G., Allende's official ID card from the Socialist Party: these are the remnants of Allende that silently haunt the present (and Guzmán). The only ruin on public display is a fragment of Allende's eyeglasses: one shattered lens and a broken earpiece. The damaged eyeglass reminds us of Allende's broken and tarnished public image, and the lens—opaque, cracked, dotted with black spots that impede vision—symbolizes the filmic (and subjective) lens through which the artist will gaze at the past, thirty years removed from Popular Unity and the dictatorship. Like the opaque lens, memory is clouded and unclear, fragmented and displaced in time and space. Its fervent desire is to reconnect with what has been irrevocably lost.

Following the opening credits, Guzmán cuts to images of Santiago today: bustling traffic, trucks, commerce (evocative of neoliberalism), and focuses on a wall from which a small bit of paint has chipped away. Facing this wall covered by a metaphorical layer of forgetfulness, Guzmán remembers that on the very same wall the Ramona Parra Brigade once painted a mural to honor Allende. As Guzmán's hand picks and scratches away at the paint, memory is shown to be a laborious process that is always jagged, fragmentary, and partial: a writing on ruins. It is precisely in this moment of chipping away toward the past that Guzmán frames the film with his subjective "I": "The appearance of memory is neither comfortable nor voluntary. It always jolts you. Salvador Allende marked my life. I would not be who I am today if he had not embodied the utopia of a freer, more just world that seized my country in those times [1970–73]. I was there, an actor and a filmmaker. The past does not pass. It vibrates and moves in accordance with the turns of my own life. Here I am in the same place where thirty years ago a simple wall near the airport said goodbye to me."

Not only does Guzmán's own personal testimony permeate the film, but many of his interviewees function as mouthpieces for statements that could have easily come from him. Ema Malig, for example, a painter who worked for Allende's campaign when she was ten years old, sits in front of a map that she painted and comments on the phenomenon of exile: "I see exile as a puzzle, as a land that has been transformed into small islands where each individual lives harboring his own landscapes and memories. I don't see exile as a huge land that we all inhabit. I think, instead, it is quite intimate." Inscribed on the map in large letters are the words ERRANCIA (errancy), DESTIERRO (exile), and NAUFRAGIO (shipwreck). The last word elliptically cites the commentary of Guzmán's college friend, Professor Ernesto Malbrán, who, at the end of *Chile: La memoria obstinada*, enthusiastically claimed that the "shipwreck" of Popular Unity would only be a momentary derailment and that the *pueblo* would rise again like a phoenix from the ashes.

Transposed into Guzmán's most recent film, the floating signifier *naufragio* is divested of any optimistic spin and comes to connote little more than the melancholy of defeat. It brings into relief each individual's need to create a mental refuge of memory, a personal utopia in which to dwell. In a sense, Guzmán's whole film is a manifestation of his own inner utopia—a space where Allende lives on, untainted and victorious, surrounded by echoes of the Canción Popular movement. It is a utopia full of snapshots, anecdotes, and sound bites, an intimate, fragmented, personal archive. It is a utopia populated by memories and feelings that, in large part, lack an analytical character. A castaway in his homeland, Guzmán prefers to focus on the intimate, happy aspects of his youth: Chile's landscape and natural beauty, the music of Violeta Parra, the experience of solidarity and revolution, and his political father Allende: "el Chicho, as we called him."

One particularity of exile is that it is often lived as a freezing in time. Even though life continues in the country from which the individual was cast out, the *patria* is harbored mentally as a snapshot of the past. In Guzmán's case, this snapshot is full of painful, melancholic moments, but also of beautiful moments that he prefers to emphasize. Moreover, the experience of feeling out of place when one returns to the lost homeland constitutes a second loss insofar as the exile finds that the nation today does not "correspond to the image constructed in memory."[14] This unresolved rift between past and present leaves Guzmán lingering in the *non-place* of exile, inclined to obsess over ruins as the only material vestiges that can facilitate his connection to an anterior utopian moment.

Consequently, the motif of physical ruins appears throughout *Salvador Allende* as a strategy for bringing the past to bear on the present. Late in the film, after constructing his intimate portrait of Allende "the man," Guzmán revisits the ruins motif via the image of a junkyard full of Allende's abandoned buses. The rusted hollow buses inspire Guzmán to interrogate the entire revolutionary endeavor. Given the internal and external forces against Allende, the director wonders if the Socialist president was becoming a political ruin in his own time, relegated like the now-rotting buses of change, movement, and progress to the dustbin of history. What could Guzmán and his *compañeros*, as militants, have done to have saved the ill-fated president or the revolution, to have changed their own fate and the fate of the nation? Guzmán's answer: a resigned and honest "nothing!" Guzmán's lesson: the reality of the present consists in little more than remains, empty rooms, and black-and-white images of a remote past whose vibrancy persists solely in the memories of the defeated.

Yet perhaps the most profound ruins in *Salvador Allende* are not the physical spaces pillaged by the military or those transformed by neoliberalism, but rather the *living human remains*, buried behind closed doors, who, like Guzmán, harbor memories in their own private utopias, oftentimes nursing romantic nostalgias, working through traumas, or wondering how things could have played out differently than they did.[15] Toward the end of the film, Guzmán shows four former

Allende supporters lined up in front of the camera in Valparaíso. One of them moves his mouth several times without speaking, as if to symbolize the muteness that trauma instills. The first man claims that Allende's supporters must have "lacked courage" to face the military. What went wrong? His is a discourse of melancholy and defeat. Another man stares blankly into the distance, removed from the present, immersed in an intimate moment of remembrance that is never communicated verbally on camera. Guzmán zooms in on this man, whose eyes are closed, seemingly more interested in filming what the man's gaze conveys than about the oral testimony being given by others in the background. The gaze captured on film once again contains the perpetual questions of the defeated: What could we have done? Could the catastrophe have been avoided? The scene posits a critical question to history, undercutting a nostalgic, at times almost hagiographic, presentation of Allende with an implicitly analytical spin (although the analysis, of course, is never fleshed out).

Based on my descriptions to this point, one might assume that nostalgia, like the romanticizing brand that Guzmán engages in frequently in reference to Allende and Popular Unity, would be an automatic impediment to critical reflection. Yet not all nostalgia should be taken as a self-indulgent practice that causes critical thought to stagnate. Svetlana Boym distinguishes between two types of nostalgia: "restorative" and "reflective."[16] Both types are similar in that they are practiced by displaced people (like Guzmán) who mediate between the individual and the collective. Moreover, both types are based in a "longing for a shrinking space of experience that no longer fits the new horizon of expectations."[17] But unlike restorative nostalgia, which hopes to rescue the past intact, to "rebuild the mythical place called home," reflective nostalgia has no such pretensions.[18] Despite being rooted in a similar longing for bygone days, reflective nostalgia wants neither to recover the past in full nor posit it as absolute truth, but rather to facilitate a meditation on history and the passage of time. Significantly, this reflective brand of nostalgia is not at odds with critical thinking precisely because the reflection on ruin and loss can awaken new "planes of consciousness" and potentialities in the present.[19]

Guzmán's film, in my opinion, seems to be trapped between restorative and reflective nostalgia, while privileging the restorative impulse. In other words, *Salvador Allende* is a filmic project marked by a profound tension between a nostalgic desire to restore the past integrally and a counter-imperative to reflect critically on and assimilate the past. As I have already described, the *restorative* impulse can be seen at many points, yet the film also contains some *reflective* elements. Let me mention one key sequence to illustrate this point. Continuing an aesthetic of *debate scenes* already begun in *Chile: La memoria obstinada* (particularly the famous schoolgirls scene), in one of *Salvador Allende*'s most significant moments, a group of ex-militants sits down to debate their actions and omissions during the Popular Unity years. One point of contention has to do with whether Allende should be remembered as a "revolutionary." Although most people at the table claim that Allende was indeed a revolutionary, one voice in the group dissents, reminding his comrades that Allende would not support armed struggle as it was called for by the MIR or many Socialists. "Our leader," he claims, "wasn't able to take charge and rise to the occasion." Faced with this challenge to Allende's political prowess, another man rebuts that such a view amounts to a "distortion of history." The scene is ultimately effective because it does not resolve the matter at hand, but leaves competing viewpoints resonating in the viewer's mind. Such reflection bridges onto other moments of the film, such as when Guzmán interviews some of today's *obreros* (workers), who wonder about how history might have been different had the *pueblo* defended its leader on September 11, 1973.

However, in keeping with the film's overall narrative tone, *Salvador Allende* ends on a largely restorative note. The final scene shows compelling footage of a poetry recital by Gonzalo Millán, who reads from his work *La ciudad* (The City), written in exile in 1979:

> El río invierte el curso de su corriente . . .
> . . . Allende retrocede hasta Tomás Moro.
> Los detenidos salen de espalda de los estadios.
> 11 de septiembre.
> Las fuerzas armadas respetan la constitución.
> Los militares vuelven a sus cuarteles.
> Renace Neruda.
> Víctor Jara toca la guitarra. Canta.
> Los obreros desfilan cantando
> ¡Venceremos!
>
> [The river changes course . . .
> . . . Allende returns to his house on Tomás Moro Street.
> The detainees walk backward out of the stadiums.
> September 11.
> The armed forces respect the constitution.
> The military returns to its barracks.
> Neruda is reborn.
> Víctor Jara plays the guitar. He sings.
> The workers march along singing
> We will conquer!]

Millán's poem is an inversion of history, a deployment of the well-known literary trope called *el mundo al revés* (the world upside-down), in which real-life events are imagined otherwise. Significantly, the film ends by citing Millán's utopian erasure

77

of the traumatic events of September 11, 1973, a poetic gesture that strives toward the tidy resolution of traumas that, via the poetic utterance, undo themselves one by one. Read in isolation, Millán's poem is clearly restoratively nostalgic.

Yet transposed into the present and taken in semiotic juxtaposition with the other elements of Guzmán's film, Millán's poem is not simply restorative. It also contains a reflective character that compels the viewer to interrogate the meanings and possibilities of its final word—*Venceremos* (We will conquer)—in the context of a neoliberal present. What might this popular leftist battle cry from Latin America's revolutionary era mean today? Can it still have consequence? If Guzmán's film, as a whole, strives to vindicate Allende as a historical figure and salvage for the present certain values associated with his legacy (equality, democracy, etc.), the challenge he implicitly puts forth has to do with how such values can inform the birth of a new emancipative politics for the left. In the end, he offers no concrete answers, only an implicit question.

Carmen Castillo's *Calle Santa Fe* (2008): Beyond the Monumentalization of History

If the predominant narrative drive of Guzmán's film is to pay homage to Allende (and to assuage personal pain) through a nostalgia that is largely *restorative*, Carmen Castillo's *Calle Santa Fe* (Santa Fe Steet, 2008) moves a little farther toward reflective nostalgia by dramatically pitting simple restoration against the need to "work through" the past in the service of present and future needs. The film documents the process through which Castillo's fervent desire to reconstitute the past *as it was* gives way to the need for new perspectives, new political articulations, and generational shift.

The girlfriend of the MIR's iconic leader Miguel Enríquez, Carmen Castillo was in the house on Santa Fe Street when DINA (Dirección de Inteligencia Nacional [National Intelligence Directorate]) agents laid siege to it on October 5, 1974.[20] Enríquez was killed, and Castillo, who was pregnant at the time, managed to escape into exile after being hospitalized for gunshot wounds. Exiled in Paris and estranged from her country, she never returned to Chile definitively. Her life, like Guzmán's and so many others, has been marked indelibly by the trauma of exile and political violence, and particularly by a sense of impotence and vacillation linked to "defeat." About her exile, Castillo remarks: "I live in a formless space." How to give narrative form to exile and how to articulate shattered subjectivity and the meanings of militancy are key questions that the film explores.

The house on Santa Fe Street is the linchpin around which the documentary's narrative emplotment unfolds. For Castillo, it takes on the monumentalized status of a fetish or an obsession. Early in the film, the house where Castillo and Enríquez lived for ten months prior to the DINA's raid represents "home"—a space of utopia, beauty, and happiness. A hyper-idealized site of memory, it metonymically (and *romantically*) embodies Chile's revolutionary moment and Castillo's entire life as a militant: "Yes, it all began in that house: the break with my country, the tearing apart of my family, my errancy. . . . My memories always stem from that house. In the living room, surrounded by weapons, Miguel reads: Victor Hugo, Cortázar, poets, and scientists. Each reading nourished our combat." As is commonplace in romanticized narratives of militancy, Chile's revolutionary moment is portrayed as an epoch of *enamoramiento*, as a collective, almost dreamlike project that was torn asunder. Just like in Guzmán's film, Castillo's documentary is traversed by an air of the *Nueva Canción*, a spirit of camaraderie, courage, and solidarity, and images of undulating masses in the streets. All of that lost, uprooted in Paris, she wanders the streets of the French capital overwhelmed by restorative nostalgia: "There are moments in which my desire to return to that house is so intense: [I want] to rekindle the fire in the hearth, to smell the fragrance of the flowers."

When she finally returns to Santiago after many years of absence, Chile's capital city (like in Guzmán's film) strikes her as a hostile, foreign environment, full of impunity, inequality, and amnesia. Santiago "revolts me" (*me da asco*), she says. A friend and former militant, Silvia Castillo, accompanies her back to Santa Fe Street so that she can see the house. She asks: "Does any of this mean anything to anyone but me?" Here, the obsessions of one individual (Castillo) conflict with the desires of the collective. How individual memories and desires might interface with collective social and political imaginings becomes a key dilemma to resolve. Yet Castillo holds firm to her individual conviction that the house *must* be recovered. She proposes to buy it from its current owner and turn it into a memory site that *monumentalizes* and pays homage to Miguel's martyrdom.

Several key scenes, however, mark a narrative progression that moves Castillo beyond fetishizing the house, beyond staying romantically and individualistically mired in the past. One of these key moments occurs when Castillo is traveling with a friend by bus through one of Santiago's shantytowns. The friend, María Emilia Marchi, claims that Castillo is out of touch with Chile's reality because she has lived in exile for so long. Her point is that Chile is not just the forgetful, neoliberal landscape full of apathy and impunity that Castillo sees with her exiled eyes. Instead, Marchi claims, there is "another Chile" in which people protest for social justice and in which the MIR's values live on, transformed. She challenges Castillo to look beyond the surface.

Although this challenge plants a seed with Castillo, her *toma de conciencia* (that is, the transformation of her character) doesn't occur until the end of the film. "How can I give shape to my memories without staying mired in the ruins of the past? How can I transmit our history [that of the MIR] to those who recognize themselves in it?" These questions are laid over images and sounds of a youth orchestra playing the MIR's anthem today. Later we hear a group of young rappers interpreting the anthem yet again. The *translation* of the anthem across space, time, and subjectivities (1969–present) is yet another way of posing the question of the MIR's legacy for our times. We then move to a rally in memory of Miguel Enríquez that is being held in a huge stadium in which the 1960s generation pays homage to their fallen hero alongside today's youth.

After that, we reach the film's climactic moment. A young man, Abner Vega, who has attended the rally, directly challenges Castillo's position about preserving the house. Yes, he says, having a space for memory is important, but at the same time, he claims, we must ask, "a space for what? Suddenly the idea of having the house doesn't get us fired up. It doesn't excite us, mainly because we feel that the homage we must pay to Miguel and our other comrades has to take place *in practice*, by trying to do what they did in the context we have been given." He goes so far as to tell Castillo that she and others of her generation aren't doing much more than *monumentalizing* the dead. Defending her position, Castillo retorts that preserving the house isn't about creating a "static" or "nostalgic" memory; it's simply about recovering the place where Miguel lived and recognizing that there's a history attached to it. The young man rebuts, pointedly: "But sometimes one has to set aside one's personal history in order to contribute to the collective cause."

How does a survivor overcome the guilt of surviving? How does one move beyond a romanticized, fetishized, individualistic, and monumentalized version of history in order to restore to history its dynamism and place it in the service of the present and future? In the film's final minutes, Mónica Echeverría Yáñez, Castillo's mother, is shown writing a letter to Carmen in Paris in which she urges her daughter to let go of some of her past "anger, hatred, and attachments." All of this leads to a dramatic moment in which Castillo finds a happy middle ground between her restoratively nostalgic yearnings and a sense of the future. Instead of buying the house and monumentalizing it, she decides to mark it with a simple plaque and hold an intimate ceremony: "I no longer felt the need to recover the house, although I did feel the need to mark the site somehow." In a gesture similar to the *Venceremos* question at the end of Guzmán's film, just as the plaque is placed on the ground, the words of Miguel Enríquez are actualized as a question and a challenge for the present: "Every defeat brings with it a heaven to be gained [*toda derrota tiene su cielo por ganar*]." Restorative nostalgia—consciously, *narratively*—cedes to its more reflective brand.

Miguel Littín's *Compañero presidente* (1971): Transposing the Past in the Present, or the Return of the Repressed

Returning to the past can be instructive. Beatriz Sarlo, in *Tiempo pasado: Cultura de la memoria y giro subjetivo, una discusión* (Past Time: A Discussion of Memory Culture and the Subjective Turn) (a book whose arguments have caused some controversy in the wake of Beverley's critique), gives us some food for thought on that point.[21] She asks: "To what extent do the ideas that moved the sixties and seventies remain in the testimonial narratives about that era?"[22] Because, in Sarlo's opinion, the revolutionary era was an overtly political, ideologically charged, and, above all, *intellectual* moment, her fear is that something of that intellectual and political content gets lost when personalized, subjective testimonies portray the past as a "postmodern drama of affect."[23] She explains that her intention is not to question the testimonial subject's legitimate (and necessary) right to speak, but rather to point out that "subjectivity is historical and [that] if we believe it's possible to capture [subjectivity] in narrative, it's the differential that matters."[24] This *differential* is crucial to my discussion precisely because works like *Salvador Allende* and *Calle Santa Fe*, both "personal documentaries," are works riddled with nostalgia (be it restorative, reflective, or both). They are works conceived from a present position of enunciation that is indelibly marked by loss, exile, melancholy, and defeat. Consequently, if we want to revisit and consider the revolutionary era through narratives whose reading is not overdetermined (or predetermined) by the melancholy of defeat, perhaps we must look elsewhere. Perhaps it is necessary to return, as Sarlo suggests, to a document from that time, perhaps to a film such as Miguel Littín's *Compañero presidente* (1971).

I saw this documentary for the first time in the winter of 2008 at the Centro Cultural de la Moneda as part of a film festival organized for the centennial of Allende's birth. After being in Santiago around this commemorative date, I got the impression that cultural production about Allende experienced a minor "boom" in 2008; many Allende-themed events were held throughout Chile in the fallen president's honor. The film festival's programming caught my attention particularly because it featured some foreign films from the early to mid-1970s that had never been seen in Chile. Those films were juxtaposed with more recent productions, such as *Machuca* (2004) by Andrés Wood and Guzmán's *Salvador Allende*, such that the festival, in its very configuration, projected a desire to balance films that narrate the past *from the present* against films that bring images from the past to bear *on the present*.

Of all the films I saw, Littín's struck me as especially noteworthy because it was not saturated—at least from the standpoint of its narrative construction—by a melancholic air of defeat. Why would it be? At the moment of filming (1971), Allende's Popular Unity project, despite the myriad impediments it faced both domestically and internationally, was still operating within, we might say, a *horizon of future possibility*. A military coup did not seem an immediate threat to the implementation of Popular Unity's platform. As we learn in the film, Allende was fully convinced that Chile's armed forces were not capable of staging a coup because historically they had been obedient to the constitution and the rule of law. The film reproduces a series of intense conversations between Allende and Régis Debray that give us a sense, when viewed from the present, of the era's deep political and intellectual character. In a certain sense, Guzmán's *La batalla de Chile* also does this, but unlike Littín's film, Guzmán's "epic" documentary is framed by the bombing of La Moneda such that its filmic narrative is already encoded with the destruction and tragedy to come. *La batalla de Chile* is emplotted and reads as the chronicle of death foretold.

Not so in *Compañero presidente*. The conversation between Debray and Allende is heated and at times uncomfortable. The central debate in the film (which undoubtedly has a propagandistic aspect) has to do with whether Chile is in the process of carrying out a true "revolution," or, instead, Allende's government is merely implementing a series of popular-democratic reforms within the bourgeoisie's historically ordained framework. Allende defends his government's revolutionary prowess at every turn, arguing that Popular Unity is not just another "Popular Front." He speaks of his admiration for Che and Fidel Castro and defends his theoretical formation in revolutionary doctrine as well as Chile's unique path to Socialism. According to Allende, the revolution must "pass through stages"; he recognizes that Chile is not yet a Socialist country but that it will get there soon. Debray plays the role of devil's advocate, asking Allende tough questions: "How can one have a revolution without arms?" As Debray notes from his own perspective, but always with tremendous admiration and respect for Allende, "At bottom, Chile is still a big question mark." The outcomes of Allende's revolution, in 1971, are unknown. The future is an open book.

Of course, when we watch *Compañero presidente* today, it is impossible to separate its reception from the history of the dictatorship. I would imagine that this is particularly true for a viewer from the revolutionary generation for whom the film could well evoke a mixture of reactions ranging from joy to nostalgia to melancholy to self-doubt.[25] I would ask, though, what might these images of intellectual debate and political possibility—which haunt the present insistently and with intention—mean for Chileans of younger generations who are eager to articulate their political demands in the present? What I find significant is precisely that after years of silencing, Littín's and other films from the revolutionary era are resurfacing in Chile and are starting to circulate again publicly in ways that seem to respond to the malaise of a political climate hungry, to echo Connery, for a sense of "futurity." I am suggesting that *Compañero presidente* is not circulating in Chile today simply as an archival piece, but rather as a crucial document whose projection has direct bearing on the present political desires of certain sectors of the population. In a certain sense, the crisis of the neoliberal generation demands that the nation contend with these images from the past and plumb their meanings in order to ask what Allende's ideals can mean for Chile today.

After Pinochet's 1998 detention in London and the 2004 Riggs Bank scandal, the ex-dictator progressively lost much of the political and symbolic clout he once held. Allende's figure, which had been silenced throughout the 1990s, resurfaced in the public arena largely due to Pinochet's political demise and a progressive opening of spaces for alternative forms of historical memory. The thirtieth anniversary of the military coup (2003) and the centennial of Allende's birth (2008) were two key moments in which Allende's ghost and its meaning came back to haunt Chile's public imagination. Understood in this context, the public circulation of films like Littín's signals, on some level, the return of the repressed in a way that generates a direct and necessary engagement with movements like that of the *pingüinos*, who vehemently protested to overturn what they saw as Pinochet's non-egalitarian reforms to Chile's educational system. In books, films, university debates, and on television, Allende's public image is gradually being revived and dignified by new generations of Chileans and a society eager to place its neoliberal present in dialogue with the "lost" ideals of its not-so-distant past.

Final Reflections

If Beatriz Sarlo's position, generally speaking, calls for a move away from narratives like *Salvador Allende* and *Calle Santa Fe* in favor of other sources (printed and visual)—perhaps like *Compañero presidente*—that return to us the "spirit of the epoch," my feeling is that the memory of the revolutionary moment does not so much require us to *set aside* romanticized, nostalgic, utopian, or melancholic narrative modes, but rather to approach them cognizant of the temporal differential that operates within their narrative logic. How these present-bound films approach the past also reveals much about the revolutionary generation's trajectory and the traumas that it suffered as a result of dictatorial genocide.

Considering films like the three examined here in juxtaposition is useful for illuminating the variegated nature of the "documents" that allow us access to history (e.g., their prejudices, their narrative operations, their silences). I agree with María Rosa Olivera-Williams's recent assessment of the problem, when she reminds us that Sarlo's problematization of first-person narratives about the revolutionary period "does not necessarily mean that every first person narrative is distorted or false," nor does it mean, I would add, that such narratives are worthless for shedding light on the density of the historical.[26] Sarlo's analysis, in my opinion, simply reminds us that first-person narratives—like all documents about the past—should be subject to critical analysis and read in their *temporal dimension*. If we truly want to understand the impact and meaning that the revolutionary moment has *in* and *for* the present, we must remember that it is crucial to "listen to all of the narratives that speak to us about that era" cognizant of their differing motivations, desires, tonalities, and subjective trajectories.[27] Only by heeding the polyphony of voices and documents about the past—I am referring not only to those documents that speak to us from a time of promise and futurity, but also to those that speak from an era of subjective crisis, self-questioning, and trauma—can we gain a true sense of historicity.

Pilar Calveiro gets it right when she argues that the memory of Latin America's revolutionary moment requires a "double movement": to recover the *historicity* of that which is remembered, with an eye toward reconstructing the attitudes, passions, debates, and ideas of that moment, while at the same time revisiting the past *in the present* to understand how that past has been rewritten by different actors, in different modes, from different perspectives, and to different ends. At the same time, it is important to revisit the past asking about the potentialities of the revolutionary moment for informing present social and political struggles. In the final assessment, it is not a question of *either/or*—of discrediting certain memory narratives while reifying others—but rather of placing individual testimonies in perspective, keenly aware of their tics, temporalities, and narrative modalities. We should try to understand the impulses behind such retellings of the past, while also fomenting a debate that does not sacrifice militancy's intellectual, conflictive, or collective dimensions. Most important, we should not deny the relevance of its continued promise.

NOTES

I would like to thank Tomás Crowder-Taraborrelli and Kristi Wilson for inviting me to write this chapter. I also want to thank my colleague María Rosa Olivera-Williams for her generosity of mind and spirit and for our many stimulating discussions of the issues treated in this chapter. Her comments have enriched my work tremendously. A special thank you goes as well to Tamara Spira, who has and continues to be one of my closest interlocutors. I presented a preliminary version of this piece on a panel titled "Memory and Revolution in Latin America: Reflections from the Southern Cone" that María Rosa Olivera-Williams organized for the June 2009 LASA (Latin American Studies Association) meeting in Rio de Janeiro, Brazil. I am also grateful to colleagues in Chile who offered valuable comments during several public presentations of this work.

1. On September 1, 2009, Chile became the 109th country to ratify the Rome Statute of the International Criminal Court. As a result of this ratification, Chile has been obliged to modify its criminal code to include the crime of genocide. However, according to prominent Chilean human rights attorney Pamela Pereira, the concept of "genocide" has not been adopted by the Chilean Supreme Court for cases stemming from the Pinochet dictatorship. The court has preferred to use the more generic term "crimes against humanity" to refer to a series of interrelated circumstances (torture, executions, forced disappearances). By labeling the crimes in this fashion, the Chilean high court has recognized the non-applicability of statutory limitations and the nonapplicability of amnesties in these cases. (Recall that Pinochet's 1978 Amnesty Law still stands in Chile.) Nevertheless, in certain cases, the Chilean courts have lessened sentences for convicted perpetrators based on the fact that the crimes occurred several decades ago. As a final note, it is worth pointing out that Judge Baltasar Garzón used the term "genocide" in a legal context in his efforts to convict Pinochet following his 1998 detention in London. For more on this, see Roht-Arriaza, *Pinochet Effect*, 44–50. I would like to thank Pedro Alejandro Matta and Pamela Pereira for providing me with this information.

2. Watenpaugh, comment made as part of the symposium "Human Rights in the Classroom," University of California, Davis, October 27, 2008.

3. Part of Chilean filmmakers' anxiety has to do with the fact that the Chilean left today is often perceived as "less socialist" than other Latin American governments (take those of Hugo Chávez or Evo Morales, for example). The idea of the "renovated socialist," who is socialist in name but upholds the tenets of neoliberalism, is frequently critiqued by more orthodox sectors of the Chilean left. Although Chile's recent governments (the Lagos and Bachelet administrations) have been socialist, one can see differences in the type of socialism that has held power in the context of Chile's consensus-based Concertación framework and other more radical forms that have taken hold elsewhere.

4. Some of the material contained in this section on Patricio Guzmán's *Salvador Allende* previously appeared in my article "Guzmán's Allende," published in *Chasqui: Revista de literatura latinoamericana* 38, no. 2 (November 2009): 48–62. I would like to thank the editors of *Chasqui* for allowing me to draw from that material to frame a larger argument here.

5. Calveiro, *Política y/o violencia*, 18.

6. Ibid., 16. All translations from the Spanish in this chapter are my own.

7. Beverley, "Rethinking the Armed Struggle in Latin America," 49.

8. For Beverley, in Sarlo's case, this "neoconservatism" consists in, among other factors: (1) "a rejection of the authority of subaltern voice and experience, and an extreme dissatisfaction with or skepticism about multiculturalism . . . and identity politics"; (2) "a defense of the writer-critic or traditional intellectual, and of his or her republican-civic function";

(3) "an explicit disavowal of the project of the armed revolutionary struggle of the 1960s or 1970s, in favor of a more considered or cautious left." See Beverley, "The Neoconservative Turn in Latin America Literary and Cultural Criticism," 76–77.

9. Ibid., 50.

10. Ibid., 52.

11. Ibid.

12. See Connery, "The End of the Sixties," 184.

13. See Richard, "La historia contándose y la historia contada."

14. Rebolledo, *Memorias del desarraigo*, 194–95.

15. I would like to thank Idelber Avelar for helping me arrive at the idea of subjectivity as ruin. Chilean writer Diamela Eltit's latest novel, *Jamás el fuego nunca*, also deals with this very issue. Two former militants are portrayed in a claustrophobic space, trying to revive a past that is far removed from the present, but whose existence undeniably determined (and continues to determine) their identities and their destinies. Its tone is of defeat, with little hope for the future in a desolate neoliberal landscape.

16. Boym, *The Future of Nostalgia*, xviii.

17. Ibid., 10.

18. Ibid., 50.

19. Ibid.

20. Castillo has written about this experience in her books, *Un día de octubre en Santiago* and *Santiago-París: El vuelo de la memoria*, the latter coauthored with her mother, Mónica Echeverría Yáñez.

21. It is not my intention to critique Beverley's reading of Sarlo in this chapter. Although I also find certain aspects of Sarlo's arguments on testimony debatable, I am interested here in rescuing a few points that I feel are worth considering in direct relation to the arguments of this chapter. A more rigorous critique of Sarlo is perhaps the subject of another article.

22. Sarlo, *Tiempo pasado*, 84.

23. Ibid., 91.

24. Ibid.

25. I am thankful to Steve Volk for reminding me that those who lived Popular Unity's defeat in the flesh are likely to receive Littín's film quite differently than someone from my generation who had not yet been born in the early 1970s.

26. Olivera-Williams, "La década del 70 en el Cono Sur." My deepest thanks go to my colleague María Rosa Olivera-Williams for sharing her unpublished work with me.

27. Ibid.

4   "The Power to Imagine"

*Genocide, Exile, and Ethical Memory
in Atom Egoyan's* Ararat

GEORGIANA BANITA

> In making *Ararat,* I wanted to show how the truth is not to be found
> in the epic scenes of deportation and massacre, but in the intimate
> moments shared by individuals—between strangers in a hallway,
> between workers on a film set, and most profoundly in the conver-
> sations between parents and their children. Any blockbuster attempt
> to amplify the event from the very private turmoil its memory
> provokes is to diminish—or at least to misrepresent—an essential
> aspect of its meaning.
>
> ATOM EGOYAN, "In Other Words"

Questioned in an interview about how members of the U.S.
Congress responded to her seminal book *"A Problem from
Hell": America and the Age of Genocide* (2002), Samantha Power made the following
confession: "I heard nothing. The Armenian community supplied Congress with
100 copies, but I still heard nothing. If it hadn't been for the Armenians, no one
would have ever heard of my book. They're the ones who have championed it.
Imagine: to be so excited just because in one book, someone writes that the
Armenian genocide actually occurred. Everywhere I go to do book signings,
Armenians appear to thank me. Adolescent Armenian boys even put up posters of
me on their walls."[1] Though signally underpublicized, the Armenian genocide of

1915 is part and parcel of any historical account of twentieth-century violence and human rights violations. In the late nineteenth century, a rapidly collapsing Ottoman Empire lost control over its Christian territories and began a systematic persecution of its Christian subjects as a result of a nationalist revival and general anxiety over the possibility of internecine betrayal. After the massacre of tens of thousands of Armenians in the 1890s and the killing or deportation of over a million between 1915 and 1922, up to one-half of the world's Armenian population was annihilated and the community in Anatolia was completely destroyed.[2] Due to the proliferation of genocide in an era devoted to the prevention of such atrocities, the need to investigate the Armenian situation within the more comprehensive "genocide studies" has intensified, yet debates continue around the historical accuracy of the "genocide" label in describing the mass deportations and slaughter of the Armenian population.

The denial of the Armenian genocide extends well beyond the initial reluctance of the European Allies in World War I and of the United States to intervene in the escalating tensions between the Ottoman Empire and its Christian population.[3] Skepticism about the legitimacy of the genocidal claim has been aided and abetted by many Western nations. As recently as October 2007, President George W. Bush urged members of Congress to reject a resolution explicitly recognizing the slaughter of 1.5 million Armenians in 1915 as "genocide." Former U.S. Secretary of State Condoleezza Rice argued that passage of the bill would severely damage diplomatic ties with Turkey, a key NATO ally in the Middle East. In her refutation of the bill, Rice refused to utter the controversial term despite being reminded of her own background as a historian and as such invested in establishing factual accuracy rather than strategically defending political allegiances.

Atom Egoyan's film *Ararat* (2002) is the first to address the Armenian genocide in great detail, even though the director prefers to see it less as a historical account of the events than as a meditation on the question of denial and its repercussions: "I think that we have to be able to find a way to stop talking about this as a film of the Armenian genocide," Egoyan insists. "It's a film about living with the effects of the denial of that event into the present."[4] Egoyan was born in Cairo to Armenian parents, who then left the country at a time of Egyptian hostility to the Armenian community and moved to the city of Victoria, British Columbia, where Egoyan grew up, in the absence of what he terms "the three pillars of Armenian identity"; living apart from the Armenian community, from its churches, and refusing to speak Armenian at home, Egoyan paved the way for his almost complete cultural assimilation.[5] The genocide was "something shadowy" that he was indeed aware of, but "only in the vaguest way."[6] It was during his studies in international relations at the University of Toronto that Egoyan reconnected with his Armenian heritage by speaking his mother tongue and gearing his research toward the investigation of the Armenian genocide and of its denial by Turkey. It was also here that he became involved in the "more political, almost militant Armenian nationalist activities through the student association."[7] Egoyan is not only conversant with the debates around what he calls "the psychology and politics of denial," but he also possesses the necessary credentials as a director to probe questions of exile, memory, and national identity implicit in any discussion of the genocide and its legacy.[8] His earlier films, *Open House* (1982), *Next of Kin* (1984), and *Family Viewing* (1987), either feature Armenian characters or refer to the genocide indirectly, while *The Sweet Hereafter* (1997) explores the issue of traumatic memory and survivor testimony in the context of a violent catastrophe that breaks apart individual lives and affects the cohesion of a community (here, on a smaller scale than in *Ararat*, the dramatic events are triggered by a disastrous school bus accident).

Ararat is more explicitly historical yet it resists the temptations of grand historical narratives in two ways. First, it problematizes the entertainment industry's ability to narrate the un-narratable by introducing a film-within-a-film that follows the standard narrative structure of the historical epic but ultimately produces cartoonish renderings of events—"a sprawling spectacle filled with stock images of pure evil, bold heroism, horrific violence, and unrelenting suffering, all punctuated by screams, close-ups of children's anguished faces, and a soundtrack that never leaves any doubt as to the desired emotional response."[9] Egoyan distances himself cautiously from this film-within-a-film by questioning not only its artistic and historical legitimacy but also the stiffness of its dogmatic style, insisting instead that multiple positions and, implicitly, multiple media differently inflect our understanding of the past.[10]

Second, *Ararat* employs intricate juxtapositions that go beyond the basic mise en abyme technique of the fictive film, also called *Ararat* and directed by Edward Saroyan (Charles Aznavour), who bases much of his script on his own mother's survivor testimony.[11] The lost identity that the film's protagonists seek to re-create or replace is wedged within the critical distance the director himself carefully maintains between historical events and their narrative reconstructions, a distance that has been theorized on the basis of Hamid Naficy's concept of epistolarity, where modes of intra- and extra-diegetic communication provide "prostheses for memory."[12] Egoyan intersperses scenes from the completed film-within-a-film or from the shooting in progress with plot lines set in contemporary Toronto, without discernable transitional segments, thus pointing out the subtle fade-outs and negotiations of memory itself both in the historical and in the personal realm. This chapter argues that in order to explain—but not explain away—the workings of historical denial, Egoyan delineates an ethical approach to memory recuperation and reconstruction, an approach that builds on the film's complex family and communal bonds and on its insistently media-conscious quality.

Mediating Memory

In this analysis of *Ararat*, Egoyan's main technologies of mediation are divided into three categories based on their narrative or symbolic proximity to historical events. To begin with, on the closest level of historical immediacy are the eyewitness accounts of Dr. Clarence Ussher, an American missionary who witnessed the atrocities and valiantly resisted all attempts by the Turks to infiltrate the Armenian community by sending in troops—allegedly to protect the Americans stationed in the area, but in fact as a Trojan horse to assault the community from within.[13] Next on a scale that runs from the factually authentic to the fictional is the engaged and passionate work of Ani (Arsinée Khanjian), an art history professor who has just completed a book about Armenian painter and genocide survivor Arshile Gorky—a book modeled on Nouritza Matossian's biography *Black Angel* (1998)—and is now lecturing about Gorky's figurative masterpiece, *A Portrait of the Artist and His Mother*, which, Ani claims, alludes to the theme of genocide through the troubling blankness around which its mystery revolves.[14] In the painting, the mother's hands are blurred, almost blotted out, either because the painter could not bring himself to paint them or because he felt that completing the painting impaired the incomplete and tentative nature of his own memories and of his fidelity to them.

The visual syncretism of the film reinforces this ambiguity. Ani's son Raffi obsessively tries to understand the mindset and motives of his father, who was killed trying to assassinate a Turkish diplomat in the naive belief that his actions would put an end to the denial of the Armenian genocide by Turkish authorities or would provide some compensation in kind.[15] In order to achieve closure and decipher what was going on in his father's mind, Raffi goes to Turkey, armed with a camcorder, on a tour of sites that are significant to Armenian historical memory. Raffi is keen to remake Saroyan's old-fashioned cinematic document into images that are less sentimental, into a more personalized vision of history that straddles the line between the sublime and its sublimation. The amateur footage of Raffi's camcorder travelogue further complicates the way in which memories or the absence of memory are communicated through media.

Meanwhile, Ani accepts a role as consultant for the film-within-a-film, whose makers have decided to include a fictional character based on Gorky and have also taken some liberties, charitably called poetic license, with details on the set and with the heroic nature of Gorky's alleged involvement in a subversive movement to liberate Van, the only Armenian town to stage a successful uprising during the genocide. Without shoehorning all of these media forms into a single notion of mediation, the film presents its visual and narrative texts as what Marita Sturken terms "technologies of memory," or objects through which memories are shared, produced, and given meaning.[16] Egoyan uses these technologies with genuine curiosity in trying to answer the question he poses to himself: "How does an artist speak the unspeakable?"[17] Through the juxtaposition of scenes from the film-within-a-film with segments of the frame story, memory appears both as the irruption of the past into the present and the bleeding of the present into the past. In Egoyan's words, "the grammar of the screenplay uses every possible tense and mood available to tell its story, from the basic pillars of the past, present and the future, to the subjective, the past-perfect, and past not-so-perfect, and the past-would-be-perfect-if-it-weren't-so-conditional."[18]

The film's reception adds a third layer of mediation. The release of *Ararat* sparked controversy when Turkish cinemas planning to screen the movie were publicly castigated and threatened to be violently besieged.[19] Indeed, Egoyan criticizes the semantic wavering that still obstructs public discourse on the Armenian genocide and sours private relationships among exiled descendants of Armenian survivors and Turks, who were raised to believe a different story. Yet *Ararat* does not operate on the principle of preventive awareness—that is, the hope that reflection on the perils of inaction will produce active involvement in conflicts to come. Rather than focusing on issues of global awareness and intervention, *Ararat* explores the expansion of witness narratives to include the experience of the distant observer, who can access atrocity only through visual media. Further complicating this stance is the film's own role as a form of mediation, accused of appropriating historical tragedy for aesthetic effect. *Ararat* proves that issues of memory, post-memory, and trauma are inextricably bound to the medium-specificity of any historical representation in an era that is characterized by an increasing collusion of events and their media afterimages.[20] The film offers a range of witness perspectives at escalating removes from the central survivor, the Armenian American painter Arshile Gorky, who occupies the space of authenticity and, this chapter argues, drives Egoyan's own aesthetic meditations.

Through Thick and Thin: The Ethics of Memory

The role of memory has always been central in relation to the Armenian genocide and has gained in urgency as the historical event recedes with each generation. *Ararat*, in fact, references a poignant reminder of the significance

91

of memory by mentioning Adolf Hitler's statement to his generals that what they were about to do (preparing the Holocaust) would be successful because hardly anyone remembered the massacre of the Armenians; that is, the grandiosity of the plan would not necessarily make it more of a landmark in public memory and historiographical discourse, because it is invariably the victorious who write the history books.[21] *Ararat's* complex cast, which includes a filmmaker, an art historian, a photographer, a painter, and an impromptu documentarian, employs the work of memory to reflect on the function of the image in establishing structures of personal belonging and identification. Along with the artistic diversity of the cast, the elliptical velocity of the editing disturbs the cohesiveness of the historical account and injects a tone of relativity about representation altogether. Yet it also implies that past and present, though rotating around a very movable axis, are tied by an ethical obligation to remember.

Between what Avishai Margalit defines as "thin" human relations ("our relations to the stranger and the remote") and "thick" relationships ("anchored in a shared past or moored in shared memory," "our relations to the near and dear"), Egoyan elaborates on the ethics of memory that arise from the invocation of particular memories by members of a "thick" community. [22] "Thick" family relations determine the multilayered plot of the film as younger characters embark on journeys of discovery driven by the tropes of fatherhood and motherhood: Celia, Raffi, and Gorky pine for their fathers, struggling to find their way back to their respective ghosts; Gorky and Raffi gravitate toward the mother figure in their artistic and self-exploratory quests. Even as he juxtaposes characters who occupy a variety of witness positions and who themselves engage in artistic and representational acts, Egoyan formulates his metanarrative reflections without losing sight of his film's artistic centerpiece, the painter Arshile Gorky and his portrayal of his mother. Aspects of Gorky's method and his artistic (self) performance bleed into the artistic impulse and self-reflective attitudes of most characters, who represent different stages of involvement with Gorky's story as a heuristic for the historical genocide itself.[23] Watching, filming, touching, discussing, and knifing the painting are actions that form a code for the extreme voyeurism of everyone's relationship to the mythical Armenian homeland or what they imagine as such.[24]

Gorky's role in the film has received only scant critical attention, despite the abundance of scholarship on Gorky himself and despite Egoyan's attempts to include in the film fragments of highbrow "art criticism" and more informal comments on Gorky's position vis-à-vis his Armenian heritage. This oversight may have something to do with the fact that in a concept-driven film featuring characters that represent discursively explicit positions, Gorky is the only one who does not utter a single word. A discussion of Gorky's transgressive act of inscribing his diasporic experience onto an artistic surface of mediation (by transplanting an image from one medium into another) is essential to any analysis of what has recently been termed the post-exilic imaginary as a form of identity politics that moves away from territorial authenticity toward forms of media-operated displacement. As Nellie Hogikyan notes, the figure of Gorky in *Ararat* offers precisely the platform on which the post-exilic condition can take shape. In the de-territorialized realm of post-exile, "thick" family ties replace spatial belonging: "In the absence of the permanence of connections, as distances grow larger between individuals and peoples, and in the absence of continuity of filiation due to migration, immediate family becomes the only possible imagined community."[25] While his film *Family Viewing* has already elicited ethical readings of how Egoyan extends intimate family concerns to the communal sphere with media technologies as a vehicle of transmission, *Ararat*'s mnemonic constellations of familial and national belonging have not yet been sounded to the full.[26]

Mythic Motherlands on Canvas, Camera, and Film

Ararat opens with close-up shots of Gorky's New York studio. The camera brushes over this room, picking up Armenian artifacts (stone crucifixes, flowers from the Van region) scattered among painting utensils, and moves in and out of focus, eventually lingering on a photograph of the artist and his mother. A source for the painting on which Gorky is working, the photograph was taken in Van (the city in eastern Armenia that had been the ancient capital of Greater Armenia) some three years before the massacre occurred. The film implies, however, that the killings began shortly after the photograph was taken, probably in an attempt to boost its claim to historical immediacy. It comes as no surprise that Egoyan should select a painter as the centerpiece of his film, which can be seen as a metabiography of Gorky, a complex meditation on the concept of mise-en-scène. Gorky's ambivalent relationship to figurative painting is also used to reflect Egoyan's own deep-seated skepticism toward images of all kinds: "I love making images," the director remarks, "yet I'm suspicious of them. . . . I am suspicious of what I am trying to add to this culture, and would expect a lot of people are as well."[27] Largely based on personal sources—photographs, drawings, and memories—Gorky's portraits apply formal solutions derived from masters such as Picasso, Ingres, and Corot to images of his past and the emotions that link him to it. His Armenian portraits, which he regarded as the beginning of his true self-expression, mark a shift from his earlier work both in style and subject matter and supply Egoyan with the only painting by Gorky that features in his film.

Ararat, 2002. Directed by Atom Egoyan.

I would like to conceptualize *Ararat*'s ethics of memory as constituted by and around the family photograph and the painting it inspires.[28] The family picture points to the "thick" relations that Margalit singled out as the basis of an ethics of memory. Multiple looks circulate in the photograph's reproduction and reading in the course of the film, reinvigorating, however obliquely, the family romance of the picture: Gorky analyzes its formal structure and probes its emotional depth while adapting it for the canvas; Ani uses the image in her lectures; and several episodes retelling Gorky's childhood in Van are also centered on the photograph.

Gorky and his mother interact primarily around the pose that the photographer demands. Through the description and narrative of his film, Egoyan thus articulates Gorky's response to the image, which is thereby transformed into what W. J. T. Mitchell calls an imagetext.[29] The text, in this case, consists of a further accumulation of images, as the film adds layer upon layer of representations meant to deepen the photograph's emotional patina. In this sense, Egoyan's film is an ekphrastic commentary on the photograph, one that tries to envision the picture not as mere illustration to the historical event or collateral artifact but as part of its essence, the very trace or remnant that gives the story its historical legitimacy. In particular, what encapsulates this idea of a historical trace is the complex symbolism of the hand as an instrument of inscription and memorization.

Much critical ingenuity has flown into interpretations of Gorky's hand symbolism and Egoyan's multiple references to hands in *Ararat*. Most conspicuously, the hands of Gorky's mother are either left unfinished in his painting or purposefully rubbed out once the portrait was completed. Blotting them out may suggest that the genocide "is an absence implied rather than revealed."[30] For Egoyan, this gesture inflicts a symbolic wound that cannot be healed even as it alleviates the pain of absence through an act of both material and spiritual reconstruction. The director writes that the "moment where Gorky rubs his mother's hands from the canvas is the closest we come to understanding the spiritual desecration of genocide, as well as the power of art to help heal such pain."[31]

Ani refers to this detail repeatedly, and at the end of one of her lectures she turns to the projected image behind her and reaches out to touch the blurred hands, made even more immaterial through the slide's holographic quality. In her elaborations on the painting and the photograph, Ani suggests that the erasure of the mother's hands points to the violent interruption caused by the genocide in the history of an ancestral people: "In his most famous painting, Gorky leaves his mother's hands unfinished, as if the history of its composition, like that of his people, had been violently interrupted. The earthly sensuality of the mother's touch is no more. Only a pure, burning spiritual light remains." By modifying the image in a gesture that entails touching the canvas with his bare hands, Gorky reclaims his past and injects himself—the artist of the present—into the time frame of the original image, thus re-appropriating it.[32] It is this reappropriation that reveals the difference staged in the film between passive remembrance and active memorization, between remembering the genocide and purposefully recalling it, pressing for responsibilities and implications.

Moreover, the reenactment of a German woman's testimony to the massacre of a group of Armenian brides contains the shot of a burning hand seen by a young Gorky hiding from soldiers, his gaze fixated on the searing flesh. And finally,

Gorky himself is depicted in the process of erasing the mother's hands on canvas, displaying the kind of physical turmoil that may have prompted his suicide. In a discussion that sees the maternal as a cipher for everything that is opposed to the forces of extermination and war, Elizabeth Swanson Goldberg interprets the symbolism of the blurred hands in the film as "the annihilation of the romantic and erotic," one among a series of visual mutilations—the German witness wishing she could dig out her eyes to remove all traces of what she saw—the last of which, Goldberg suggests, is Gorky's suicide.[33]

However, it is too simple to equate erasure with the loss or impairment of memory, despite the easy connection one might draw between the blotting out of the painting and such often-cited notions as Nadine Fresco's "absent memory" or Henri Raczymow's "memory shot through with holes."[34] Rather, the erasure of the hands allows us to reconsider the image (both as photograph and as painting) in light of Roland Barthes's discussion of the punctum—that incongruous element that occasions a shock of recognition, a personal response to a detail that is both attractive and repelling: "Punctum is also: sting, speck, cut, little hole—and also a cast of the dice. A photograph's punctum is that accident which pricks me (but also bruises me, is poignant to me)."[35] The blurring of the hands marks a literalization of Barthes's description of the punctum as incision or clipping. Not only does it interrupt the contextual reading of the painting against the narrative background of the historical events (what Barthes would call studium), but it also disturbs the flat surface of the image and embeds it into a different—affective—narrative, thus operating the transition from merely observing to noticing, from knowing the history of the people depicted to realizing the abominable drama of their fate. Despite its authentic testimonial quality, for Gorky the photograph circumscribes the tension between presence and absence, life and death that is the constitutive core of his relationship with his mother. Erasing her hands is his attempt to break that equilibrium and tell a more complicated story that the comparatively simple technique of photography can barely approximate.

Genocide and the Pathologies of Recollection

The enigmatic story Gorky seeks to tell is marked by what Sigmund Freud terms "traumatic neurosis," which implies the return of the traumatic event after a period of delay: "The time that elapsed between the accident and the first appearance of the symptoms is called the 'incubation period,' a transparent allusion to the pathology of infectious disease. . . . It is the feature one might term *latency*."[36] Gorky's trauma as a survivor of the genocide can thus be described as "the successive movement from an event to its repression to its return."[37] By first witnessing the burning of the brides and the hand engulfed in flames, then erasing the hands of his mother, Gorky shows that even though the harrowing memories burned themselves into his psyche, they can be recalled only through a willful act of forgetting. An event, as Cathy Caruth argues, can only be traumatic as a result of a latency period in which memories are suppressed, which explains how the Armenian genocide itself has traversed a period of invisibility in the memory of its people and in public discourse, only to emerge with greater force as a result of that repression.

In his article "Truth and Testimony: The Process and the Struggle," Dori Laub recounts the story of a little boy living in a Krakow Ghetto who was smuggled out when his parents heard that all children would be rounded up for extermination. As a parting gift, his mother offered him a photograph of herself as a student, which the child later used for prayer, in lieu of a crucifix, pleading with his mother to come and take him back and urging for the war to be over.[38] By the same token, the picture of his mother is not only a surrogate witness for the young Gorky but also an iconic presence that resonates with images of Armenian church carvings in Raffi's video footage of his journey to Turkey and later in Ani's academic lectures: "Arshile Gorky was born in a small village on the shores of Lake Van. From the shores of this village, the island of Aghtamar was in plain view. Gorky, as a child, would go to this island with his mother, who would show him the detailed carvings on the walls of the church." In showing Celia his footage of these carvings, Raffi retraces the metamorphosis of the image "from the memory of this place . . . from the photograph, to the sketch, to the painting" in a palimpsestic curve that shows to what extent transmedial representation can also demarcate a nation's historical stratifications.

Indeed, many of *Ararat*'s narrative segments are organized around a series of flashbacks that, to paraphrase Caruth, provide a form of recall that operates at the cost of willed memory and conscious thought.[39] By switching from images of Gorky in his studio to episodes of his life in old Van, Egoyan reveals how the painter's traumatized psyche relives the insistent realities of the past without recourse to active recollection.[40] Such pathologies of memory are often noted in patients with various forms of post-traumatic stress disorder (PTSD), whose conscious recollection is often impaired but who nevertheless frequently experience "intrusive thoughts, nightmares, or flashbacks" and the relentless resurfacing of "unbidden repetitive images of traumatic events."[41] The image of the burning hand thus occupies a space to which willed access is denied, so the event vividly and paradoxically returns as a signifier of amnesia, crystallized in the metaphor of the mother's blank hands. The visual mutilation of the mother's body is therefore closely tied up with Gorky's ability to recover the past but not to have access to it—to have it but not to properly hold it. By extrapolation, the massacre of the Armenian people is not only obstructed by repression or amnesia, but is essentially constituted by its lack of integration into consciousness. However, present in the photograph and the painting, Gorky seems to believe, there is still a gaping hole, a point of dissolution at the heart of the story that can only be told elliptically, as it presents itself rather than as the mind recalls it.

Egoyan's own eclectic use of media replicates this piecemeal reappearance of memory as a flashback and short circuit of recollection. His multiple re-enactments of the genocide convey both the brutal truth of the historical event and the subtler truth of its incomprehensibility. Similarly to Claude Lanzmann, who began working on his film of Holocaust testimonies by admitting the very impossibility of telling the story, Egoyan challenges our expectations of what it means to access the past, suggesting that historical truth may be transmitted through the refusal of certain frameworks of understanding (such as linear narrative or realism), a refusal that becomes a creative form of reconstruction.[42] The "refusal of understanding," which Lanzmann deems to be "the only possible ethical and at the same time the only possible operative attitude," is compounded by Egoyan's multiple approaches to mediation.[43] With Lanzmann we listen; with Egoyan we watch and struggle to gain access to a historical catastrophe as witnesses from afar. More important than the two individuals portrayed, the photograph, like a classical painting, "at once depicts a scene *and the gaze of the spectator*, an object *and* a viewing subject."[44] The viewing subject, in this case, acts as witness not only to the precarious situation of the mother and child before the Ottoman clampdown on the Armenian population but especially to the genocide itself, which is the photograph's inscribed future.

"Part of the genocide's damage," Lisa Siraganian observes, "has been to leave younger generations without a meaningful symbol of memorialisation."[45] Indeed, on his trip of emotional and cultural reconnaissance, Raffi recognizes the erasure of "not just the land and the lives, but the loss of any way to remember it." To compensate for this absence, survivors and their progeny resort to desperate acts of fetishization, whereby genocide paraphernalia (such as the button that Gorky's mother sewed back onto his coat or the pomegranate seeds that sustained Saroyan's mother on the death marches and now serve to bear witness to her son of "luck and the power to imagine") function as prosthetic memory devices.[46] Both the photograph and the painting belong to this list of fetishized artifacts, whose materiality is tested not only by Gorky rubbing the canvas with his bare hands, as if in an attempt to restore organic contact through which affect can be nurtured or to mold the flesh of the past, but also by Raffi's confused girlfriend, Celia, who transfers her anger at her stepmother's refusal to accept responsibility for the (suicidal or accidental) death of Celia's father by taking a knife to Gorky's symbolically saturated painting. Both of these gestures are part of a performative ritual that underpins the entire film and manifests itself in a number of interactions between the iconic images featured in the film and their interpreters.

Ethical Memory as Performance

Egoyan's narrative de-focalizations, despite their seeming pre-occupation with history, disrupt linear temporality, working with repetition, circularity, and prolonged time. The action takes place on several planes (Gorky's studio, Saroyan's set, the airport terminal, Mount Ararat as seen by Raffi, etc.) and the film cuts back and forth from one setting to another, intermingling their respective time frames. The transpositions among these temporal levels are effected through performative means, which raise questions about the ethics of not only remembering the past but also re-*acting* to it. The most significant element of this performative code is the pose—that of the mother and child waiting for their picture to be taken for the benefit of the (absent) father; the pose of the actors suddenly interrupted by Ani storming onto the live set and spoiling the scene of Ussher's heroic acts among the villagers in Van; the pose of Gorky himself as imagined by Ani against the promotion poster for Saroyan's film *Ararat*.

On his way back from Turkey, carrying canisters of film for a shady figure he met there, Raffi is held at Canadian customs and subjected to a lengthy interrogation by a customs officer who suspects Raffi of being a drug dealer smuggling drugs into the country. The Toronto airport is not only used as the backdrop of this questioning—which "foregrounds the act of telling and hearing a personal narrative" as well as the validity of narrative as a discourse of victimization and ascription of guilt—but it also features as a liminal place where cultural luggage is exchanged and identities verified.[47] In the closely controlled environment of the airport and its sanitized climate of enforced security, surveillance, and organized anticrime, every individual carries out an impersonation of what the system expects him or her to be. Failure to carry out the exact prescriptions of behavior or act according to the scripts of patience, submission, and discretion results in immediate questioning and even withdrawal of freedom. The exception in Raffi's case only confirms the rule. Raffi plays his part so successfully that he manages not only to defeat the system by being released despite carrying large quantities of heroin over the border, but to do so while staying within the bounds of his acting role as a potentially suspect but not yet suspicious object of scrutiny.

Another highly performative moment in the film takes place between Raffi and Ali (who plays the part of a particularly gruesome Turkish officer, Jedvet Bey, in the film-within-a-film), two contemporary Canadians, one with Armenian roots, the other of Turkish descent. Asked how he feels about playing Jedvet and pushed to admit that the genocide happened, Ali delivers a succinct yet complicated answer: he is not Turkish, but Canadian, living in a young country where he must both remember his heritage and move beyond ancient enmities. In this particular instance, remembrance and affect are sparked by impersonation as a form of historical transposition. Raffi is moved not only by Ali's performance but also by impersonation itself as testimonial procedure. Or, to put the question to Egoyan: "Can an actor, who is only playing a role, give the viewer the critical distance needed to understand an event? Can a director? Can a film? Who has the authority— be it moral, spiritual, or artistic—to tell a story?"[48] In Egoyan's film, many stories are told by an academic, Ani, who also carries out a complex performance in which she aligns her own personal history with the interests of the Armenian community in a way that deftly employs the complexity of transmediation. Ani's stepdaughter Celia regularly appears at Ani's lectures, where she offers combative responses to the statements put forward by her stepmother, whom the young woman holds directly responsible for her father's death and regards as a highly histrionic self-performer.

Multiculturalism and Amnesia

In a commentary on one of his own poems, poet and scholar Lorne Shirinian acknowledges the tendency to create connections and continuity in a web of thin relations by accepting non-relatives as family surrogates "despite knowing full well that such forms of intimacy were impossible."[49] When David, the customs officer at Toronto airport, releases Raffi after discovering that the young man was attempting to smuggle heroin into the country (most likely un-knowingly), he does so by considering the situation of his own son, whose coming out precipitated a family crisis. By substituting an unknown Canadian traveling to Turkey to recover his Armenian heritage for his own son, David highlights the flexibility of thick relations and their status as a plausible foundation for larger social unity and less direct networks of kinship. As in Egoyan's *Calendar* (1993), whose photographer protagonist never seems able to accommodate a received and pre-determined Armenian identity, *Ararat* posits various inflections on what exactly constitutes cultural and emotional affiliation to the Armenian past. Egoyan never discards belonging as a form of cultural identity, yet he refuses to prescribe how one attaches oneself to one culture and how those attachments manifest them-selves in everyday life. This seems at odds with Canada's official policy of multi-culturalism, which often appears to exoticize ethnic attachments.

As many critics have observed, *Ararat* is as much about contemporary Canada as it is about the Armenian genocide, a clear-headed reflection on historical memorization and a critique of cultural issues plaguing contemporary Toronto.[50] "In Cannes, the film was hijacked by the political agenda between Armenia and Turkey," Egoyan remarked. "I'm really excited about the Toronto screenings, because it is very much a film about living in that city, in Canada. It's about how we, as Canadians, must fight and struggle to place ourselves in our country. It's not easy. You know, the folkloric, smiley-face aspect of multiculturalism is one thing. I was a part of it, in a way, with travelling around with *Next of Kin*. But it's hard work to create a tolerant, multicultural society like ours. It's an achievement. It's sacred."[51] Edward W. Said once remarked in an interview with Canadian journalist Robert Fulford that Canada is unique among modern nations as one that has turned the idea of exile into an institution. According to Said, Canadian multiculturalism policy domesticated the aches of exile and encouraged only superficial remembrance manifested in exterior cultural practice, while the pain of exile still goes unrelieved and unexpressed. That a new nation would encourage its citizens of various backgrounds to actively preserve their origins and cultural practices while simultaneously subscribing to the codes of contemporary Canadianness struck Said as "intellectually untenable, seriously dislocating and uncomfortably alienating."[52] The half-Turkish actor who plays the part of Jedvet Bey proposes that historical tensions be forgotten and the Canadian mosaic celebrated, an apparently benign suggestion that the film turns on its head. For the Armenian diaspora, memory is necessary as an act of recall and of mourning, often inflected by rage and despair. In this sense, *Ararat* stages the predicament faced by many Canadians of remembering their cultural roots while not being incapacitated by this memory.

The animosity sparked by artistic memorization is thus an integral part in the formation of identity for the Armenians living in Canada, for the director himself, and for a considerable section of the cast—also selected to be of Armenian descent. The film's Armenian characters are often at cross-purposes as far as their personal commemoration practices are concerned. Raffi does not understand Saroyan's failure to take Ali to task for his flippant rejection of historical data on the Armenian genocide, while Ani and Celia cannot find any common ground or sympathy for each other's need to see their losses acknowledged and mourned. Such rifts instantiate what Kai Erikson classifies as the public repercussions of trauma: "Sometimes the tissues of community can be damaged in much the same way as the tissues of mind and body, . . . but even when that does not happen, traumatic wounds inflicted on individuals can combine to create a mood, an ethos—a group culture, almost— that is different from (and more than) the sum of the private wounds that make it up. Trauma, that is, has a social dimension."[53]

Within a community, trauma seems to force open the fault lines that run silently through the larger structures of that group, dividing it into fragments. This is not to say that after so many decades and their dissipation throughout the world, the Armenians' plight can still be regarded as a form of collective trauma. Rather, memories of and belated reactions to the historical events slowly and insidiously work their way into the Canadian community to which the survivors and their children now belong. The social organism traumatized by the genocide is less the original Armenian community (which was, of course, torn asunder, though not subjected to trauma in its sense of a nonimmediate shock emerging sometime after exposure) but the post-exilic Canadian community that the film's characters are part of.

To conclude, what *Ararat* shows is that we understand the Armenian genocide through the diverse range of representational coordinates that determine what and how we see, how we process visual detail, and what meaning we give it. Throughout, Egoyan's temporally vertiginous film, fraught with oblique and unresolved questions, carries out a structural distancing through nested narrations that demonstrate how one medium takes up residence within another. What this chapter has been arguing is that the switch from the photographic image to the painting and to film codifies the shift from authentication to representation and, as such, the transition from direct memory to a form of ethical recall. This recall draws its sharpness not from faithfulness to an event but rather from the desire to have lived it—dramatizing the memory envy endemic to the torment not of survivors but of their descendants, who did not have to survive anything except the very absence of the genocide as a caesura in their own lives. This chapter has shown how Egoyan uses structural and medial memorization to reveal the affinities of post-exilic experience with trans-medial modes of representation along both narrower and larger circles of belonging. *Ararat*, then, is both a very private working-through of issues relating to the self as well as to family intimacy and a public statement on the permeability of boundaries between thick and thin relations in an age of visual screens that defy such fixed dimensions.

NOTES

1. Wasserman, "Dialogue with Samantha Power," 222. Samantha Power is a lecturer in human rights and foreign policy at Harvard's John F. Kennedy School of Government, where she previously worked as founding executive director of the Carr Center for Human Rights Policy. Power's study of twentieth-century genocides includes discussions of the Bosnian Serbs' eradication of non-Serbs, the Armenian genocide, Saddam Hussein's slaughter of Kurds in northern Iraq, and the systematic extermination of the Tutsi minority in Rwanda. In taking too long to "muster the imagination needed to reckon with evil," she argues, the United States has consistently forfeited their tremendous ability and moral obligation to

curb massacres, deportations, and other atrocities that were eventually emboldened by U.S. inaction: "No U.S. president has ever made genocide prevention a priority, and no U.S. president has ever suffered politically for his indifference to its occurrence. It is thus no coincidence that genocide rages on." Power, *"Problem from Hell,"* xxi.

2. Melson, *Revolution and Genocide*, 145.

3. Turkish authorities have been suppressing awareness of the genocide by revising history to omit accounts of the event and even engaged in censorship not only on Turkish ground but also by using their international leverage to prevent the release of a feature film focusing on the stories of survivors. On this issue see Siraganian, "Telling a Horror Story, Conscientiously," 135; Smith, Markusen, and Lifton, "Professional Ethics and the Denial of Armenian Genocide."

4. Romney, *Atom Egoyan*, 173.

5. Egoyan, "In Other Words," 887. In his introduction to the published script of *Ararat*, Egoyan elaborates on his Armenian heritage: "My grandparents from my father's side were victims of the horrors that befell the Armenian population of Turkey in the years around 1915. My grandfather, whose entire family save his sister was wiped out in the massacres, married my grandmother who was the sole survivor of her family." Egoyan, *Ararat*, vii.

6. Ouzounian, "Dealing with the Ghosts of Genocide."

7. Naficy, "The Accented Style of the Independent Transnational Cinema," 191.

8. Porton, "The Politics of Denial."

9. Markovitz, "*Ararat* and Collective Memories of the Armenian Genocide," 236.

10. Mediation as metaphor and structural design runs through Egoyan's entire oeuvre. Jonathan Romney begins his introductory overview of the director's work by pointing to Egoyan's intense interest in questions of visual transmission and imagery: "His characters rarely confront each other directly: more commonly, they watch each other through windows, or stare at each other as images on screens. They seem capable of apprehending each other only through television, video, and surveillance systems—ways of looking at others that are invariably also indirect ways of looking at themselves." Romney, *Atom Egoyan*, 1.

11. Lisa Siraganian interprets the film-within-a-film as Egoyan's answer to the potential rejoinder that he failed to offer a basic outline of the events themselves or that he, as an Armenian director and the grandson of genocide survivors, may not be in a position to provide a balanced, nonpartisan representation of the story: "Egoyan's film is not Saroyan's film because the distinction enables Egoyan to create a strategy to answer and dismiss within the film itself the charge of falsification." Siraganian, "Telling a Horror Story," 148. I would argue, however, that the film-within-a-film in fact illustrates *Ararat*'s central metaphor of double (or multiple) representation, whereby one artifact mirrors another in bridging the gap between documentation and representation.

12. Naficy, *An Accented Cinema*; Baronian, "History and Memory."

13. Ussher, *An American Physician in Turkey*.

14. Matossian describes Gorky's painting as an "homage to his mother," Shushan Adoian, who died of starvation and illness after their family was forced from their home during the genocide. See Matossian, *Black Angel*, 93–99.

15. The incident is based on Armenian terrorist activity against Turkish civilians and diplomats in the 1970s and 1980s, for which two diasporic organizations were primarily responsible: the Justice Commandos for the Armenian Genocide (JCAG) and the Armenian Secret Army for the Liberation of Armenia (ASALA). See Siraganian, "Telling a Horror Story," 135.

16. Sturken, *Tangled Memories*, 9.

17. Egoyan, *Ararat*, viii.

18. Egoyan, "In Other Words," 900.

19. Ibid., 904. Turkish groups also protested against the film's American distributors, complaining that Egoyan was disseminating anti-Turkish propaganda; see Romney, *Atom Egoyan*, 173.

20. There is a growing body of literature that contests Marianne Hirsch's concept of postmemory, defined as "the experience of those who grow up dominated by narratives that preceded their birth, whose own belated stories are evacuated by the stories of the previous generation shaped by traumatic events that can be neither understood nor recreated" (Hirsch, *Family Frames*, 22). My own position is also mildly critical of her terminology to the extent that she relies too much on the implications of "memory" in the structure and definition of her new concept, restricting the reform to the prefix "post-." A closely related term, that of post-exile, will inform my argument and carries many of the same conundrums. What connects Hirsch's term to my argument is her gesture of replacing recollection through an act of imaginative investment and creation—which perfectly describes Gorky's creative rituals of memorization.

21. Power cites a larger portion of Hitler's statement than Egoyan does: "It was knowingly and lightheartedly that Genghis Khan sent thousands of women and children to their deaths. History sees in him only the founder of a state. . . . The aim of war is not to reach definite lines but to annihilate the enemy physically. It is by this means that we shall obtain the vital living space that we need. Who today still speaks of the massacre of the Armenians?" Power, *"Problem from Hell,"* 23.

22. Margalit, *The Ethics of Memory*, 7.

23. Incidentally, Raffi's video contains the image of a mother carrying her child in a clear—albeit unintended—echo of Gorky's painting, which thus seems to be haunting the film. Romney notes that "the mother and child were actually discovered by chance by the cameraman who shot the video material for Egoyan in Turkey." Romney, *Atom Egoyan*, 183.

24. I borrow the term "voyeuristic" from a statement by Egoyan concerning his film *Calendar*; he describes his relationship to the "dreamed historical homeland" of Armenia as "voyeuristic" and very abstract. See Egoyan, "Calendar," 93. The pattern of visual dissociation is reinforced in *Calendar* by the male protagonist's profession as a photographer.

25. Hogikyan, "Atom Egoyan's Post-Exilic Imaginary," 196. See also Parker, "Something to Declare," 1046–47: "The governing metaphor for history in *Ararat* is the intergenerational embrace."

26. See Shapiro, *For Moral Ambiguity*, 79.

27. Erbal, review of *Ararat*, 957.

28. Marianne Hirsch has referred to verbally described photographs as prose pictures and to photographs that make up narratives as visual fictions. See Hirsch, *Family Frames*, 272. The hybrid form of *Ararat* combines these strategies.

29. Mitchell, *Picture Theory*, 89.

30. Burwell and Tschofen, "Mobile Subjectivity and Micro-territories," 127.

31. Egoyan, *Ararat*, xi.

32. The reverse takes place in Egoyan's short film, *A Portrait of Arshile* (1995)—consisting of footage of his son named after the Armenian painter—where the commentary uncannily locates Gorky's mother in a museum, "where she now stares from a gallery wall into a land she never dreamed of."

33. Goldberg, *Beyond Terror*, 182.

34. Fresco, "La Diaspora des cendres"; Raczymow, "Memory Shot through with Holes."

35. Barthes, *Camera Lucida*, 27.

36. Freud, *Moses and Monotheism*, 84.

37. Caruth, *Trauma*, 7.

38. Laub, "Truth and Testimony," 70–71.

39. Caruth, "Recapturing the Past," 152.

40. By replicating the structure of traumatic replay, Egoyan may have sought to transfer traumatic effects onto the viewer, in keeping with his tendency to reflect thematic aspects of his films in their formal structures. For instance, the nonlinear structure of Egoyan's experimental film *Diaspora* (2001) effects a form of displacement by seeking to alienate viewers from any stable referent and thus forcing them to experience time, space, and disorientation in a diasporic manner.

41. Krystal, "Animal Models for Post-Traumatic Stress Disorder," 6; Greenberg and van der Kolk, "Retrieval and Integration of Traumatic Memories with the 'Painting Cure,'" 191.

42. Lanzmann, "Le Lieu et la parole," 295.

43. Ibid., 279.

44. Burgin, *Thinking Photography*, 146.

45. Siraganian, "Telling a Horror Story," 151.

46. Another such object is Mount Ararat itself, which Egoyan refers to as "the most fetishized symbol" for the Armenian nation, which "freezes the multiplicity of meanings of what Armenia is." Naficy, "The Accented Style of the Independent Transnational Cinema," 219, 224.

47. Siraganian, "Telling a Horror Story," 147.

48. Egoyan, "In Other Words," 893.

49. Shirinian, *Landscape of Memory*, 40.

50. Romney argues that Egoyan uses city backdrops as empty signifiers or zones of absence and to illustrate a sense of rootlessness that he associates with the multicultural makeup of Canadian society. See Romney, *Atom Egoyan*.

51. McSorley, "Faraway, So Close."

52. Ibid.

53. Erikson, "Notes on Trauma and Community," 185.

Part II

Coloniality and Postcoloniality

5 Massacre and the Movies

Soldier Blue *and* *the Sand Creek Massacre of 1864*

PAUL R. BARTROP

Introduction

The late 1960s and early 1970s was a period in which filmmakers extended the boundaries of what they saw as their role in helping to shape public awareness of major social and political issues. Films such as *M*A*S*H* (Robert Altman, 1970) and *Catch-22* (Mike Nichols, 1970), for example, were iconoclastic antiwar movies inspired by opposition to the Vietnam War (though neither were set during that conflict), in which the establishment was ridiculed and the heroic image of American greatness was shown to be far less monolithic than earlier images had portrayed. Appearing the same year as these two movies was *Soldier Blue*, a stereotype-breaking "revisionist Western" in which the usually heroic U.S. Cavalry on the frontier is shown in a far more contemptible light. Directed by Ralph Nelson, it is a fictionalized treatment of the events leading up to, and culminating in, the Sand Creek massacre in Colorado on November 29, 1864. Starring Candice Bergen, Peter Strauss, and Donald Pleasence, the movie is a stinging indictment of white American expansion into Native American lands during the nineteenth century, and presents, in graphic terms, the filmmakers' view that this was accompanied by merciless genocide.

This chapter considers some of the more important issues revolving around the portrayal of the massacre in film. It explores the depiction of the historical

Sand Creek, seeking to ascertain just how far the film can be construed as accurate history or a fictionalized stereotype. The most fundamental of questions regarding filmic portrayals of historical issues can be considered in any such treatment. Is the movie true to the historical reality (so far as it can be understood) on which it is based? Is the movie useful in providing an understanding of what massacres can "look" like? And finally, how effective can graphic depictions of massacres—such as *Soldier Blue*—be for a new generation of viewers seeing such images for the first time? These are generic questions, all of which will be touched on here as a starting point for what can become broader areas of investigation at a later time.

The Background

The destruction of indigenous peoples throughout the Americas represents one of the greatest and most extensive human catastrophes in history. The pace and magnitude of the destruction varied from region to region over the years, but it can safely be concluded that in the two and a half centuries following Christopher Columbus's "discovery" of the Americas in 1492, probably 95 percent of the pre-Columbian population was wiped out—by disease as well as by deliberate policy on the part of the Spanish, the French, the English, and, ultimately, by the American-born heirs of those colonizing nations.

The process was often characterized by violent confrontation, deliberate massacre, wholesale annihilation, and, in several instances, genocide. Many indigenous peoples in North America were completely, or almost completely, wiped out, for example, the Yuki of California (destroyed by white encroachment and sustained mass murder) and the Beothuk of Newfoundland (destroyed by population collapse following a steady withdrawal from the white presence). Given this, it is important that care is taken when employing the term *genocide* relative to colonial expansion: each and every claim must be assessed individually and on its merits. In some instances, genocide might be unequivocal; elsewhere, despite a sudden or enormous population collapse, the crucial ingredient of the colonizers' intent would not appear to have been present. Often, populations declined as a result of diseases that arrived with the colonizers, and the deaths that occurred were not anticipated. On other occasions, lethal diseases were deliberately introduced for the purpose of wiping out a population. If we were to generalize—not an easy task when considering a continent-wide phenomenon occurring over several centuries—it could be said that colonial expansion in North America saw attempts at clearing the land of indigenous populations; of forcibly assimilating these same populations for racial, religious, or ethnic reasons; and of intimidating the survivors so they would retreat before the advance of the colonizers so that capitalist economic development could take place.

Overall, we are looking at a horrific case (or, rather, series of cases) of mass human destruction, in which millions of people lost their lives. And the destruction did not stop once most of the people had died or been killed; U.S. policies of population removal, dispossession of lands, forced assimilation, and confinement to reservations meant that in a vast number of cases, even the survivors were denied the opportunity to retain their identity as distinct peoples.

The foundations of indigenous destruction were many, and they varied from place to place. The quest for land, religious conversion, development of concepts of racial inferiority and superiority, displacement, and population transfer undertaken in the pursuit of "progress" on the frontiers of European or American settlement— all of these had their place in the devastation of the Native Americans. Individual murders, occasional massacres, and wholesale annihilation in long-term campaigns facilitated violent destruction. That genocide of specific Native American groups took place is beyond doubt; but this must be tempered by the qualification that not all destruction or population collapse occurred as the result of a deliberate intent on the part of the colonists. On those occasions where intent *can* be detected, a case for genocide might be prosecuted, but the disintegration of the Native American world was not a monolithic event, and must, therefore, be examined carefully and thoroughly, with an eye to the particularity of each people, region, and time period, and without preconceived opinions.

European colonization was frequently characterized by the establishment of settler communities that resulted in the displacement, absorption, or destruction of preexisting communities. In the history of the United States, large numbers of American-born settlers left their original homes to start new outgrowth communities or to reinforce those of their kin already there. In so doing, they took over land— sometimes quite brutally—already occupied by Native Americans. Genocidal massacres of the latter were not infrequent, and ongoing oppression or neglect has in numerous cases persisted to the present day. Colonialism, as it impacted Native American populations, also led to the suppression of local languages, religions, and folkways, as the settlers looked for ways to consolidate their rule and ward off what they perceived as threats to the expansion of "their" territory in the new land. The human cost was devastating and long-lasting for the Native American populations being taken over by the colonizers, and the injury done to their sense of identity and self-worth has, in many cases, yet to be resolved.

The term *genocidal massacre* was introduced in 1981 by noted political scientist and genocide scholar Leo Kuper, in his seminal work *Genocide: Its Political Use in the Twentieth Century*. Noting that the annihilation of a section of a group in a localized massacre (for example, in the wiping out of a whole village of men, women, and children) contains some of the elements of a genocide, Kuper sought to find a way to give such massacres their proper place within a model of genocide while recognizing that such events did not, *by themselves*, constitute genocide.[1] He thus found the notion of genocidal massacre particularly useful when describing colonial situations, identifying a clear affinity between colonialism and genocide. While even an aggregation of genocidal massacres did not necessarily connote a policy of genocide, nonetheless the motives that underlay such massacres were, in their time-and-place circumstances, motivated by a genocidal intent. For Kuper, therefore, the genocidal massacre, while not necessarily equating with genocide, was a convenient device for explaining the many examples of destruction that took place during the process of territorial acquisition.

The Massacre at Sand Creek

To appreciate the crucial role of state intent when trying to arrive at a determination for or against genocide—and in particular, of genocidal massacres—in colonial settings, we may consider an instance that took place in the Colorado Territory of the United States on November 29, 1864. Here, Colonel John M. Chivington, commanding the Third Colorado Volunteer Cavalry Regiment, led an attack against a Cheyenne village under Chief Black Kettle. Those doing the killing had been given clear instructions that were worked out in advance and communicated unequivocally.

Colorado in 1864 was, in the words of historian David E. Stannard, "the quintessence of the frontier west."[2] Incidents between Indians and white settlers resulted in escalating rounds of violence, but the settlers were able to cloak their attacks in the legitimacy of organized military force. The period of 1861 to 1865 was a time of bloody civil war for the United States, and as its soldiers in the western part of the country were recalled for active duty against the Confederacy, their places were taken by militia forces raised in the territory itself. Actions against the Indians were, henceforth, undertaken by uniformed volunteers—local men acting under orders from the territorial government. As one historian has viewed it, many of these citizen soldiers were frontiersmen with a deep contempt for Native Americans; an illustration is recalled of how one of these detachments fired shells into a Sioux camp for artillery practice.[3]

Despite such wanton violence and the refusal of the Indian bands to be cowed, by the early 1860s, some measure of accord had arrived in the form of limited peace treaties agreed to between the white authorities and certain Indian chiefs—in particular, for our purposes, with the southern Cheyenne chiefs Black Kettle and White Antelope, who had agreed to white demands for the cession of a substantial area of land near Denver. American scholar James Wilson describes what followed: "The other Cheyenne chiefs, however, rejected it (something which, as autonomous band leaders, they were perfectly entitled to do), and in the spring and summer of 1864, hoping for a pretext to take the land by force, members of the Colorado militia launched a series of indiscriminate raids against Cheyenne camps. They were commanded by Colonel John Chivington, a Methodist preacher and rabid Indian-hater who was notorious for publicly advocating the murder of Native American children on the grounds that 'nits make Lice.'"[4]

Chivington did not just hate Indians; he was also obsessed by them. In the spring of 1864, prior to leaving on a military expedition to track down a group accused of stealing settler-owned cattle, he issued an order "to kill every Cheyenne they found and take no prisoners."[5] The Third Colorado Volunteers and their commanding officer were thus made for each other, as the government of the Colorado Territory had established this militia unit "exclusively for the purpose of killing Cheyennes, Arapahos, and any other native people they might encounter over a 100-day period."[6] The volunteers themselves were keen to carry out their mandate: they included "a large number of rowdies and toughs recruited from the mining camps and Denver saloons, and they sought action and the notoriety they would gain if they smashed the Indians before their hundred-day enlistment period expired."[7]

When Chivington ordered that the Third Colorado militia kill all the Cheyenne, a regular U.S. Army Major who was commanding Fort Lyon, Edward Wynkoop, invited Black Kettle and White Antelope to bring their people closer to the fort for their protection. Chivington, in turn, arranged for Wynkoop to be replaced "on the grounds that he was too 'conciliatory.'"[8] Wynkoop's replacement, Major Scott Anthony, "encouraged the Indians to remain near the post, in order—there is no doubt of this—to have them available for a massacre."[9] If Chivington was to use his Third Colorado Volunteers for the purpose they were intended, moreover, he would need a pool of likely victims close at hand; the hundred days' muster for which the troops had signed on would run out before the end of 1864, and the episode with Major Wynkoop had already taken up a good deal of September.

The area in which the Cheyenne were to be "protected" was about forty miles to the northeast of Fort Lyon, on a nearly dry watercourse named Sand Creek. The Indians, numbering over two hundred men and five hundred women and children, had been required to surrender any weapons they possessed and accept what has been described as "de facto internment status."[10] They were thoroughly defenseless. Chivington decided to wipe out the Indians encamped at Sand Creek. His men, having signed on to become Indian fighters, had not seen much action, and were being looked on with derision by the people of Colorado as nothing but paper heroes. After a forced march in a blizzard, the Third Colorado militia arrived at Fort Lyon on November 27, 1864, determined to press home the attack. As one account has recorded, "Several officers remonstrated, declaring that the Cheyennes had been led to understand that they were prisoners of war. Chivington responded, as one of the protesters recalled, that he believed it to be right and honorable to use any means under God's heaven to kill Indians that would kill women and children, and 'damn any man that was in sympathy with the Indians.'"[11] Having his way, Chivington then led his men off toward Sand Creek.

Surrounding the camp before dawn on the morning of November 29, the Third Colorado's assault group, comprising some seven hundred men and four howitzers, took the Indians by complete surprise. Black Kettle pleaded with his people to keep calm, and hoisted both an American flag and a white flag of truce above his quarters. As the Indians realized what was happening, the troops began to open fire on them. The ensuing massacre was so horrific that some of Chivington's own men would later turn in evidence against him for allowing such abhorrent acts to take place. The soldiers were indiscriminate in their killing, as an interpreter, John Smith, would later testify: "[The Indians] were scalped, their brains knocked out; the men used their knives, ripped open women, clubbed little children, knocked them in the head with their guns, beat their brains out, mutilated their bodies in every sense of the word."[12] Major Anthony wrote later: "We, of course, took no prisoners"; it was obvious to everyone at the scene that this would be a total annihilation.[13]

Not only was mutilation taking place everywhere; all prisoners captured were summarily executed as soon as they surrendered. Angie Debo has shown how one lieutenant "killed and scalped three women and five children who had surrendered and were screaming for mercy; a little girl was shot down as she came out of a sand pit with a white flag on a stick; mothers and babes in arms were killed together."[14] The massacre continued for some five miles beyond the Sand Creek campsite, as the soldiers, many of whom were drunk on liquor or bloodlust, pursued those who had tried to run away. When Chivington and the Third Colorado returned to Denver, they exhibited more than a hundred scalps,[15] the gruesome booty of a death toll that may have numbered up to two hundred[16]—of whom two-thirds were women and children, and nine were chiefs. Black Kettle, the only one of all the "peace chiefs," escaped, though he was killed in a later massacre.[17]

The Sand Creek massacre did not bring an end to Cheyenne resistance to white encroachment, for by the end of December 1864, Black Kettle and other survivors had been able to spread word of what had happened to allied Indian nations on the Great Plains. Sioux, Arapaho, and Cheyenne united to try to avenge Sand Creek and keep the murderous white destroyers at bay, but, as subsequent developments would demonstrate, they were not successful. The American Civil War ended in 1865, regular U.S. troops returned to the West, and the conquest of the Indians became a foregone conclusion. One last massacre—of Big Foot and his Sioux at Wounded Knee in December 1890—would see the whites' military triumph complete.

To what degree can we consider the Sand Creek massacre an act of genocide? The issue has more than just historical interest; as with all such questions, the matter of responsibility has to be confronted—and if it can be shown that the United States was, at this time, possessed of a government that practiced or condoned genocide, then we can determine what the character of that government was, and, through this, what the nature of its laws was at a particular time in history. It might even be possible to draw some tentative conclusions about the assumptions on which modern America was based.

The actions of Colonel Chivington and the Third Colorado Volunteers were not only open; they were also eagerly advertised, with malice before the event and triumph after it. These actions were, moreover, committed by a military force raised by the government of the region for the express purpose of killing every Indian on whom it could lay its hands. Chivington's orders came directly from John Evans, the governor of Colorado, and were endorsed by a popular clamor throughout the territory. Far from breaking the law, Chivington was carrying it out—and this was not confined to the territorial government. When a later investigation into the massacre was conducted by the U.S. Congress, not only was it found that the people of Colorado endorsed Chivington's attack, but no action was taken against him at the federal level for murder or exceeding his orders. Four decades later, President Theodore Roosevelt called the Sand Creek massacre "as righteous and beneficial a deed as ever took place on the frontier."[18]

Sand Creek was clearly a genocidal massacre undertaken as part of a larger campaign of genocide against the Cheyenne and Arapaho, in which the objective was that none would remain alive. It was, in its purest form, an act committed with intent to destroy, in whole or in part, an ethnic or racial (or, perhaps, by their own sense of self, national) group, through a deliberate policy of killing its members. The United Nations Genocide Convention's very terms provide an explicit frame of reference in which Sand Creek can be understood.

Moreover, Sand Creek undoubtedly was a case of genocidal massacre in the sense intended by Leo Kuper. It was justified in the eyes of the perpetrators by reference to a need to "punish" the victims for the latest violation of a nonexistent peace, and it brought an overwhelming use of modern firepower to bear against people who were undefended noncombatants. Those who brought death and devastation to the people at Sand Creek were enforcing the law's decree, and in doing so were carrying out policies instituted by a genocidal administration. Sand Creek took place with the full sanction of the state, which acted as the major force in fomenting genocide against the target population.

Soldier Blue

The first filmic depiction of the massacre at Sand Creek was *Soldier Blue*, made in 1970. It was a fictionalized treatment of the events leading up to, and culminating in, the massacre; and it was a stinging indictment of white American expansion into Native American lands during the nineteenth century. It presented, in graphic terms, the filmmakers' view that this was accompanied by merciless genocide. While the movie was controversial owing to its disparagement of the near-sanctification of the "Manifest Destiny" argument in the United States, it was also equally controversial for its explicit depictions of genocidal violence, including the rape of women, mutilation, and the savage murder of children. Further controversy resulted from the message the movie was sending at a time when U.S. soldiers were fighting an unpopular war in Vietnam, and while the country was still reeling over the court-martial of Lieutenant William Calley for his role in overseeing a massacre of Vietnamese civilians at My Lai on March 16, 1968. *Soldier Blue*, within the context of the Vietnam War, was thus a movie that held up a mirror to U.S. society and showed that genocidal massacre was not only possible but had already happened on U.S. soil in the past.

Based on the book *Arrow in the Sun* by Theodore V. Olsen, the film is an attempt at showing, in unflinchingly graphic and close-up detail, the horror and pointlessness of mass murder on the frontier, in a climactic scene devoted to portraying sheer bloody slaughter of the most vicious type. The images of carnage remain vividly grotesque and etch the movie into an audience's memories; it is, in the words of an unnamed reviewer, "An ending that shows no mercy to the viewer."[19]

The film is thus most famous for its ending, a highly realistic attempt at reproducing the butchery of the massacre itself. But most of the movie deals with the journey to manhood of a young and naïve soldier, Honus Gant (Peter Strauss), who is educated into the reality of life on the frontier by Cresta Mary-Belle Lee (Candice Bergen), a young white woman who had earlier been captured by a Cheyenne raiding party, taken as wife by Chief Spotted Wolf (Jorge Rivero), and initiated into the tribe. Her general attitude to the United States has been influenced by her exposure to the other side of white expansion, and she is clearly unsympathetic to the U.S. Cavalry or the extension of white settlement into Indian lands.

The plot is subtle, but relatively simple. Cresta has been promised in marriage to a cavalry officer, and a cavalry detachment of twenty-two soldiers, transporting her and a paymaster's strongbox filled with gold to a frontier fort, is attacked and massacred by the Cheyenne. Only two survivors remain: Honus, who survived the battle because he had been removed from the main part of the corps on picket duty, and Cresta. Together, they set out to reach the fort on foot. As they travel onward, Honus is torn between his growing affection for Cresta and his disgust at her frequently expressed anti-Americanism.

The appearance of an important linking character in the film, a gunrunner by the improbable name of Isaac Q. Cumber (a double joke from the scriptwriters; the joke is located in both "IQ"—his doesn't appear to be all that high—and in "Q. Cumber"—as in "cucumber," which, he states, was his father's lasting gift). Cumber (Donald Pleasence) is an unscrupulous and sadistic character; he holds Honus and Cresta captive when they realize he is selling guns to the Indians. After they manage to escape, their love blooms, though she leaves him when she sees that nothing can come of their relationship due to her impending—presumably forced—marriage. Found by scouts of the U.S. Cavalry, she learns of a planned attack on a Cheyenne village a few miles away, the same village, it turns out, that was her home when living with Spotted Wolf. Cresta runs away to warn the Cheyenne of what she has learned; in the meantime, Honus is found by soldiers and taken into custody for desertion. With Honus back in the army, trying to warn his commander of the peaceful nature of those he is about to attack, and Cresta back with the Indians encouraging them to flee or prepare for defense, the film's finale is thus set up.

The fifteen minutes or so of the massacre scenes rank as being among the most violent ever shot in a major American movie. Children's limbs are mutilated, men and women are scalped, women and children are beheaded, women get raped and are tortured—we see one woman raped prior to having one of her breasts hacked off—and in other ways the soldiers brutally destroy the village and people living in it. The cavalry commander, Colonel Iverson (a mask for the real Chivington), issues an order to "burn this pestilence," which the men of his command take as an order to carry out what in a later age would certainly be described as crimes against humanity, war crimes, and genocide. A feature of the scene is when soldiers come on a ravine into which large numbers of women (including Cresta) and children have sought refuge; dragging Cresta out of the line of fire (with the command "get that white woman out of there"), they then open fire at point-blank range, killing dozens. When an appalled and quite distraught Honus then

Soldier Blue, 1970. Directed by Ralph Nelson.

sees Cresta, as she sits numbly among the bodies holding the corpse of a child, she asks him, "Got a prayer, Soldier Blue? A nice poem? Say something pretty." It is an extremely graphic, and, for many, disturbing scene.

And this is not the end of the horror. As viewers still recoil from what they have just seen, the next scene shows Colonel Iverson addressing his troops with a stirring concluding speech: "To each of you, to officer and soldier alike, I offer my most profound admiration, my deepest affection, my overwhelming gratitude, for a job well done. You men here today have succeeded in making another part of America a decent place for people to live. We have given the Indian a lesson he will not soon forget. But more than that, you men will hold your heads proud when this day is mentioned." The revulsion an audience is supposed to feel at this statement, following the massacre scene, serves as a sledgehammer blow to the sensibilities of even the most hardened of movie watchers.

Owing to its extreme violence, particularly the horrific final massacre, for decades only a severely edited form of the movie could be seen in its television or VHS format. Throughout the world, it teetered on the edge of an "X" rating, though usually it received an "R" for cinemas. Often, it might then be further reedited down to a "PG" rating, with much of the violence cut. Although it was a massive hit in Great Britain and much of the rest of the world, *Soldier Blue* was not a popular success in the United States when it appeared in 1970, despite its titillating promotional material showing a naked squaw tied with her hands behind her and its tagline that proclaimed it as "the most savage film in history!" The picture's groundbreaking violence was of course a major factor in this, but another reason for the film's mixed reviews was on account of the fact that the cavalry on this occasion was the diametric opposite of the usual image of "good guys" riding to the rescue. It rendered *Soldier Blue* as one of the most radical films in the history of American cinema up to that time.

Clearly, *Soldier Blue* does not deal with the typical images of "good Americans and bad Indians." It is unique within its genre because it was the first Western of its kind to really paint the army as inherently evil. It showed a very dark side of the expansion of American influence into the West and of how genocide was committed in the name of freedom and democracy—two terms that are sullied by the actions of the Colorado troops.

Conclusion

Soldier Blue was not a typical Western-genre movie. Previously, the prevailing image portrayed in Hollywood films was one of "savage" Indians attacking peaceful white settlers, though some path-breaking films had appeared before 1970. Two exceptions that stand out were *Broken Arrow* (Delmer Daves, 1950), which depicted white savagery against Indians, and *The Searchers* (John Ford, 1956), which showed that indiscriminate white racist obsession could be destructive—and totally unacceptable. These were, however, ahead of their time. Contemporaneous with *Soldier Blue* was an equally controversial movie, *Little Big Man* (Arthur Penn, 1970), which took the story of one man's observations of (and participation in) the "pacification" of the West to a personal level. Later, the release of *Dances with Wolves* (Kevin Costner, 1990) showed how far the notion of "the White Man's Indian" had moved away from the stereotypical idea of "savage" Indians and "upright" whites.[20] Earlier Western-genre films often depicted Native Americans in conflict with the whites and were thoroughly ethnocentric portrayals that left little room for doubt that the "Injuns" deserved all they got—with the exception of the occasional "Noble Red Man," who was elevated to a near-status of "honorary white" for as long as he was useful to the plot. Angela Aleiss, who has examined the history of Native Americans in Hollywood movies, has shown that even this stereotypical view was never as monolithic as it first appears, though of course the impact of the earlier negative view of Native Americans has had such a profound impact on broader attitudes throughout the history of motion pictures.[21]

When looking at the relationships between the Native Americans and the American whites during the period between 1607 (with the settlement of James-town in Virginia) and 1890 (with the massacre at Wounded Knee Creek, South Dakota), the time-and-place circumstances of the filmmakers must always be kept in mind. The culture surrounding those involved in making movies, as it is with those who write fiction, poetry, or music, is an inescapable part of the creative process. Like it or not, there was always going to be a stark contrast between depictions of Indians in film and the reality of their historical experience, and in this regard, *Soldier Blue*, made in the United States in 1970 during a time of national uncertainty, an unpopular war, and a serious questioning of the values of an older generation, can be said to be a movie that heightened the plight of Native Americans and brought it before an audience that was ready to be receptive to its message. *Soldier Blue*'s appearance, along with that of some others from the same period, meant that the previously negative, culturally demeaning, and destructive image of Native Americans—and the elevated, exaggerated views of the heroism character-izing white settlement—were never to be the same again.

NOTES

1. Kuper, *Genocide*, 45.
2. Stannard, *American Holocaust*, 129.
3. Wilson, *The Earth Shall Weep*, 272.
4. Ibid., 273.
5. Debo, *A History of the Indians of the United States*, 191.
6. Churchill, *A Little Matter of Genocide*, 228.
7. Utley and Washburn, *Indian Wars*, 206.
8. Wilson, *The Earth Shall Weep*, 273.
9. Debo, *A History of the Indians of the United States*, 194.
10. Churchill, *A Little Matter of Genocide*, 231.
11. Utley and Washburn, *Indian Wars*, 207.
12. Ibid.
13. Debo, *A History of the Indians of the United States*, 195.
14. Ibid.
15. Ibid.

16. Wilson, *The Earth Shall Weep*, 274.

17. David E. Stannard has compiled a number of eyewitness accounts of the Sand Creek massacre, many of them from soldiers who had themselves been directly involved. These accounts make for gruesome reading. See Stannard, *American Holocaust*, 132–33.

18. Ibid., 134.

19. See http://www.learmedia.ca/product_info.php/products_id/727.

20. The term "White Man's Indian" was introduced and popularized by Robert F. Berkhofer; see his *The White Man's Indian*.

21. Aleiss, *Making the White Man's Indian*.

6   The Other in Genocide

Responsibility and Benevolence
in Rabbit-Proof Fence

DONNA-LEE FRIEZE

Phillip Noyce's *Rabbit-Proof Fence* (2002) depicts the true story of the removal of mixed-descent Australian Aboriginal children from their home under the biological absorption plan conducted in Western Australia in the twentieth century in the interwar period. Molly Craig, her sister, Daisy, and cousin, Gracie, were forcibly removed by police from their family in Jigalong to a government settlement 1,500 miles away from their home. Under the watchful eye of the Chief Protector of Aborigines in Western Australia, A. O. Neville, the girls managed to escape from the Moore River Settlement, intent on walking home to their family. Their home was situated along the rabbit-proof fence—a rabbit barrier stretching the length of Western Australia, which the girls used as their guide. The girls eluded the tracker and police, all employed or encouraged by Neville to return the escapees to the settlement. Eventually, Gracie was recaptured, but Molly and Daisy finally arrived home to their family in Jigalong.

The victims of child removal (which occurred for the most part in the twentieth century) are referred to as the Stolen Generations, a term coined by Peter Read in 1981.[1] The debates surrounding these policies in Australia—regarding removal and voluntary "capture," in order to assimilate some Aborigines into "white" society—are beyond the scope of this chapter, but such issues nevertheless impinge on a reading of a film that depicts genocide as the forced removal of children rather than mass murder. Moreover, the depiction of genocide as the intention to destroy a group through the means of forcible child removal forms an essential part of a discussion of Emmanuel Levinas's philosophical theory of responsibility.

Article 2 (e) of the "Convention on the Prevention and Punishment of the Crime of Genocide" (CPPCG) states that the forcible transference "of children from one group to another," with the intention to destroy a particular group in whole or in part, constitutes genocide.[2] The state government administered a biological absorption policy that insisted, as a matter of supposed good faith, that mixed-descent Aboriginal children were deemed "half-caste" and could "breed out" the colors through intermarriage with "whites," which evokes another definition of responsibility: an imperialistic morality that claims what I am doing for you is beneficial for both of us.

In Levinas's terms, this ontological responsibility borders on a supercilious and debasing view of Others that insists you are an extension of me, and, in the case of biological absorption, demands that you *resemble* me.[3] For Levinas, the capitalized "Other" always edicts my responsibility and respect and is never regarded as an extension of me: to regard the Other as such would be unethical. This notion of the Other, and the embracing of the Other's otherness, underpins Levinas's concept of ethical responsibility. Indeed, responsibility is an issue that frames *Rabbit-Proof Fence*. The normative grasp of the term *responsibility* contrasts with Levinas's ethical understanding of "responsibility," which is to be always *for* the Other.

Noyce's film highlights the essence of these two forms of "responsibility" as ethical (Other) and ontological (other). This chapter argues that the film juxtaposes the ontological with ethical senses of responsibility and highlights the genocide of the Aborigines as a process of biological absorption. Responsibility obfuscated as duty—portrayed in the film as genocide—reflects the challenge posed by Levinas's theory of the ethical. Through this dichotomy of responsibility-as-ethical, and responsibility-as-dutiful, the Levinasian thesis of the ethical over morality motivates this viewer of *Rabbit-Proof Fence* to examine how a policy of apparent benevolence of the law is transformed into genocide.

Responsibility and Duty

> Duty, service, responsibility. Those are our watchwords.
>
> NEVILLE, *Australia's Coloured Minority*

With the release of *Rabbit-Proof Fence*, five years after the publication of the report titled *Bringing them Home*, the issue of the Stolen Generations passed from public debate to popular culture.[4] Art often mirrors contemporary concerns, rather than the historical event it depicts. Thus, in many ways, Noyce's film is a product of the polemic in Australia regarding the debates about the Stolen Generations.[5] Were the instigators responsible for the *forced* removal of the children and the subsequent tragic consequences? Was there an intention to destroy the group in whole or in part? How does the issue of intent differ from the motive behind the benevolence of the government? Although these questions are not explicit in the film, the issues they raise through the subtext of responsibility shed light on some answers. Through a reading of Levinas's theories of responsibility in relation to the Other, it is argued that *Rabbit-Proof Fence* portrays the Stolen Generations as victims of genocide, whose perpetrators confused notions of intent, motive, duty, and responsibility.

Neville's first words to Molly Craig, the "watchwords" previously quoted, are unexceptional unless contextualized. Molly and her sister and cousin are forcibly removed from their mothers to be "re-educated" and absorbed into "white" society along with other Aboriginal children at the Moore River Settlement in 1931. The next day, Neville summons Molly, along with other children, and inspects the color of their skin. Molly cautiously approaches Neville, who attempts to calm and appease her with those words. The "watchwords" are anathema to Molly, whose lifestyle, customs, and values are as far removed from the "white" Australian ideals as is her home in Jigalong from the settlement. In addition, the agglomeration of the three "watchwords" creates the Other as a cluster of additional others. What occupies the ideology behind the "watchwords" are paradigms of responsibility, illustrated in one striking sequence in the film.

The children's mothers and grandmothers wail in grief at the end of a harrowing abduction sequence that Noyce finds difficult to complete. Neville's voice-over from the following sequence overrides the wailing. *Rabbit-Proof Fence*, therefore, acknowledges Neville's responsibility for the sorrow, as well as Neville's complete disregard for the chaos he has caused. The chief protector's treatment, summed up in the sentence that overlaps and connects the sequences, is confronting: "As you know, every Aborigine born in this state comes under my control."[6] Toward the end of the film, in an act of empowerment, the film counters this imbalance. Shot from high overhead, looking down on his meticulous desk, Neville confronts his inability to capture the two girls who escaped the settlement. The real life Molly Craig's voice-over is now the authoritative narrative.

Rabbit-Proof Fence reveals Neville's values by focusing on the chief protector's attention to detail, order, and, hence, delivery of method, in the way he re-creates his methodical and bleak office. Levinas writes: "Consciousness of my injustice is produced when I incline myself not before facts, but before the [O]ther."[7] In his subservience to order, Neville remains blind to the equitable right of the other to be Other.

In a lecture to the Perth Women's Service Guild about the "problem" of "half-caste" Aboriginal children, Neville presents a pictorial slide show. His demonstration reveals how he dehumanizes people into a group of clustered others. The group, selected for obliteration, is the "half-caste." In order to authenticate his argument (his eugenics), Neville shows the guild a slide of three generations: grandmother, daughter and son, who were "mated" with "white" men until "no sign of native origin is apparent." In light of the previous abduction sequence, Neville's logic is abhorrent. He states, with the pointer indicating each "generation": "Three generations—half-blood grandmother, quadroon daughter and octoroon grandson. . . . The continued infiltration of white blood finally stamps out the black color."[8] While the guild women politely sip tea, a female Aboriginal domestic servant—filmed through the long-boxed projector leg—stands in the back of the room. When Neville confidently displays the slide of the Moore River Settlement—the intended destination for the group of predominately female "half-castes" training for domestic labor—he states, "Ladies, most of you will be familiar with the work that we are doing here—the training of domestic servants and farm laborers—and I want to thank you for your continuing support." Sardonically, Neville is filmed from the servant's point of view.

This sequence deals explicitly with genocide but *not* as mass murder, rather, as genocidal biological absorption, with intent to destroy the Aborigines. There is a juxtaposition of the ideology of Neville's genocide with images of mass annihilation, which subliminally reinforce the genocidal notions of the chief protector's policy. Tony Hughes D'aeth points out often-repeated images in films about genocide, in particular, the Holocaust: the barbed wire (rabbit-proof) fence, the shaving of a girl's head at the settlement, and "the 'selection' scene, where Neville separates out the children to be taken."[9] In addition to this, the film includes sequences of everyday clothes replaced by white uniforms; sparse, foul food; and the suppression of customary language and religion. The "dutiful care" sits uncomfortably with issues of unethical responsibility.

Levinas is not advocating an ungovernable responsibility when he argues that "the responsibility for the [O]ther cannot have begun in my commitment, in my decision," rather, he proposes that the decision to be responsible does not begin with a commitment.[10] In other words, nothing can induce me to act responsibly. *Before* the commitment to duty, I am *in essence* responsible for you. Levinasian responsibility goes beyond obligation and laws that govern duty. Ethical responsibility does not seek reciprocity nor is it content with its apparent accomplishment, in, for instance, altruism. In other words, Levinasian responsibility does not seek to return the favor. To suggest that the Other should do for me as I have for her or him goes against Levinas's "descriptive rather than prescriptive" attempts to depict the asymmetrical relationship with the Other.[11] Responsibility is not based in epistemology, but rather, as Tim Woods explains, is a "philosophy of *absolute altruism*."[12] A "benevolent" responsibility as enacted by the chief protector, nurses, and police in *Rabbit-Proof Fence* negates this "absolute altruism" as this form of "goodwill" refuses to engage with the otherness of the Other.

The sequences with Neville often take place within his meticulous office, which overlooks (and looks down on and thus dehumanizes) groups of Aborigines queuing for requests, who are conspicuous in their bright, elegant clothes. The camera lingers on them, as if to emphasize their *poverty* (in the Levinasian sense, poverty is the vulnerability of the Other), while Neville is content to see the Aborigines as an extension of his busy and meticulous timetable.[13] Neville believes he is responding to his duty, but he has no time to dawdle or delay. His task, as Chief Protector of Aborigines, is an obsession, a preoccupation of responsibility and duty whose result is persecution and, ultimately, genocide. The Aborigines request Neville's consent to marry, to visit their children in the settlement, and even for new shoes. Disgruntled, Neville informs his secretary that a women applying for a new pair of shoes already received a new pair a year ago. More disturbingly, the secretary describes the applications as "nothing out of the ordinary," but a customary function of his official duties. Here, the disengagement with the ethical Other and ethical responsibility is elucidated.

Levinas strips responsibility of its customary meaning. In *Rabbit-Proof Fence*, the form of responsibility that might be considered as benevolent is depicted as being counterproductive. This is not because the means do not justify the ends (that is, the responsibility the chief protector and the local protectors have is negated by the girls' escape) but rather that the vision of their responsibility is unethical. As Neville executes his duty, he expects the captors to respond obligingly, lawfully, and "responsibly." In other words, he expects reciprocity. Conversely, Molly's sense of responsibility toward her sister and cousin is not overt in the film, but it emerges subtly. It is not until the end of the film that Molly articulates her responsibility in a very moving piece of cinema. At twilight, after their nine-week walk home, Molly and Daisy run into the arms of their mother and grandmother as Molly sobs repeatedly: "I lost one, I lost one." Facing the camera, in her grandmother's arms, Molly's tears glisten as the insufferable loss of her cousin, recaptured during the walk home, overwhelms the exhaustion of the 1,500-mile trek. Molly's sense of ethical responsibility overrides the joy of reuniting with her family. In saying "I lost one," Molly could have said, "I lost an Other." Her words do not suggest reciprocity. As Jane Lydon comments, "One of the film's most moving ironies is the contrast it makes between Neville's admonition to Molly to mind her duty, and Molly's own sense of responsibility to her kin."[14] Her sense of responsibility toward her cousin is her "persecuting obsession" and is illuminated in this moment in the film.[15]

Cinematic effects expose the girls' very Otherness; indeed, there is never a sense that the audience can *know* the girls. The lack of epistemological information about the girls distresses some reviewers, as the classical narrative of a Hollywood film apparently requires such an exposé. As Matthew Dillon observes, "We travel several thousand . . . [miles] with the girls without coming to know them much better than we did at the start."[16] Conscious of capturing the essence of their Otherness, Noyce frames the girls walking toward the camera as if they are approaching the audience. For the audience to pretend to know these Others would be tantamount to the violations of the chief protector, who claimed exhaustive knowledge of his captives.

Indeed, Levinas argues we cannot *know* the Other. The Other does not equate with knowledge or the *satisfaction* of completion of knowledge: I cannot *know* responsibility. Zygmunt Bauman articulates this: "'*The duty of us all*' which I know, does not seem to be the same thing as my *responsibility* which I *feel*."[17] The duty, in fact, with which the film engages is static and rigid. Inflexible duty can never go beyond itself because it always adheres to and is constrained by an external law. Indeed, Neville dutifully held positions in Aboriginal administration in Western Australia for twenty-five years.[18] Duty, it seems, is akin to loyalty, bereft of the ethical. However, the ethical, by its very Levinasian meaning, must be fluid, because the Other *always* fluctuates and surprises. In the film, the adherence to order and duty obscures a fear—an anxiety regarding the loss of freedom. In order to capture the Other and limit the Other's freedom, the local protectors literally confine the victims by entrapping them in cars, trains, and cages. Levinas comments that the "responsibility for another [is] an unlimited responsibility which the strict book-keeping of the free and non-free does not measure."[19] For the local protectors, freedom, executed through their responsibility to assimilate the other, precedes the obligation to the Other, and enables a "strict book-keeping of the free and non-free."

Even Neville's title suggests a (misguided) duty—Chief *Protector* of Aborigines— where the protection it would seem envelops the state's sense of fear of an other. The protector, however, carries a conviction that he is responsible for the moral upbringing of the "half-castes," and through this conviction, is "rightfully" protected by "universal" law. Nevertheless, the Levinasian responsibility is sempiternal, never complete, as Alphonso Lingis points out: "[The self] is from the start responsible, with a responsibility it will never catch up to, ever in deficit."[20] The duty of the removal of the children to the settlement is fulfilled; the responsibility of myself to you is always in question, and *always* in deficit.

The Ethical and the Moral

> Morality is what governs the world of political "interestednesses," the social interchanges between citizens in a society. Ethics [the ethical], as the extreme exposure and sensitivity to another, becomes morality and hardens its skin as soon as we move into the political world of the impersonal "third"—the world of government. . . . If the moral-political order totally relinquishes its ethical foundation, it must accept all forms of society, including the fascist or totalitarian, for it can no longer evaluate or discriminate between them. . . . In some instances, fascism or totalitarianism, for example, the political order of the state may have to be challenged in the name of our ethical responsibility to the [O]ther. This is why ethical philosophy must remain the first philosophy.
>
> LEVINAS, interview in Kearney, *Dialogues with Contemporary Continental Thinkers*

Levinas shows that he is reluctant to rely on a moral world order, enacted through politics, to sustain an ethical world. He does not dismiss outright the value of a moral world but cautions us to the dangers of solely relying on morality to deliver a truly ethical framework.

The moral world of Neville—in his "benevolence," governed by a didactic and racist ideology masked as righteousness—is bereft of the ethical. Because of its paucity of the ethical, this moral world is, as Levinas states, open to all types of discrimination and genocide. The film challenges the premises of Neville's apparent moral world, and the Levinasian ethical theory illuminates this process. Implicit in the film is not only Neville and his agents' inability to perceive the dichotomies of right and wrong but also the incapacity to perceive what they *can* do (the ethical) and what they *should* do (the moral). The Superintendent of the Jigalong Depot, Arthur Hungerford, and Constable Riggs supply rations to the Aborigines and observe the events in the community with a vigilance that borders on stalking. The ostensible benevolence—the supply of rations—in fact creates the nexus to Neville's policy, because in the course of their duties, they inform the chief protector of the community's "secrets." This is how Neville understands that Molly's younger sister, Daisy "is promised to a 'full blood.'" As Neville writes, the mixed-descent Aborigine must not partner "with full-bloods [as she or he] is liable to prolong the process of absorption until there are no more virile full-bloods remaining alive."[21] This is why Riggs, the seemingly benign local protector, steals the three girls from their families. The film depicts Riggs' actions as dutiful and moral according to the ideology of the day, but categorically unethical.

Rabbit-Proof Fence, 2001. Directed by Phillip Noyce.

Indeed, Levinas differentiates between the notions of moral choices and the ethical. Colin Davis observes that according to Levinas: "Choices are made by conscious subjects, whereas the responsibility that Levinas finds at the core of the relationship with the Other cannot be accepted or rejected in an act of conscious volition."[22] In other words, ethical responsibility is an element of my *response* to the Other, whereas benevolence, in the form of duty, is a conscious decision. Although one can make moral choices and be ethical, in the film, the benevolence shown by Neville and his agents cancels out any response to the Other and makes the moral choice unethical.

Noyce juxtaposes audio and visual components in the sequence at the settlement, mentioned earlier. As Molly approaches Neville for the inspection of her skin color, she is filmed in extreme close-up, inviting the viewer to engage with her poverty (in the Levinasian sense), and, her very Otherness. Neville's voice-over counters this engagement: "We're here to help and encourage you in this new world." Sounding as if they are spoken in an echo-chamber, blanketed by Molly's heavy breathing, and music suggesting disaffection and a portending, intimidating "new world," Neville's benevolent words contrast with the genocidal policies of the state. In addition, Neville can only *gaze* at Molly, observing only her corporeal self. His "morality" conflicts with his unethical actions and behavior.

The law in *Rabbit-Proof Fence* not only provides the approbation for the implementation of genocide, but also justifies the very act by obfuscating the crime as "benevolence." In 1978 Levinas wrote that "all philosophical literature today, identifies the ethical with the Law." For Levinas, however, the Law is a result of the ethical "obligation toward the [O]ther."[23] By acting within the law, the perpetrators in the film are under the impression that they are responsible. During the abduction sequence, Riggs holds a legal document that severs Maude (Molly's mother) from Molly and Daisy. She loses any rights over her children. During the horror of this sequence, shot claustrophobically close to the ground, with its pounding music and wails from the mothers and children, the piece of paper—the Law—is not elevated as altruistic morality, but rather is wielded as power. In his uniform, Riggs embodies the law. In an earlier sequence in the film, Noyce frames Riggs's rifle in perfect alignment with his leg, filmed from boot to face, portrayed as an extension of the law and a hunter of "half-castes." As Riggs surreptitiously watches, Molly and her family delight in the capture of a goanna. While he perceives a group destined to be absorbed, the shots of Molly's family reveal a familial relationship. The implicit message behind this sequence is that both Riggs and the family are legally engaged in hunting.

How does Levinas's theory of responsibility and the ethical over morality inform an understanding of genocide committed by "forcibly removing children from one group to another"?[24] According to Davis, the "ethical relationship which Levinas finds at the core of subjectivity does not imply that humankind or society is inherently or necessarily moral."[25] The implied morality from the perpetrators in the film does not presuppose an ethical responsibility. Benevolence is not necessarily altruistic and morality may be dutiful, but these traits are not always ethical. In the perpetrator's ontological world, the protectors are, as Levinas writes, "free to refuse the other . . . [even though they] remain forever accused, with a bad conscience."[26] Indeed, Noyce's film signals a society of ignominy.

Conclusion

Although no mass murder is depicted or implied in *Rabbit-Proof Fence*, Noyce effectively portrays the actions of Neville and his agents in Western Australia in the interwar period as "genocide" according to the CPPCG. The multilayered ideologies of duty and benevolence obfuscate the intent to destroy a group of Australians through the forced removal of children from their families. In addition, the film skillfully links the ideas of duty and responsibility through the intentions of Neville with the ethical responsibility of Molly. The notions of responsibility revealed in *Rabbit-Proof Fence* all point to a dichotomous relationship between ontology and the ethical. The model of responsibility as advocated by the "benevolent" protectors suggests a struggle between Neville's actual forcible seizure and Neville's apparent goodwill—realized in the film in the abduction sequence and, perversely, through the ordered, hierarchical, and homogeneous structure of the settlement. By spurning the Other, Neville and his agents *create* separation, under the guise of sameness or assimilation. As Woods appropriately argues in relation to the Levinasian ethical thesis, "The advent of peace cannot be brought about by an interaction built on the basis of ontology, because that very model of consciousness is underpinned with the notion of a struggle."[27] The representation of methodical "white" Australians contrasts with the apparent disorganization and haphazardness, not only of indigenous Australians but also of the harsh terrain they traverse. The varied, natural landscape the girls travel to reach home counterpoints the attempt at neutrality and sameness in the artificial world created at the Moore River Settlement.

Levinas contends that the difficulty in assessing the call to duty in law is that morality is historically, socially, and culturally relative. This relativism, Levinas argues, implies "a hierarchical system of values . . . [and its] own rational justification within itself."[28] Likewise, the institutions governed by Neville locate this "rational justification." Conversely, *Rabbit-Proof Fence*'s vision rejects this moral relativism, elevating instead the primacy of the ethical responsibility of the Other, in the context of the dehumanizing dimension of genocide. Moreover, Neville's desire to "eventually forget that there were ever any aborigines in Australia" is not only indicative of his genocidal intentions but also symptomatic of the perpetrator's denial of the Otherness of the Other.[29]

NOTES

1. See Read, *The Stolen Generations*. For two opposing views on the Stolen Generations, see Tatz, "Confronting Australian Genocide," and Brunton, "Genocide."

2. United Nations Office of the High Commissioner for Human Rights, "Convention on the Prevention and Punishment of the Crime of Genocide." Article 2 reads: "In the present Convention, genocide means any of the following acts committed with intent to destroy, in whole or in part, a national, ethnical, racial or religious group, as such: (a) Killing members of the group; (b) Causing serious bodily or mental harm to members of the group; (c) Deliberately inflicting on the group conditions of life calculated to bring about its physical destruction in whole or in part; (d) Imposing measures intended to prevent births within the group; (e) Forcibly transferring children of the group to another group."

3. I acknowledge Pam Maclean's contribution to these thoughts. Levinas defines ontology as "the struggle to be" an obsession with being, a fixation with myself, as a metaphor for self-obsession. See Kearney, *Dialogues with Contemporary Continental Thinkers*, 60.

4. Human Rights and Equal Opportunity Commission, *Bringing them Home*.

5. For a thorough review and discussion on this issue, see Tatz, *Genocide in Australia*, and Tatz, *With Intent to Destroy*, 67–106.

6. Neville was the "guardian of all Aboriginal and half-caste children." See Manne, "Aboriginal Child Removal and the Question of Genocide," 12.

7. Levinas, *Collected Philosophical Papers*, 57.

8. As Bartrop points out, "these were real terms, employed by leading public servants." See Bartrop, "The Holocaust, the Aborigines, and the Bureaucracy of Destruction," 77.

9. Hughes D'aeth, "Which Rabbit-Proof Fence?"

10. Levinas, *Otherwise than Being or Beyond Essence*, 10.

11. Davis, *Levinas*, 49, 51.

12. Woods, "The Ethical Subject," 56, emphasis mine.

13. Levinas writes, "The disclosing of a face is nudity, non-form, abandon of self, ageing, dying, more naked than nudity. It is poverty, skin with wrinkles, which are a trace of itself." See Levinas, *Otherwise than Being or Beyond Essence*, 88.

14. Lydon, "A Strange Time Machine," 147.

15. Levinas declares that the responsibility for the Other is a "persecuting obsession . . . [and] could never mean altruistic will, instinct of 'natural benevolence.'" See Levinas, *Otherwise than Being or Beyond Essence*, 111–12.

16. Dillon, "Summertime Blues," 35.

17. Bauman, *Postmodern Ethics*, 53.

18. Charlton, "Racial Essentialism," 37.

19. Levinas, *Otherwise than Being or Beyond Essence*, 124.

20. Levinas, *Collected Philosophical Papers*, xviii.

21. Neville, *Australia's Coloured Minority*, 56.

22. Davis, *Levinas*, 80.

23. Levinas, *Collected Philosophical Papers*, 183.

24. United Nations, Office of the High Commissioner for Human Rights, "Convention on the Prevention and Punishment of the Crime of Genocide."

25. Davis, *Levinas*, 84.

26. Levinas, *Collected Philosophical Papers*, 64.

27. Woods, "The Ethical Subject," 54.

28. Hand, *The Levinas Reader*, 237.

29. Neville, quoted in Manne, "Aboriginal Child Removal and the Question of Genocide," 219.

7 Genres of "Yet An Other Genocide"

Cinematic Representations of Rwanda

MADELAINE HRON

Seventeen years ex post facto, "Rwanda," or the misnomer "the Rwandan genocide," had become a catch-all phrase to signal the failure of Western interventionism and international human rights discourse.[1] The horrific events of 1994, when, in one hundred days, more than 800,000 Tutsi and moderate Hutu were slaughtered as the world stood by and did nothing to stop it, irrevocably transformed celebratory fifty-year-old declarations of "never again" into the cynical current caveat of "yet again"—with regards to Darfur, the Congo, or future genocides.[2] At the same time, Rwanda became a "hot commodity" in Western popular culture, with the mass production of scholarly studies, novels, testimonials, films, and documentaries. In particular, in the wake of the ten-year commemoration of the atrocities in 2004, there was an explosion of cinematic representations of the events, with the wide release of such feature films as *Hotel Rwanda*, *Shooting Dogs*, and *A Sunday in Kigali* and the production of numerous documentaries, such as *Shake Hands with the Devil: The Journey of Romeo Dallaire*, *Mothers Courage*, and *Rwanda: Living Forgiveness*. This attention is incongruously ironic when we consider the Western media coverage of the 1994 events or its commemoration ten years later. At the height of the killings in April 1994, the Big Three TV networks (ABC, CBS, NBC) together allotted Rwanda only 32 minutes, or 1.5 percent, of news time.[3] Despite profuse apologies in the wake of the genocide, only one Western leader attended the ten-year commemorative ceremonies in Kigali.[4] As a Rwandan observer noted during those commemorative ceremonies, "We've come to expect nothing of the world. So far, the world has not disappointed us."[5]

133

How then do Western cultural products represent the terror and atrocities of the genocide in Rwanda? How do they address the lingering trauma or living conditions of survivors in post-genocide Rwanda? How do they reconcile the failures of the West, both during the genocide and post-genocide? These are some of the questions explored in this chapter, which examines recent films and documentaries about Rwanda, a cinematic corpus that has been, as of yet, largely overlooked. This chapter investigates how these Western cultural representations shape popular understandings of the Tutsi genocide and its aftermath, while also deliberating their effects in social discourse.

The importance of cinematic representations about Rwanda cannot be underestimated. Because of their wide distribution in the West, films and documentaries have largely informed, in their most generic terms, Western perceptions about *itsembabwoko*—the Rwandan term for the 1994 Tutsi extermination campaign—as well as, more broadly, popular understandings of genocide and post-genocide.[6] Furthermore, these films effectively reaffirm Western discourse about non-Western others. Generic tropes drawn from feature films about Rwanda now often resurface in recent Hollywood films about Africa. For instance, the depiction of Hutu killers—as a crazed mob dressed in colorful clothing, who sing and yell as they wield their murderous weapons—has since been replicated in *Blood Diamond*, *The Last King of Scotland*, and *Casino Royale*, as recognizable, brutally barbaric, yet exotically carnivalesque "African bad guy" figures. Moreover, the effects of these films are not only apparent in cinema, but also in the public forum. Activism about Darfur often refers back to films about Rwanda; most prominently, actor Don Cheadle from *Hotel Rwanda* and activist Adam Sterling have in fact initiated a widely publicized campaign called "Hotel Darfur," which was later changed to the better known campaign "Darfur Now."

This chapter therefore outlines some of the generic conventions of films about Rwanda. Unquestionably, the greatest challenge facing filmmakers wishing to portray the Tutsi genocide is the issue of genre. Until 2004, there was no established film genre associated with this "other" genocide, just as there is, as of yet, no explicitly definitive genre of the human rights narrative. As Kay Schaeffer and Sidonie Smith have noted in *Human Rights and Narrated Lives*, what may be termed "the human rights narrative" draws on tropes and models from a variety of genres, such as Holocaust literature, the Latin American *testimonio*, contemporary life narratives, and postcolonial novels.[7] In *Human Rights Inc.*, Joseph Slaughter draws particular attention to the bildungsroman in shaping both historical human rights legislation and our popular discourse about human rights today. In like manner, this chapter will show that films about Rwanda draw on conventions from a variety of genres and models, including Holocaust films, colonial ethnographies, love stories, and

Christian redemption myths, to represent these events. Concomitantly, these films struggle with the bildungsroman model; its ideals of progress, social assimilation, and narrative resolution resist, if not counter, the reality of genocide and its aftermath.

Moreover, this chapter posits that, in the wake of mass production for the decennial, films about Rwanda have become distinct genres themselves. Commemorative narrative films and documentaries, produced from 2003 to 2007, may be easily sorted into three categories. First, there are "retrospective" accounts, which focus solely on the genocide itself, in an attempt to portray it. Most feature films about Rwanda are retrospective, including the blockbuster Hollywood film *Hotel Rwanda* (George, 2004), the U.K. film *Shooting Dogs* (Caton-Jones, 2005), and Canadian films *Sunday in Kigali* (Favreau, 2006) and *Shake Hands with the Devil* (Spottiswoode, 2007), as are a number of widely available documentaries, such as *Ghosts of Rwanda* (Barker, 2004), accessible online on PBS's website.[8] Second, in contrast, there are "post-genocide documentaries," or lesser-known independent documentaries that solely deliberate on activities after the genocide, namely the return of the killers and *gacaca* (village justice), such as *In Rwanda We Say . . . The Family That Does Not Speak Dies* (Aghion, 2004), *Rwanda: Living Forgiveness* (Springhorn, 2004), and *A Killer's Homecoming* (Volker, 2004). Finally, a couple of works, namely the film *Sometimes in April* (Peck, 2005) and the documentary *Shake Hands with the Devil: The Journey of Romeo Dallaire* (Raymont, 2004), are, as this chapter argues, "interpenetrative": they attempt to merge the present and the past, the terror of the genocide and its lingering trauma for survivors.

"Yet An Other Genocide": "An Impossible History"

Though distinct in genre, all of these films manifestly contend with shared cinematic concerns: fundamentally, the aesthetic, narrative, and ethical difficulties of representing genocide or graphic violence. Numerous scholars have pointed to the impossibility of representing or conveying genocide or mass atrocity (e.g., Caruth, Walker, Kaplan). Others have deliberated the "aesthetics of murder" that are appropriate or even possible on screen, or that are necessary to jolt us from "compassion fatigue" or "states of denial," given the contemporary currency of suffering in media today.[9] All of these dynamics are manifestly of concern in representations of the genocide in Rwanda.

More crucially, however, the Tutsi genocide raises the problematics of representing *yet another* genocide, in this case moreover, *an other, non-Western* genocide. As "genocide," the Tutsi extermination campaign transhistorically refers back to the "originary" genocide, the Holocaust, and so seemingly always subsists as a specter of this "real" genocide. Thus, just as scholars and officials allude to "tropical Nazi genocide," the "African Holocaust," or "anti-Nazi pogroms,"[10] films about Rwanda also draw numerous cinematic conventions associated with Holocaust films. Although on one hand, these Holocaust-like tropes may enable general viewers to better grasp the gravity of the 1994 extermination campaign, on the other hand, they also serve to obfuscate or relativize the specificity of Tutsi genocide and the particular post-genocide experiences of survivors.

In similarly relativist terms, the Tutsi genocide all too easily becomes conflated with the "African genocide." As South African actress Pamela Nomvete explains, "it's *the* African story. Any African knows it. They understand it."[11] In this worldview, Rwanda comes to symbolize the history of the West in Africa: its colonial or neocolonial politics, its inaction and belated response during atrocities, its pathetic apologies, or its facile forgetfulness ex post facto. Yet, just as Rwanda may epitomize the repeated racism perpetrated by the West on Africa, it may also educe "all those unpleasant, racist feelings about Africa,"[12] so often reproduced in media about Africa. Stereotypically, in films we see "TIA" or "This is Africa": a primitive and savage, albeit exotic, continent, characterized by "the 4Ds" (danger, death, disease, and desperation).[13] In this reductionist view, Tutsi are "just other dead Africans," to cite reporters in *Shooting Dogs*.

Within this complex matrix, Rwanda also signals *the failures of the West*: its failure to prevent genocide, as well as, correlatively, the failures of Western rationalism, neocolonialism, and humanitarianism. The plethora of Western representations about Rwanda suggests that the 1994 events connote a "traumatic memory" for the West, which, even after fifteen years, "cannot be assimilated but occurs only belatedly in its insistent and intrusive return," be it for Western politicians, scholars, writers, and filmmakers.[14] Clearly, the "trauma" of complicit Western bystanders in no way compares to the experience of traumatized survivors, yet films about Rwanda, which deliberate Western disillusionment, guilt, or shame, may have a tendency to self-reflexively, if not self-absorbedly, focus on Western perspectives on the genocide or on Rwanda's significance in terms of Western discourse.

Interrelated with these politics of representation is the issue of the "cultural capital of trauma victims."[15] Cultural critics have argued that the "politics of pain" or "wounded attachments" are a means to gain agency and authority in public discourse.[16] Representations of Rwanda, therefore, urge us to consider the representation of suffering in these films. Who are the victim-subjects gaining authority in these films: Rwandans or Westerners, survivors or bystanders, victims or perpetrators? How is the experience of Rwandans represented in these films?

Given these diverse, often-irreconcilable, discursive frameworks, the specificity of the Tutsi genocide and the particular experience of survivors is easily lost or dismissed. As Cathy Caruth explains, victims of mass atrocity carry "an impossible history within them, or they become themselves the symptom of a history that they cannot entirely possess."[17] For Rwandans, this "impossible history" carries all of the aforementioned cultural connotations, as well as irreconcilable features of their own history. Though it manifestly culminated with 1994 events, Rwanda's history extends from precolonial Rwanda to current conditions post-genocide. As such, it includes Belgian colonial practices, previous instances of Tutsi cleansing campaigns (in 1958, 1963, 1973, and in the 1990s), the exile of Tutsi to Uganda or Tanzania, the post-genocide exodus of Hutu killers to Zaire and the Congo, and further massacres post-1994. In other words, this "impossible history" encapsulates the whole history of Rwanda, a history that is largely misunderstood and, most often, wholly dismissed in the West. Strikingly, none of the films or documentaries surveyed for this chapter mention the Rwandan term for the 1994 extermination: *itsembabwoko*. When considered in its sociocultural and historico-political specificity, however, it is clear that *itsembabwoko* differs drastically from the Holocaust or an "African" model of genocide.

The particularities that characterize *itsembabwoko* are its transparency, ubiquity, and brutal intimacy. Where there exists only a single, two-minute film clip of actual killings in World War II concentration camps, there are hours of video footage of slaughter in the streets of Kigali, of beatings, beheadings, close-ups of the living dead, as well as innumerable photographs of corpses decomposing on roadsides, in churches, or floating in rivers.[18] There was no ambiguity or secrecy in the Tutsi extermination campaign: hate propaganda was spewed on public airways by radio RTML, which even directed killers to the next murder site. Unlike in the Holocaust, where mass murder was concealed in undisclosed concentration camps, killings in Rwanda took place in broad daylight, everywhere—in churches, streets, fields, and swamps, everywhere. There were no "concentration camps" in Rwanda, no separation or transition between the space of life and death. Most problematically during *itsembabwoko*, neighbors slaughtered neighbors. Unlike Nazis and Jews, or Africans and Muslims in Sudan, Hutu did not differ from Tutsi in faith, upbringing, or culture; rather, most inhabited the same hills and shared the same culture and values. Most appalling though, is the sickening proximity the killers had to their victims, and their vicious means of killing. Instead of gassing them or shooting them, most killers hacked their victims to death with machetes or other farming implements.

Finally, *itsembabwoko* differs drastically from the Holocaust because of events post-genocide. Unremitting attention on 1994 events usually dismisses the ramifications of *itsembabwoko* or current conditions in post-genocide Rwanda. Though Rwanda is often described as an economic success story, as its economy is growing twice as fast as those of the United States or Europe, most Rwandans lack access to basic social programs such as education or health care.[19] Humanitarian aid for survivors, once so copious, is drying up; numerous centers assisting victims of trauma, rape, and HIV/AIDS have been forced to shut down. For instance, writer and survivor Esther Mujawayo founded Avega, an organization supporting some 10,000 women rape victims dying of AIDS. However, no international sponsor was willing to come forward with the estimated $100 a month for antiretroviral drugs per woman. As Mujawayo notes, "The world is watching again. The UN just let people die, and now it's watching as the survivors die."[20]

Most contentious, however, is the issue of post-genocidal justice. After 1994, an estimated 120,000 people were imprisoned in Rwanda, suspected of participating in killings, just as 60 *génocidaires* were indicted by the International Tribunal in Arusha for crimes against humanity. To date, fifteen years later, only twenty-three of these *génocidaires* have been prosecuted, often because of Western countries' unwillingness to extradite them.[21] In Rwanda itself, since 2002, some 70,000 prisoners, convicted or accused of participating in the atrocities, have been set free. These returning killers were told to return home and live peacefully with their neighbors—often their former victims. They were also to testify at *gacaca*, a form of Rwandan restorative village justice. In *gacaca*, if a killer confesses his crimes and asks for forgiveness, with sufficient veracity for the judges, he is free to live within the community, though he might have to pay a fine or perform some community service. For Rwandans, herein lies the most important difference between Jewish and Tutsi victims: after the Holocaust, no one expected Jews to live peacefully next door to their Nazi killers. Rather, the Holocaust brought about the creation of the State of Israel. Rwandan survivors, however, must learn to live side by side with their killers, despite their grief, memories, trauma, hostility, or penury.

Films and documentaries about Rwanda are therefore faced with the thorny task of addressing the "impossible history" of *itsembabwoko*, in its many historical and culturally specific nuances, both during and after genocide. Concomitantly, they also contend with the complex matrix of cultural connotations associated with Rwanda: that of "yet another Holocaust," "the African story," or "the failure of Western interventionism." Finally, as films, they are also inscribed within specific generic, narrative, and aesthetic conventions, ranging from the Holocaust film to the ethnography, the African disaster narrative to the bildungsroman. Driving all of this, there must be compelling visual aesthetics and emotive narrative storytelling; as critic Geoff Pevere explains, films about Rwanda cannot be "just documentary, or just feature film; they must insert the personal and political into the historical to make these things matter to us."[22]

Retrospective Revisionism

Most feature films about Rwanda (*Hotel Rwanda*, *Shooting Dogs*, *Sunday in Kigali*) are "retrospective accounts," in that they focus solely on the genocide. As such, these fictional accounts must render the history of *itsembabwoko* coherent, accessible, and engaging for Western viewers. In so doing, films often curtail the history of Rwanda to a few weeks in 1994, thus depicting *itsembabwoko* apolitically and ahistorically as an inexplicable catastrophe. The Hollywood blockbuster *Hotel Rwanda* exemplifies this trend; there is hardly any historical or cultural explanation for the genocide. The viewer is thrust *in media res* into what appears to be a "disaster movie," which concludes before the end of the genocide, when hero Paul is "liberated" in a refugee camp and reunited with his family. The history of Rwanda pre-genocide is completely dismissed in these films; post-genocide is sometimes alluded to in a concluding coda (*Shooting Dogs*) or in a frame story (*A Sunday in Kigali*). Notably, the most widely available retrospective documentary, PBS's *Ghosts of Rwanda*, never mentions previous pogroms of the Tutsi and completely overlooks the developing situation in post-genocide Rwanda; it basically reproduces PBS's *Triumph of Evil* produced six years earlier. In these revisionist retrospective accounts, therefore, *itsembabwoko* is neither a long-standing, planned extermination campaign nor an event with serious ramifications; its depiction rarely deviates from disaster films about "TIA" ("This Is Africa").

A greater difficulty presented by *itsembabwoko* is how to make its brutally intimate slaughter visually palatable and even aesthetic on screen, so as not to shock audiences into "states of denial," or, with repeated imagery, induce "compassion fatigue."[23] In order not to alienate viewers, the atrocities of genocide are minimized, judiciously edited, or intimated by allusion. In the PG-13 rated *Hotel Rwanda*, for instance, all the action is contained within the walls of the Hotel des Mille Collines. Only one scene points to the horror beyond the walls of the hotel: a murky sequence set in early morning fog, wherein the hero Paul and his driver cannot drive forward because of all the corpses strewn on the road. In other films, particularly harrowing scenes of killing serve as the climax of the film: a close-up of a killing at a barrier in *Shooting Dogs*; a protracted massacre in a school in *Sometimes in April*; and a lengthy rape sequence, intimated by silhouette, in *A Sunday in Kigali*.

However, the greatest problem underlying these fictionalized representations of genocide is most certainly that of narrative structure; in fictional films, the narrative structure typically follows a generic pattern (episodic plot development, climax, and denouement) that largely corresponds to the pedagogical model of the bildungsroman. Genocide, however, manifestly counters the bildungsroman and its ideals of progress, community-building, or positive resolution; instead, genocide signals the failure of discourse. In order to contravene this problem, noticeably, all these feature films revolve around love stories set in the backdrop of genocide—be it mild crushes (*Shooting Dogs*), passionate love affairs (*Sunday in Kigali, 100 Days*), or marriages that withstand the atrocities (*Hotel Rwanda, Sometimes in April*). In this way, the complete destruction and dehumanization that genocide engenders is somewhat attenuated by the enduring love and indomitable faith in another human being. The conventions of the romance narrative also enable these films to reach some form of final resolution or catharsis; such conventions manifestly counter the real-life consequences of *itsembabwoko*. However, when adopting the *thanatos/eros* trope, these films risk reproducing stereotypes about Africa as a racialized space of danger and exoticism. This danger/exoticism is best exemplified in the interracial love affair in *Sunday in Kigali*: dark, beautiful, and docile "Gentille only lives for [white] Valcourt" and so achieves "a love story like in the films, a white love story, the dream of many Africans."

Furthermore, retrospective films also adopt generic narrative and thematic conventions from the Holocaust genre to characterize *itsembabwoko*. On a basic level, most of these films follow the generic narrative structure of the Holocaust texts: movement from the home to the "concentration camp," arrival in the camp, conditions in the camp, episodic killing growing in intensity, and eventual escape or liberation.[24] Notably, most of the action in these films is confined to "concentration camp" like spaces—be it the Hotel des Mille Collines, schools, or churches. Only *100 Days* is set in rural Rwanda, among the forests of Kibuye, and only *Sometimes in April* showcases the space of the marsh—uncontained spaces where most of the rural population hid for months on end, enduring daily raids, among rotting and decomposing dead bodies. The ubiquity and extent of the atrocities in *itsembabwoko* is thus curtailed. In addition to the concentration camp space, we also note the repeated image of the Holocaust-like "transport convoy"—the UN truck—which in this case does not signal death, but white salvation. In *Hotel Rwanda*, often termed "the Black *Schindler's List*," we even discern subtle allusions to *Schindler's List*. For instance, the cover of the *Schindler's List* DVD features an adult male hand holding the hand of the little girl in red. This scene is replicated in *Hotel Rwanda*: as hero Paul departs the hotel in the UN convoy with his wife Tatiana and their children, the camera zooms in on their firmly clasped hands. Similarly, the pivotal corpses-in-fog sequence in *Hotel Rwanda* also recalls the climactic scene in *Schindler's List*: the burning and burying of victims' bodies after the destruction of the Warsaw Ghetto. In that scene, Schindler gags into his white handkerchief; similarly, Paul hides his face into his white shirt, sobbing.

Given the prevalence of such Holocaust motifs, it is thought provoking to consider elements from the Holocaust genre that are missing in these feature films.

First, there is never any systematized "selection" process: roll calls, triage, or ordered lists of Tutsi to be killed. Though the ethnic cleansing of the Tutsi was highly organized even before the genocide started, in feature films, the genocide is often reduced to a confused chaos—again, stereotypical of "TIA" or "backward, un-civilized Africans." Only at *barrières* do we note a differentiation between Hutu and Tutsi, or a close-up of an identity card; however, this selection process seems highly haphazard, as whites are often at equal risk of being killed as Tutsi victims (e.g., the conclusion of *Shooting Dogs*). More saliently, there is never any recuperation of victims of this selection process; *Schindler's List* markedly revolves around this "list"—the naming and recognition of individual Jewish survivors. Aside from Paul Rusesabagina in *Hotel Rwanda*, all the characters in feature films are fictional; there is certainly no attempt made to pay tribute to individual victims of the genocide. Most important, perhaps, Holocaust films often seek to recuperate Jewish culture, since its annihilation was the target of the Nazi cleansing campaign. *Schindler's List*, for instance, is framed by Sabbath scenes and punctuated by Yiddish and Jewish cultural references. By contrast, in these films, just as Rwandans have little history, they have little culture. In *Hotel Rwanda*, there is not one single reference to traditional Rwandan culture, not even a single word in Kinyarwanda (even inscriptions on the wall are in English).

Ostensibly, feature films about *itsembabwoko* are not so much about Rwandans—more specifically, about Tutsi victims of the genocide—as they are about the West and the failure of the West to respond to human rights violations of genocidal proportions. Ironically, most feature films "whitewash" this "African genocide" by featuring white heroes. Spottiswoode's film, *Shake Hands with the Devil*, focuses on real-life Canadian hero General Romeo Dallaire, already the subject of a few documentaries (e.g., those by Raymont, Silver, and the Holocaust Museum). *Shooting Dogs* presents us with Joe, an idealistic, but self-preserving, aid worker; frustrated Belgian leader Delon (modeled on Belgian Colonel Luc Marchal); and, finally, the savior figure of Father Christopher (loosely based on Catholic Priest Vjeko Curic), who sacrifices his own life to save Tutsi children in his school. Finally, *A Sunday in Kigali* (adapted from Courtemanche's novel *A Sunday at the Pool in Kigali*) showcases the heroism of reporter Valcourt, who understands more about the genocide than his Tutsi lover Gentille, who is subsequently captured and gang-raped, because she failed to heed Valcourt's sage warnings to leave Kigali.

In these films, experiences of Tutsi, as either victims or survivors, are secondary to the sufferings of the white hero and thus reflect the trend characterizing recent Hollywood films about Africa (*The Last King of Scotland*, *Blood Diamond*, *The Constant Gardener*): "white guides / black pain" or "black suffering dramatized on white faces."[25] To exemplify, Gentille's repeated gang-rapes are intimated by her silhouette moving in shadows, yet during her ordeal, we watch Valcourt's face contorting and his body writhing in pain. The agency ascribed to Tutsi victims—in relation to their white saviors—is thus often extremely problematic, as it derives from fatalist victimhood. For instance, in one of the most poignant scenes in *Shooting Dogs*, the remaining Tutsi kindly request that the departing Belgians shoot them all, as they would rather die quickly from Western bullets than slowly from machete wounds. The conclusion of *A Sunday in Kigali* is even more disturbing; after her rape, Gentille is left disfigured, and, more importantly, "no longer a woman"—as her genitalia had been excised. At her behest, Valcourt smothers her with a pillow and kills her. By showcasing this assisted suicide, the film suggests that women who have suffered as much trauma as Gentille have no possible future. In reality, of course, thousands of women in Gentille's situation have had to continue surviving in post-genocide Rwanda. More implicitly, both of these scenes suggest that if whites cannot save Tutsis by granting them life, at least they can take up the savior role by enabling them to die in peace.

Even when these films do feature a black hero, such as in *Hotel Rwanda* and *Sometimes in April*, this hero is problematic. In both instances, the Rwandan protagonist is a Hutu, representative of the "just" or "good Hutu," a characterization that Tutsi victims find deeply troubling. Eager to avoid Manichean Hutu/Tutsi binaries, such films often end up relativizing crucial ethnic differences or banalizing the suffering of Tutsi victims or the heroism of Tutsi survivors. For example, in *Hotel Rwanda*, a Western photojournalist points to two prostitutes, one Hutu and one Tutsi, to emphasize that, physically, they "could be twins." Of course, this prostitute example wholly dismisses the issues of class, social mobility, and socio-economic status that led to divisionism among Hutu and Tutsi. Similarly, the Hutu hero from *Hotel Rwanda*, Paul Rusesabagina, is a highly contentious figure, a "manufactured hero" according to Rwandan authorities.[26] For many Rwandans, Rusesabagina is not the "ordinary man" he claims to be in his autobiography; rather, he represents the type of Hutu who could save Tutsi, because he was friends with the genocide masterminds.

The on-screen representation of Paul Rusesabagina is similarly troubling. In *Hotel Rwanda*, Colonel Oliver describes Paul as "the smartest man here. You've got them all eating out of your hands. You could own this hotel. Except for one thing. You're black. You're not even a Nigger, you're African." Though Paul is "the smartest man around," the most diplomatic and politically savvy, he also ironically irons his shirts in the middle of a genocide, bills the refugees in his hotel for their stay, and holds umbrellas for departing whites in a rainstorm. The cinematic representation of Rusesabagina is thus none other than that of the perfect colonial subject. Innately intelligent, docile, and having internalized colonial structures—these were characteristics that urged Belgians to educate Tutsi in the first place. Except, of course, Rusesabagina is Hutu. Though in *Hotel Rwanda*, he's just a black African, a victim of racism, not an actor in ethnic conflict.

In all, feature films draw on various genres and diverse generic tropes—be it the love story, Holocaust tropes, white-savior figures, or Africanized colonial subjects—to minimize the failure of the West. Though it may be convenient to dismiss these films because of their generic conventions and dubious truth-value, it is important to recognize the impact of these models on the representation of Africa and human rights issues. Moreover, despite its shortcomings, each of these films has redeeming features. For instance, the quasi-pornographic and racist film *Sunday in Kigali* is the only film that addresses the issue of AIDS in Rwanda. By virtue of such differences or resistances to generic norms, each of these films jolts us into awareness about the particularities of *itsembabwoko* and its complicated human rights implications.

To conclude, a pause is needed on just such an exception among these retrospective accounts: *100 Days*, directed by journalist Nick Hughes in 2001 (thus several years before the "Rwandan genocide film" prototype *Hotel Rwanda*), the only feature film cofunded by Rwandans. Unlike other narrative films, *100 Days* is set solely in rural Rwanda (in Kibuye) and narrated wholly in Kinyarwanda with subtitles. The generic norms of Western-based films are countered in various ways in *100 Days*, most significantly in its representation of the politicized, human rights dimensions of *itsembabwoko*. It is unequivocally pro-Tutsi, and its plot scathingly condemns the role of the church and the French, depicting them as perpetrators of crimes against humanity. Finally, it resists any form of bildungsromanesque evolution or resolution: it concludes with the estrangement of the two lovers, because heroine Josette is pregnant with the baby of her priest-captor—a powerful comment on real-life conditions in post-genocide Rwanda. Unfortunately, perhaps because this independent film was produced in Rwanda and is thus more inaccessible, or because it does not fit nicely into more generic, if not revisionist, representations of *itsembabwoko*, *100 Days* remains relatively unknown in the West. However, when analyzed comparatively in relation to the generic models it transcends, *100 Days* enables viewers to grasp some of the cultural and historical specificity of the Tutsi genocide in more complex political, ethical, and human rights dimensions.

Reconciling Post-Genocide

An alternate understanding of *itsembabwoko*, particularly of its aftermath, is also presented in the many "post-genocide" documentaries produced in the wake of commemoration, including *In Rwanda We Say... The Family That Does Not Speak Dies* (Aghion, 2004), *Killers* (Keane, 2004), *A Killer's Homecoming* (Volker, 2004), *Rwanda: Living Forgiveness* (Springhorn, 2004), *Keepers of Memory* (Kabera, 2004), *Through My Eyes* (Kabera, 2004), *In the Tall Grass* (Metcalf, 2006), *Mothers Courage* (Kalinda, 2005), and *The Diary of Immaculée* (LeDonne, 2006). All these films deliberate experiences of survivors ten years after *itsembabwoko*. Specifically, many focus on the return of killers to their home villages after the 2002 amnesty and on the process of Rwandan restorative village justice or *gacaca*. Though they represent a substantial corpus, like *100 Days*, these films have been largely ignored by film critics, perhaps because of their subject matter, or because of their inaccessibility.[27] Unlike widely circulated narrative films, many of these documentaries were only aired as TV specials in 2004, or are only available as educational material, though some are also accessible online.[28]

In their depictions of traumatized survivors and *gacaca*, these documentaries manifestly engage with the complex dynamics of representing racial and epistemological otherness. In so doing, however, they often reveal generic Western perspectives on Africa and non-Western others. Like narrative films, these documentaries are largely ahistorical and acultural: the history of the genocide is usually condensed to less than three minutes of explanation and symbolized by the iconic image of rows of white skulls. The viewer is transported to the rural countryside, often to an unnamed location, without any explanation of the ethnic history in that particular region, though regional distinctions were crucial during the killings.[29] Because these documentaries focus on the killer's return, like in feature films, there is disproportionate emphasis on Hutu perpetrators as opposed to Tutsi victims. Most important, these documentaries often further relativize Tutsi–Hutu distinctions by additionally blurring differences between victims and perpetrators: killers are generally depicted as ordinary farmers, eking out their existence in the fields, undifferentiated, in every respect, from their victims and their families. Except when in quiet tones, these men confess to killing their Tutsi neighbors out of duress, because they had no choice. Their confessions are accompanied by testimonials of traumatized, frustrated, or angry survivors. Sometimes, therefore, it is difficult to discern the "good guy" or "bad guy" in these documentaries—which, in certain instances, is the premise of the documentary.

While the Western perspectives presented in these documentaries are in many ways analogous to those in retrospective films, there are also critical differences. First, none of these films depict whites on screen, though manifestly, Westerners, be they whites or Westernized Africans, are behind the camera, directing the action, conducting interviews, or editing the material in ways that speak to Western cultural and aesthetic conventions. Most saliently, there are very few allusions to the

Holocaust in these documentaries, because the history of post-genocide Rwanda in no way corresponds to events post-Holocaust. Therefore, all these films must somehow address Rwanda's diverging history, its particular cultural practices or legal epistemology. In so doing, however, most of these documentaries revert to hackneyed Western hermeneutical formulas for representing racial and cultural otherness: colonial primitivism and Christianity. These discourses are enabled by the underlying ethnographic aesthetics in these films, ethnography being traditionally deployed to highlight oppositions between the primitive and the civilized.

Anne Aghion's *In Rwanda We Say . . .* first aired on Sundance TV in 2004. It nicely illustrates the ethnographic gaze prevalent in these films and, associatively, its primitivist, colonial connotations. Like many post-genocide documentaries, Aghion's film thematically focuses on the contested return of an accused killer to his unnamed rural village. Though it is manifestly set sometime after 2002 in the Rwandan countryside, because of formulaic ethnographic clichés, the action seems set outside time and space. The camera mainly showcases scenes of daily life in the village—such as farming, herding, or making manioc—and so the movie more resembles a colonial travelogue or National Geographic special than a portrait of a twenty-first-century country ravaged by mass murder. Accompanying these nostalgic pastoral scenes are multiple interviews—with the killer, his family members, neighbors, and school children—presented here in Kinyarwanda with translated subtitles. Overall, this compilation of seemingly unedited interviews seem circuitous, if not confusing and contradictory, and appears to foster the representation of "backward," rather than traumatized, survivors post-genocide. Aside from a brief introduction, the narrator and interviewer are conspicuously absent, so we never know what questions were asked of the survivors, and in what context. The film's climax is not *gacaca*—alluded to by a brief sequence of a pre-*gacaca* sensibilization campaign—but the reflections of schoolchildren, Rwanda's next generation. The various scenes of classrooms of teenagers in khaki school uniforms recall colonial films about education and progress. Most important, the children's clear, logical, and uplifting rationalizations, deftly edited for maximum impact, starkly contrast with the confused, tormented, or rancorous remarks of the illiterate adults, and thus point to Rwanda's optimistic future.

The most powerful scene in Aghion's film offers a self-reflective critique of such invasive ethnographic praxes. In it, two women comment on the presence of the whites in their village who question them about their traumatic experience: "How can one ask us what the return of the prisoners stirs up in us? We saw them return that's all. How are we supposed to feel? Yes, it's true our killers have returned. [. . .] But why are they asking us this? These Whites. They ask if we are happy, if we feel plenitude—Why?" We never know if these women speaking in

Kinyarwanda are unaware of the camera or consciously resisting its intentions. In either case, their reflections poignantly testify to the commodification and banalization of survivors' pain in many of these documentaries.

Ralf Springhorn's *Rwanda: Living Forgiveness* (2004) perhaps best exemplifies another trend, also underlying Aghion's film: the need for optimistic closure through reconciliation. This openly Christian film follows three returning prisoners who find open acceptance, forgiveness, and even brotherly love in their community. Though both victims and perpetrators acknowledge they still feel great pain, they also testify that through forgiveness, they have found hope, community, and thus a means of creating an affirmative future. The film's last example spotlights a victim/perpetrator couple (the guilty man killed fourteen members of his victim's family) who travel the countryside and its prisons, preaching the Gospel message and enacting their story in film and performance. Positing positive closure, this film argues that Rwanda's past wounds can only be healed by acceptance, forgiveness, and reconciliation, as openly advocated by the Christian faith.

Though these documentaries portend to depict post-genocide realistically by virtue of their ethnographic realism, most of them dismiss the post-genocide problems. Only select documentaries, such as Daniela Volker's inaccessible *A Killer's Homecoming*, draw attention to the complex problems arising on the killers' return.[30] Volker's film wholly sidesteps the issue of *gacaca*, which we learn will not happen for a few years because of backlogs. Rather, it focuses on the story of Théofile, who, on returning from prison, charges his wife Odette with bigamy and demands custody of his children. Odette has remarried since her husband's incarceration, as her husband was tried and convicted of killing members of her family. Indeed, Théofile confesses to killing his mother-in-law and his six-month-old niece; nonetheless, he wants his own children and his wife back, and so takes her to court. Aside from this seemingly absurdist court battle, the documentary also explores the bizarre motives for Théofile's murders, as well as the psyche of his children, who learn of their father's crimes as they prepare to live with him.[31] This depiction of the traumatized wife and children who bravely, but unsuccessfully, attempt to reason or reconcile with this murderer wholly contrasts with both Aghion's and Springhorn's vision of Rwanda's future. In the end, Théofile loses his bigamy and custody case, yet the viewer is left with the deeply disturbing portrait of an unrepentant killer, an absurdist civil legal system, and traumatized survivors.

Very few of these documentaries address survivors' trauma as compellingly as Volker does. Generally, in these accounts, there is no intimation that the psychic wounding of survivors might be traumatically repeated or remain unresolved. Instead, these documentaries suggest that the traumatic sequelae of *itsembabwoko* will disappear in generation, precluding any forms of "postmemory."[32] Furthermore, there is often little room for any distortion, fantasy, or falsification in these documentaries. Yet, as Janet Walker explains, in the "traumatic paradox," traumatic memories range from veridical accounts to false memories to "fantasies propped on reality."[33] None of these vicissitudes of memory are reflected in Aghion's or Springhorn's documentaries, seemingly implying that the psyches and experiences of traumatized Rwandans are not as complex as those of Western victims. While Volker overtly points to such distortions and fantasies in her content, the film's narrative structure remains linear, and its aesthetics never stray from stark realism. In order to observe more creative representations of traumatic memory, we must turn to "interpenetrative" films about Rwanda.

Interpenetrative Perspectives

Peter Raymont's documentary *Shake Hands with the Devil* (2004) and Raoul Peck's narrative *Sometimes in April* (2005) are both interpenetrative films in that they vacillate between the past and present, or between 1994 and post-genocide. In so doing, both also attempt, through different aesthetics, to reflect the complex history of *itsembabwoko* and the polyvalent experience of traumatized survivors post-genocide. As such, both films depart from conventional Hollywood or realist documentary praxes and thus exemplify "trauma cinema" defined by Walker as films characterized "by disturbance and fragmentation. . . . of narrative and stylistic regimes" that seek to "'disremember' by drawing on innovative strategies for representing reality obliquely by looking to mental processes for inspiration and by incorporating self-reflexive devices to call attention to the friability of the scaffolding for audiovisual historiography."[34]

Raymont's *Shake Hands with the Devil: The Journey of Romeo Dallaire* (2004) is a powerful interpenetrative film that follows UN General Romeo Dallaire's first return to Rwanda, ten years after his mission in 1994, for the decennial commemoration. While the film may be criticized for its focus on white hero Dallaire, the film is remarkable in its detailed representation of *itsembabwoko*, in particular, its meticulous application of archival footage, as well as its captivating portrait of a traumatized witness to genocide.[35] The film was shot on location, in exact sites that most affected Dallaire during the genocide, and so it never strays from situated specificity. Its predominant cinematic technique, though simple, is highly effective: Raymont intercuts shots of present-day Rwanda with images of the genocide—thus intimating Dallaire's own traumatic experiences of return; as Dallaire explains, "past images just keep on exploding in front of me. Digitally clear. In slow motion." Michele Hozer's fluid editing and montage of these crosscut scenes convincingly engages the viewer to vicariously experience Dallaire's traumatized point of view.

Raymont's exploitation of archival film footage is also particularly forceful. It is obvious that researcher Patrick Reed painstakingly surveyed the vast repertoire of footage about Rwanda to judiciously select those that were most suitable for each scene. Instead of, as in other films, deploying a photo montage, Raymont draws on actual available video footage, from such rare sources as Belgian colonial raciology documentaries, reports for TV stations, and even personal video by Rwandans and UN soldiers. Consequently, scenes that have become almost cliché in representations about Rwanda are defamiliarized through a shocking reality effect. For instance, the evacuation of the Europeans, particularly from the Don Bosco School, is a common trope in both films and media reports about Rwanda. A 1994 article from *Time*, for example, presents a photo of a white woman in pink who seems so frightened when leaving Don Bosco School that she must be carried away by French soldiers.[36] Here, however, the soundtrack offers us actual facts about this scene: this Quebecois woman in pink was not distressed, but rather she was resisting evacuation; she did not want to abandon the orphans she was caring for to face their death. The soldiers are therefore dragging her to the convoy against her will, while hissing to the crowd, "It's up to you to solve your own problems."

Another powerful sequence is that of killing in Kigali streets, as filmed by Nick Hughes in 1994, in the course of an afternoon, for more than twenty-two minutes. This sequence was broadcast for less than ten seconds in newscasts in 1994, and is also often replicated, albeit briefly, in films about Rwanda (it was re-created on a TV screen in *Hotel Rwanda*). Here, however, to intimate Hughes's lengthy footage in *Shake Hands with the Devil*, the scene seems interminable and is reproduced throughout the documentary. Also intriguing is rare UN archival footage of the Amahoro Stadium, where some 16,000 people were saved. As Dallaire explains, "No one in the West could understand how a stadium could shelter thousands for weeks. It was like a concentration camp." Ironically, after Hurricane Katrina, viewers now understand the dynamics of such a Rwandan "concentration camp." Finally, most harrowing are images of the living dead—bodies still quivering or eyes still moving—like the one shot by a reporter featuring a seemingly dead child, whose eyes then turn to interrogate the camera. In all, throughout this film, special attention is paid to the plethora of evidence of genocide, footage of Hutu training camps, extermination lists, and Dallaire's desperate faxes—in all, the ample evidence proving that indeed *itsembabwoko* was a planned and organized genocide. Dallaire's January 6 fax to the UN is even included in the booklet accompanying the DVD.

Generally, however, for Western viewers, the success of this documentary largely depends on the affecting characterization of traumatized General Dallaire. Dallaire's frank words and his unrehearsed movements poignantly reveal the depth of his lingering trauma. In the first few minutes, this high-ranking officer admits that he is stuffed full of drugs to survive, and later he candidly elaborates on the post-traumatic stress disorder (PTSD) he suffered on his return, eloquently describing it as a ceaseless swirling spiral or a crushing vice.[37] Throughout the film, the camera helps viewers grasp this trauma, with silent close-ups or fragmented and intercut scenes. For example, during the climactic scene, at the killing site of the ten Belgian soldiers, Dallaire stops midsentence, staring, and, discomfortingly, there is no sound or movement; thus the viewer clearly grasps Dallaire's anxiety as "the mound [of dead soldiers] came back." In other difficult scenes, we note that the general reverts to his native French or clings to his wife for support.

Manifestly, however, *Shake Hands with the Devil* explores the trauma of a white Westerner, moreover a UN general; the trauma of Rwandan survivors is only intimated. In the end, this leads us to speculate whether such an involved documentary, with such deft cinematography, laborious archival research, careful editing, and on-location shooting, would ever be produced about a Tutsi survivor. Moreover, both the camera's movements as well as the viewers' understanding largely depend on Dallaire's untranslated words and culturally comprehensible gestures. It is questionable whether such unmediated cultural translation would even be possible in the case of a non-Western victim of trauma.

Oppositely, in his narrative film *Sometimes in April*, Peck vies to convey the experience of ordinary Rwandans post-genocide in his fictionalized tale of two Hutu brothers who have completely different experiences in the genocide. One, Augustin, a soldier, escapes, while his entire family is killed off, as he was married to a Tutsi woman. The other brother, Honoré, a radio broadcaster at RTML, is implicated in the genocide and in the murder of Augustin's family. The story, set in 2004, oscillates between flashbacks of genocide and the 2004 present, as Augustin travels to Arusha to visit his brother, and as his new wife Martine prepares to testify before *gacaca*. Though Peck's fictionalized film is not a documentary, Peck nonetheless attempts to be painstakingly accurate. For example, he replicates evidence taken from Gizosy Memorial, copies of lists, or Hutu ten commandments from *Kangara* magazine. Some of the film's most graphic scenes also reconstruct archival footage, such as the evacuation and slaughter at Don Bosco School or the massacre at Ntamara Church. The film itself was shot on location in Rwanda and employed 5,000 Rwandan extras.[38] Peck provided several on-site psychologists to deal with the cast's trauma. Finally, he even used some of their experiences to develop the story line; the swamp scene, for example, was based on the actual experience of a crew member.

Peck's film is thus noteworthy because of its subtle blending of truth and fiction, testimonials and imagined stories, in other words, his performative re-creation of actual events complemented with archival evidence. Both Rwandan scholars and general viewers are thus never quite sure what elements of Peck's are accurate accounts and which ones are "fantasies propped on reality." The cinematography thus reflects the content of the films, as the audience is never sure about the truth-value in the brothers' distorted, truncated, and fragmented accounts. Moreover, by focusing on various characters in a noncontinuous chronology, *Sometimes in April* offers us a glimpse of polyvalent experiences of genocide, while intimating divisive, ambiguous, or traumatized human relations in Rwanda post-genocide.

Framing Conclusions about *Itsembabwoko*

To conclude, the frame story in *Sometimes in April* succinctly sums up the diverging trends in commemorative films in Rwanda. *Sometimes in April* opens on a classroom scene of Rwandan children silently watching Clinton's famous 1998 apology on a TV, a scene frequently reproduced in commemorative films. On watching the media clip, one of the girls quietly asks, "Could it have been stopped?" Another girl quickly reprimands her with the terse reply, "That's all in the past." The film closes on another classroom scene: this time the kids are laughing uproariously at a black-and-white clip in German; it's a scene from Charlie Chaplin's controversial film *The Great Dictator*.

These two scenes deftly identify some of the prevailing tendencies in films about Rwanda explored in this chapter. In retrospective films, we observe the repeated query "could it have been stopped?" in exhaustive examinations of *itsembabwoko*. By contrast, in post-genocide documentaries, through ethnographic depictions of reconciliation, these concerns are dismissed as "that's all in the past." Furthermore, the intertexual reference to *The Great Dictator* draws us back to the "originary genocide" of the Holocaust, just as the children's laughter at this untranslated adaptation points to the need for narrative resolution, emotional catharsis, and, in an optimistic worldview, precluding "yet another genocide." Correspondingly, Clinton's speech calls to mind the tacit, complicated, multifaceted role of the West and the media, both during *itsembabwoko* and now post-genocide—as actors, witnesses, archivists, producers, and disseminators of knowledge. Finally, however, there is also the focus on children, or Rwanda's future generations.

In the end, how will future generations—both in Rwanda and the West—understand the Tutsi genocide and its aftermath, given its various cinematic representations? As shown in this chapter, retrospective narrative films about Rwanda offer us a curtailed understanding of *itsembabwoko*, a representation more in line with Holocaust films, disaster films, or Hollywood films about Africa. By contrast, post-genocide documentaries largely reproduce colonialesque forms of ethnography,

150

while advocating education or facile reconciliation. What will be the residual effect of these films? These films downplay the atrocities, "whitewash" 1994 events with white protagonists, Africanize or Christianize the Rwandan experience, or relativize Tutsi/Hutu differences. Most problematically, how will the heroism or trauma of Tutsi victims—the victims of this extermination—be memorialized? Feature films offer only infantilized, exoticized, or colonial models of survivors, and even post-genocide documentaries mitigate their lingering trauma.[39] Throughout this chapter, films have been identified that transcend these generic patterns, such as Hughes's *100 Days* or Volker's *A Killer's Homecoming*; however, it is questionable whether Westerners or Rwandans will have access to these hard-to-find independent films. More widely available, Raymont's and Peck's interpenetrative films reflect more innovative aesthetics and narrative thematics that represent the post-genocide period more accurately and compellingly, and thus offer models for yet other representations of Rwanda. However, already past the seventeenth commemoration of *itsembabwoko*, it is debatable whether further, more nuanced films about Rwanda will be produced. Or whether now, this canon of "Rwanda films" has become the generic means of formulating "yet another genocide" and thus the continued, disappointing failure of Western media and human rights interventionism.

NOTES

1. While no one would term the *Shoah* the "German genocide" or the *Ermeni Soykırımı* (the Armenian genocide) the "Turkish genocide," ethnic cleansing is all too often ascribed to the whole Rwandan population, instead of its Tutsi victims. Here I will therefore refer to "the genocide in Rwanda," "the Tutsi genocide," or *itsembabwoko*, the Kinyarwanda term for 1994 events.

2. For the declarations of "never again," see "The Convention on the Prevention and Punishment of the Crime of Genocide," from December 9, 1948, and the "Universal Declaration of Human Rights," from December 10, 1948.

3. Moeller, *Compassion Fatigue*, 283.

4. In particular, Bill Clinton's fifteen-minute visit to Kigali Airport in March 1998, at the height of the Monica Lewinski scandal, was often reproduced in media and film about Rwanda. Only Belgian Prime Minister Guy Verhofstadt was present at the ten-year commemoration, as ten Belgian peacekeepers were also killed in the genocide.

5. From Raymont's documentary, *Shake Hands with the Devil: The Journey of Romeo Dallaire*.

6. *Itsembabwoko*, a compound word meaning "killing" of "a people/clan," was coined post-1994. Before that, massacres were referred to as *itsembatsemba*, "to kill, and kill again," as well as other euphemisms, such as *gukora*, meaning "work."

7. Schaffer and Smith, *Human Rights and Narrated Lives*, 15–23.

8. Please note the distinction between the 2007 narrative film *Shake Hands with the Devil* and Raymont's 2004 documentary on the same topic, *Shake Hands with the Devil: The Journey of Romeo Dallaire*. To clarify, I refer to either Spottiswoode's film or Raymont's documentary.

9. Kleinman, "The Appeal of Experience," 10; Moeller, *Compassion Fatigue*; Cohen, *States of Denial*.

10. Boutros-Ghali, *Unvanquished*, 132; Scherrer, *Genocide and Crisis in Central Africa*, 209; Prunier, *The Rwanda Crisis*, 199.

11. Interview with Pamela Nomvete, a South African actress who plays Martine in the featurette in *Sometimes in April*.

12. Quoted by UN Special Envoy Stephen Lewis in Raymont's *Shake Hands with the Devil*.

13. "TIA" is a refrain from the Hollywood blockbuster *Blood Diamond* (Zwick, 2006).

14. Whitehead, *Trauma Fiction*, 12.

15. Kleinman, "The Appeal of Experience," 10.

16. Hron, *Translating Pain*, 51–64; Brown, *States of Injury*, chap. 3.

17. Caruth, *Trauma*, 5.

18. I refer to Reinhart Weiner's personal film footage of an *Einsatzgruppe* firing squad.

19. Kielburger and Kielburger, "A Vision of Stability in Rwanda," AA2, describes Rwanda's economic success.

20. Hilsum, "Rwanda's Genocide Could Have Been Prevented," 23.

21. France, for example, is home to ten of the fugitives appearing on the indictment list of the International Criminal Tribunal for Rwanda, but is refusing to hand them over to Rwandan authorities.

22. Commentary in featurette in Raymont, *Shake Hands with the Devil*.

23. Cohen, *States of Denial*; Moeller, *Compassion Fatigue*.

24. Reiter, *Narrating the Holocaust*.

25. Calhoun, "White Guides, Black Pain," 32.

26. George, "Smearing a Hero," A25.

27. To exemplify, E. Ann Kaplan refers to one such post-genocide documentary about Rwanda to explain her notion of "vicarious empathy." See Kaplan's *Trauma Culture*. Unfortunately, though she elaborates on the conflicting emotions this film provokes for her and her students (92–93), she never mentions the name of the documentary or that of the filmmaker.

28. TV specials aired on such channels as Discovery, Sundance, and VisionTV; *Rwanda: Do Scars Ever Fade?* (Freedman, 2005) is available on freedocumentaries.com.

29. For instance, at the border of Tanzania or Uganda, the Tutsi Rwandan Patriotic Front advanced rapidly; by contrast, in the West and North, killings were greater and more protracted. In the central Bugesera region, a 1959 and 1973 Tutsi deportation site, ethnic differences were exaggerated and killings proceeded very quickly.

30. Only aired twice on BBC2 in the spring of 2004, *A Killer's Homecoming* is unavailable on VHS or DVD.

31. Théofile claims to have killed his victims because they asked him to. According to Joseph, Odette's new husband, other killers could have done the job, but Théofile insisted on doing it himself, because he didn't want to share his famous banana beer with other killers.

32. Hirsch, *Family Frames*, 22.

33. Walker, *Trauma Cinema*, 12.

34. Ibid., 19.

35. See Razack for criticism of the pathos-laden heroization of Dallaire at the expense of Rwandan victims of the genocide.

36. "Rwanda: Anarchy Rules," photo by Bernard Delaterre, 46.

37. Notably, Dallaire's testimonial compelled the military to recognize PTSD and create an educational video of it in the 1990s.

38. There has been much media attention about the fact that *Sometimes in April*, *Sunday in Kigali*, and *Shooting Dogs* were filmed in Rwanda (by contrast, *Hotel Rwanda* was filmed in South Africa). Usually such reports highlight the fact that Rwandan survivors were traumatized (e.g., Lacey, Milmo). In Hatzfeld's interview collection, *La Stratégie des antilopes*, survivors, specifically referring to the filming of *Sometimes in April*, contradict this claim and report that it was in fact foreign cameramen who most consulted psychologists after harrowing killing scenes (118–19).

39. Regarding feature films, see the Tutsi schoolgirl Rachel in *Shooting Dogs*, Tutsi love interest Gentille in *A Sunday in Kigali*, and colonial exemplar Paul Rusesabagina in *Hotel Rwanda*.

Part III

Visual
Documentation
and Genocide

8 The Specter of Genocide in Errol Morris's *The Fog of War*

KRISTI M. WILSON

Any military commander who is honest with himself, or with those he's speaking to, will admit that he has made mistakes in the application of military power. He's killed people unnecessarily—his own troops or other troops—through mistakes, through errors of judgment. A hundred, or thousands, or tens of thousands, maybe even a hundred thousand. But he hasn't destroyed nations.

ROBERT S. MCNAMARA,

interview in *The Fog of War*

When I started it [*The Fog of War*], it was about history. It was about events that occurred 40, 50 or even 60 years ago. But as we continued to work on it, suddenly it became more and more obvious that we were making a movie about today.

ERROL MORRIS,

interview in Ryan, "Making History"

In virtually every modern instance of mass murder, beginning, it appears, with the Armenians, the key element—not the only element but the key element, which has raised the numerical and psychic level of the deed above the classic terms of massacre—has been the alliance of technology and communications.

ARLEN,

Passage to Ararat

Introduction: The End of the "Good War," Channels of History, and the Specter of Japan

On any given day, with the click of the remote, one can revisit the glories of World War II on the History Channel. Featured shows, such as *Patton 360, Battle 360, Hero Ships, Dog Fights, Lost Worlds, Hitler's Eagles Nest Retreat*, and more, offer a never-ending celebration of American bravery during the "good war": "our all-American war in which we fought the bad guys to a standstill because they forced us to do it."[1] The near ubiquitous range of World War II program offerings, website forums, video games, and gift shop items available on the History Channel's companion website attests to Andreas Huyssen's concern that the act of preserving memory at all costs has usurped the act of envisioning the future in Western societies.[2] More specifically, the type of memory discourse that produces such entities as the History Channel relies explicitly on marketing strategies whose packages include as much mythology as reality about the United States' range of political dealings in foreign affairs in general:

> The geographic spread of the culture of memory is as wide as memory's political uses are varied, ranging from a mobilization of mythic pasts to support aggressively chauvinistic or fundamentalist politics . . . to fledgling attempts, in Argentina and Chile, to create public spheres of "real" memory that will counter the politics of forgetting pursued by postdictatorship regimes either through "reconciliation" and official amnesties or through repressive silencing. . . . The fault line between the mythic past and the real past is not always that easy to draw—one of the conundrums of any politics of memory anywhere. The real can be mythologized just as the mythic may engender strong reality effects.[3]

In his tireless efforts to convince lawmakers and politicians of the importance of his newly invented term, "genocide," Raphael Lemkin referred to the dangerous aspects of the politics of memory as occurring in "the twilight between knowing and not knowing."[4] For example, while the History Channel promotes a version of history in which the United States acts as a leader in the Allied fight against the perpetrators of the Holocaust (and, by extension, leaders in the fight against the horrific crime of genocide), the historical record suggests a radically different story.

According to Samantha Power, from the Armenian genocide, to the Holocaust, to Pol Pot's killing fields, to Saddam Hussein's murder of Northern Iraqi Kurds, to Bosnia, to Rwanda, American policymakers have turned a blind eye to genocide and have embraced a rhetorical stance of avoiding the term in general: "Yet notwithstanding all the variety among cases and within U.S. administrations, the

U.S. policy responses to genocide were astonishingly similar across time, geography, ideology, and geopolitical balance. . . . [Lemkin] believed a 'double murder' was being committed—one by the Nazis against the Jews and the second by the Allies, who knew about Hitler's extermination campaign but refused to publicize or denounce it."[5]

Even after the extent of Nazi war crimes was exposed at the Nuremberg Trials, the United States refused to ratify the Genocide Convention of 1948, opting instead to lose itself indefinitely in debates over definitions.[6] At issue were actions that qualified as genocide (physical, cultural, colonial, biological, and political genocide, for example), as well as the question of intention to destroy. Although Ronald Reagan finally signed onto the Genocide Convention in 1987, American lawmakers are still deeply conflicted by the term *genocide*. Newly elected President Barack Obama marked the anniversary of the Armenian genocide in 2009 by avoiding the term, opting instead to use "great atrocities." Elsewhere, he has used terms like "massacre" and "the terrible events of 1915" to address the Armenian genocide without tainting political relations with the Turkish government. The Obama administration avoided acknowledging the term once again in the context of the 2010 Armenian Genocide Resolution in the U.S. House of Representatives.

The Fog of History

Nowhere is the United States' problematic relationship to history and notions of genocide better exemplified than in its atomic bombing of Hiroshima and Nagasaki and firebombing of Japanese cities at the end of World War II. This chapter argues that in his 2003 documentary, *The Fog of War: Eleven Lessons from the Life of Robert S. McNamara*, Errol Morris offers U.S. viewers in particular a different model than popular venues, such as the History Channel, for understanding the complicated and paradoxical position of the United States at the end of World War II, having liberated Europe from the Nazis and, almost simultaneously, having annihilated hundreds of thousands of Japanese civilians through firebombing and nuclear bombing campaigns. Rather than offer a historical panorama (complete with "objective," omniscient narration and a plethora of interviewees), Morris isolates Robert S. McNamara and prompts him, during sixteen hours of interviews, to look back over his military career and offer some sort of rationale for his involvement in controversial military actions that scholars such as Leo Kuper and John W. Dower consider to be genocidal in nature.[7] Thus, an ethic of personal responsibility clashes with the rhetoric of avoidance that has for so long characterized mainstream historical accounts of the end of the war. *The Fog of War* posits a connection between U.S. military imperialism, capitalist expansionism, a Bush era continuity of aggressive cold war nuclear age politics, and an overall rupture of the United States' rhetoric of World War II heroism in favor of a repositioning of this identity as a nation with an ongoing, complex relationship to the concepts of history, war crimes, just and unjust wars, and genocide.

In his book on the Allied bombings of German cities, *On the Natural History of Destruction*, A. G. Sebald suggests that in the West (in particular in the German context), we have failed to give the "horrors of air war" significant historical and literary attention, perhaps because "the need to know was at odds with a desire to close down the senses" and, in the case of the new Federal Republic of Germany, move forward with reconstruction.[8] Kuper more explicitly condemns such horrors in both the Eastern and Western contexts as acts of genocide committed on both sides during World War II: "The changing nature of warfare, with a movement to total warfare, and the technological means for the instantaneous annihilation of large populations, creates a situation conducive to genocidal conflict. This potential was realized in the Second World War, when Germany employed genocide in its war for domination; but I think the term must also be applied to the atomic bombing of the Japanese cities of Hiroshima and Nagasaki by the U.S.A. and to the pattern bombing by the Allies of such cities as Hamburg and Dresden."[9]

And yet, Mary Nolan's historical tract on memory and air wars suggests that it is dangerous to compare the German victim-centered perspective on air wars (a perspective that has been around since the end of the war but has experienced a renaissance in popularity in Germany since 2002) with a Japanese counterpart.[10] A quick glimpse at the historical record of photographic and filmic images of the air wars over Japan at the end of the war offers a possible explanation for the bizarre fact that in contemporary Western parlance, "'air war' . . . in the current debate usually means only the Anglo-American saturation bombing of German cities from 1942–1945."[11] Such a truncated notion of "air wars" is out of step with what we know historically to be an ambitious U.S. propaganda campaign to characterize the Japanese people as a "bloodthirsty and ruthless type" in order to indoctrinate "U.S. soldiers into believing that even means such as incendiary bombing against civilian targets were acceptable, given the despicable nature of the German and Japanese people."[12]

There is plenty of Japanese film and photographic documentation of the devastation of Hiroshima and Nagasaki; however, film and photographic evidence in the Western context has been largely kept at arm's length. As Barbie Zelizer suggests, images are generally confined to the anonymous mushroom clouds in the sky, signaling the end of the war more than exposing any ground-level physical destruction: "*Life* depicted two shots of mushroomlike clouds under the general title 'The War Ends.' There were 'no injured Japanese in these photographs, no doctors and nurses treating the ill and wounded, no funeral pyres, no one mourning.'"[13] Films with explicit footage of the victims, such as Ogasawara's and Matsukawa's *Hiroshima*, were banned in the United States until the mid-1970s.[14] On the other hand, in Japan, U.S.-produced propaganda films like Norman Taurog's *The Beginning or the End* (1947) circulated in the theaters to try to convince American citizens that the bombs were a necessary part of ending the war.[15]

This lack of availability of images of the destruction of Japan at the end of the war has its parallel in a general lack of information about the Tokyo Trial, during which one of the eleven judges accused the Allies (United States) of genocide. Whereas the trial of Japanese high officials was mirrored on the Nuremberg Trials of Nazi officials, the official transcript of the proceedings remained "substantially inaccessible to a wider public," which stood "in striking contrast to the Nuremberg judgment, which was published in both English and French, together with the proceedings, running to 42 volumes."[16] The full proceedings of the Tokyo Trial were only published in 1981, with the exception of the dissenting judge's opinion (Justice Radhabinod Pal of India), which was published in 1953 at his own expense. Although the trial resulted in death sentences for seven of the defendants (two former prime ministers and five generals) and jail sentences for the remaining twenty-one, Justice Pal insisted that all of the defendants were innocent on all counts based in part on the logic that the absence of any discussion of Western colonialism or the United States' use of the atomic bombs on Japan rendered the trials a joke.[17] Tokyo Trial Justice B. V. A. Röling suggested that even in the Japanese context of immediate reconstruction, the topic of the bombing of Hiroshima and Nagasaki, although on the minds of most of the Japanese population, was off-limits in his discussions with General Douglas MacArthur:

> It was what you might call a very delicate issue. It would have more or less implied our criticism. . . . We would have been confronting him with an issue that was a very difficult one throughout the trial. I sometimes had contact with Japanese students. The first thing they always asked was: "Are you morally entitled to sit in judgment over the leaders of Japan when the Allies have burned down all of its cities with sometimes, as in Tokyo, in one night, 100,000 deaths and which culminated in the destruction of Hiroshima and Nagasaki? Those were war crimes." I am strongly convinced that these bombings were war crimes. . . . And that is forbidden by the laws of war, for sure. So why discuss it with the General? That would have been only embarrassing, I think.[18]

Röling's reluctance to discuss the bombing of the Japanese cities at the end of the war on the grounds that it would be embarrassing for MacArthur marks a general pattern that has persisted in the way in which we continue to collectively mythologize

The Fog of War, 2003. Directed by Errol Morris.

this moment in time through silence and lacunae. Christopher Joon-Hai Lee's work on teaching U.S. history and notions of "empire" in the present day suggests that even as late as 2006, educational paradigms in the West have still failed to respond to Justice Pal's charges that the official record of the end of World War II in Japan should include a discussion of Western colonialism and U.S. aggression.[19] He indicates that it is difficult to educate students about "new imperialisms" (resulting from the end of the cold war and the 1990s rise of global capitalism) because contemporary historical discourse is marred by a failure to understand earlier moments in which notions of empire intersected with American history. Lee suggests that educators who wish to address the topic of "new imperialisms" take recourse in the past as a prerequisite for situating "contemporary social, political, and economic trends."[20] Morris's 2003 documentary film, *The Fog of War: Eleven Lessons from the Life of Robert S. McNamara*, seems to answer Lee's call. It is a film concerned as much with America's present as its dark past in Japan. Morris makes use of archival footage to create a dual sense of McNamara's presence on screen. He addresses audiences both as a young, ambitious military career man and as an elder statesman looking back on his actions. One can hardly reconcile the slightly doddering man in an overcoat at the end of the film with the strutting, confident Kennedy protégé at its beginning. The common thread that binds the two consists in McNamara's distinctive voice, his sharp memory, and an unmistakably quality of his gaze that, at times, threatens to undermine his discourse.

Technological Genocide/White Collar Genocide

The issue of American guilt concerning Japan is still a controversial topic six decades after the bombings, as evidenced by the awkwardness, shame, and embarrassment, at times, with which McNamara recounts his understanding of the relationship between technology, mass killing, and ethics. As if to echo Lee's concern that we have not learned from the past, the first interview scene with McNamara features his perspective on historical lessons: "Any military commander who is honest with himself, or who knows who he's speaking to, will admit that he has made mistakes in the application of military power. He's killed people, unnecessarily, his own troops or other troops, through mistakes, through errors of judgment, a hundred, or thousands or tens of thousands, maybe even a hundred thousand, but he hasn't destroyed nations, and the conventional wisdom is don't make the same mistake twice. Learn from your mistakes. And we all do. Maybe we make the same mistake three times, hopefully not four or five. . . . There'll be no learning period with nuclear weapons. You make one mistake and you're going to destroy nations."

McNamara continues by stating that he is at an age where he can look back and "derive conclusions" about his actions during periods of deep uncertainty and war. In fact, at the time *The Fog of War* was filmed, McNamara had successfully repositioned his military history so that he was now an authoritative antinuke crusader who preached the immorality of nuclear weaponry as a foreign policy tool. But what about McNamara's actions at the end of World War II? Morris indicates early on in the film that he will return to the moral question of what it means for "a hundred thousand" people to die in one night on McNamara's watch. In fact, the documentary's title suggested that the term "the fog of war" will be itself interrogated, under Morris's microscopic lens, just as McNamara's "personal commitment to persuading others about the perils of the future [will prove to be] threatened by the remains of the past."[21]

Michael J. Shapiro argues that in order for the type of military rationality that paves the way for the "fog of war" rationale to be wrenched from its comfort zone in the "institutional perspectives and practices" that generate perpetual wars, the actual bodies and carnage that result from the lethally "effective and efficient" war practices have to emerge.[22] He suggests that Errol Morris's use of Philip Glass's dissonant soundtrack, his camerawork, and style acts as a counterpoint to McNamara's continual attempts to derive enlightened lessons from his previous actions. In fact, Shapiro suggests that there is a powerful element at play in this film, at the limits of the rational and proportional, that threatens to rupture the narrative at all times. Where McNamara uses abstract geopolitical rhetoric ("nations were not lost"), Errol Morris emphasizes bodies, exposing the cruel distancing effect of such rhetoric in a manner that unearths the emotional impact of McNamara's recollections about the firebombing and nuclear bombing in Japan, making them visceral and real.[23]

Morris seems to draw on Kuper's ideas about the explicit relationship between technological change and genocide at the onset of his film.[24] McNamara, compared by some to Adolf Eichmann, is introduced as a technological whiz kid, and Morris couches his exploration of McNamara's culpability in mass killing in an overall context of military technological expansion.[25] Accordingly, the first sequence consists of stock footage in which we see McNamara preparing a very large map for a televised address to the nation. "Is this chart at a reasonable height for you?" he asks the cameraman. He then begins his address, "Earlier tonight . . . ," only to cut himself off to speak to the cameraman once, "let me first just ask the TV, are you ready?" He wants to make sure that the camera angles are at appropriate heights to capture his message and the map positioned behind his podium. As the credits roll over Glass's somber soundtrack, we see a long series of archival footage depicting the technology of war on an American aircraft carrier ship, as men go through the detailed steps of preparing for an aerial bombing campaign: maps are consulted, the ship's guns are pointed out to sea, and bombs are assembled and delicately loaded. This series of shots ends with McNamara, a couple of generations older, expressing a similar concern over the transmission of his image. The elder McNamara looks off camera (presumably toward Errol Morris) and demands: "Let me hear your voice level to make sure it's the same."

If American historical familiarity with the devastation wreaked by its fire-bombing and nuclear bombing of Japanese cities has been characterized by fog or opacity, Morris more than makes up for such a gray zone with a thunderstorm of archival film and photograph footage, most of which is drawn from U.S. military sources and CBS televised "Reports." The voiceover in one of the reports calls McNamara the "most controversial person ever to hold the position of Secretary of Defense" because he was the first civilian to hold government control over the military. We see shots of McNamara working out equations with a pen on a white-board while the voiceover talks about how his critics call him a con man, "an IBM machine with legs." The words "brainy," "self-made," "cold logic," "unshakable," "effective," "efficient," and "whiz-kid" pop out from a montage of popular magazine and newspaper articles on McNamara's ascent to Pentagon power, followed by a long archival shot of the young, well-dressed genius filing past a line of paparazzi as he makes his way from the car to what looks like his first day on the job. The subtextual comparison between McNamara and a Hollywood actor walking the red carpet at an awards show could not be clearer. And yet, in spite of Morris's emphasis on McNamara's star qualities and intelligence, the tension between technological ingenuity and the criminal use of such knowledge is ruthlessly maintained.

Morris's approach to the topic of criminal uses of technology consists largely in an overall discussion of the cold war. As some critics have pointed out, McNamara's memories, while astute and perhaps rehearsed, are oddly nonlinear: "McNamara's recollections have a retrogressive circular movement projected backward and that returns in memory, gathering the remains to return to a momentary place anew. . . . [He] must return, recollect, and clear the fog that has confused him and so many others of his generation."[26] Accordingly, Morris sandwiches the film's most devastating and visually stunning sequences about destruction in Japan anachronistically between McNamara's recollections of the Cuban missile crisis and the Vietnam War. The nuclear question in the context of the cold war is the primary focus of the start of the film, with earlier specter of Hiroshima and Nagasaki looming eerily, almost silently, in the background.

Although the Cuban missile crisis was a frightening moment in U.S. history, it provides a safe starting point for American audiences because nuclear attack was avoided through a combination of luck and diplomacy. Morris makes use of archival footage of nuclear missiles being readied during the crisis as we hear audio tapes of McNamara talking to John F. Kennedy: "I don't know quite what kind of world we'll live in after we've struck Cuba. How would we stop at that point? I don't know the answer to this." As McNamara attempts to bring the primary lesson derived from this crisis—that nuclear war will destroy nations—to a close, several opaque, black-and-white images of modern Japan fade in and out, subtly reminding us of the lacunae in McNamara's discussion and foreshadowing the sequence to follow. Morris's choice to run the images under McNamara's meditations on the Cuban missile crisis muddles McNamara's message that the United States had been capable, at the time, of teaching the world a valuable lesson about the benefits of dialogue, negotiation, and empathy (this first section of the film is titled "Lesson #1: Empathize with Your Enemy") over brute force. The images reveal a complete detachment on McNamara's part between the risk of nuclear war during the Cuban missile crisis and the relatively recent nuclear bombing of Japan, making the claim that he would not know what kind of world he would live in seem ridiculous.

McNamara's "retrogressive recollections" in this sequence form an out-of-sync, illogical argument about the dangers of nuclear warheads, based on the illusion that the world had never experienced such devastation. The Cuban missile crisis/cold

The Fog of War, 2003. Directed by Errol Morris.

war segment ends with cockpit footage of a nuclear explosion. As bright light fills the pilot's window, we hear McNamara's words: "I think the human race needs to think more about killing . . . about conflict. Is that what we want in the twenty-first century?" This flash takes us back to the end of World War I in McNamara's memory-scape, to the "war to end all wars," around the time when McNamara discovered his love for philosophy courses at the University of California, Berkeley, ironically, the same department in which Errol Morris studied philosophy.

McNamara reaches the topic of Japan at his own pace, after he has discussed his transition from being a Harvard Business School professor to becoming an Air Force statistician, where his technical training in analysis and statistics would implicate him in what he describes as a disproportional killing of Japanese civilians and what other scholars call, quite simply, a genocide. McNamara's recollections of the firebombing of Japanese cities, such as Yokohama, Tokyo, Toyama, and many others, using the B-29 bomber planes exemplifies the type of geopolitical rhetoric theorized by Shapiro. The fact that his voice cracks halfway through the sentence—"On a single night we burned to death one hundred thousand Japanese civilians—men, women, and children"—is telling, however, of its fragility and ultimate failure to convince. Morris lingers on footage of Tokyo engulfed in flames while he asks off-camera, "Were you aware this was going to happen?" To which McNamara responds with one of the most often-quoted lines from the film, words that echo those of Eichmann: "Well, I was part of a mechanism that in a sense recommended it."

A startling animated, aerial photography segment accompanies the rest of McNamara's confession/disclaimer, in which we are made to feel as if we are falling from the sky among a sea of bombs over a Japanese city along with his handwritten, now scrambled, calculations: "I analyzed bombing operations and how to make them more efficient, i.e., not more efficient in the sense of killing more, but more efficient in weakening the adversary. . . . Now I don't want to suggest that it was my report that led to—I'll call it the firebombing. . . . I don't want to suggest that it was I that put into [Curtis] LeMay's mind that his operations were totally inefficient and had to be drastically changed, but anyhow that's what he did." The close-ups of McNamara's signatures on several official-looking documents juxtaposed with the sky-diving numbers sequence mirror the vertiginous logic of his rationale for what amounted to technological genocide.

While McNamara essentially contradicts what he has said elsewhere about the combination of firebombs and nuclear bombs over Japan, Morris makes an explicit visual comparison between the proportion of Japanese major cities that were destroyed by fire and what the equivalent cities might have been in the United States in a series that flashes the name of a major U.S. city for each image of a Japanese one that burned, along with the percent of the city that went up in flames. "Tokyo is roughly the size of Los Angeles," McNamara says during this sequence. "Proportionality should be a guideline in war," he goes on. "Killing 50 to 90 percent of the people of sixty-seven Japanese cities and then bombing them with two nuclear bombs is not proportional in the minds of some people to the objectives we were trying to achieve. . . . Why was it necessary to drop the nuclear bomb if LeMay was burning up Japan?" McNamara's powerful rhetorical question undermines his own rationale for the atomic bombings of Japan offered as late as 2005 in *Foreign Policy*: "Why did so many civilians have to die? Because the civilians, who made up nearly 100 percent of the victims of Hiroshima and Nagasaki, were unfortunately 'co-located' with Japanese military and industrial targets."[27]

McNamara goes on to contradict the United States' innocence in perhaps the most powerful moment of the film: "LeMay said that if we lost the war, we'd all have been prosecuted as criminals. And I think he's right. He, and I'd say I, were behaving as war criminals. . . . But what makes it immoral if you lose and not immoral if you win?" The age-old question—"doesn't might make right?"—first raised by Thrasymachus in a discussion with Socrates in Plato's *Republic*, appears again in this dialogue between former philosophy students, McNamara and Morris.[28] McNamara's stutter, as some have referred to his ideological slippage in *The Fog of War*, does not amount to an apology but a condemning insider's statement about what Justice Pal had referred to at the time of the Tokyo Trial as unacknowledged atrocities committed by the United States. Morris's camera lingers on this moment, floating slowly across McNamara's questioning face, as if to suggest that if anything, the human race has not evolved since ancient times but has simply seen empire after empire evolve and self-destruct, sadly demonstrating that the victor in the dialogue between Socrates and Thrasymachus still proves to be the latter.[29]

NOTES

1. "As a nation, we constantly revisit World War II in song, on radio, on TV and in the movies, in novels and history books. In both pride and sorrow, we remain a nation that is always 'lookin' for the old Arizona.'" Basinger, *The World War II Combat Film*, xii.

2. Huyssen, "Present Pasts," 21.

3. Ibid., 26.

4. From Raphael Lemkin's unpublished autobiography, quoted in Power, *"A Problem from Hell,"* 35.

5. Power, *"A Problem from Hell,"* xvi and 28.

6. "The United States was not among the eighty-four nations which ratified the convention by 31 December 1978. In recent hearings before the Senate Foreign Relations Committee, reference was made to earlier objections *inter alia*, that the American Constitution prevented ratification because genocide was a domestic matter, and though the committee dismissed the arguments, the United States has still not ratified the convention. If a relatively stable country such as the U.S.A., which took a leading role in the Nuremberg Trials and the Genocide Convention, has reservations about ratification of the Convention, one can understand the reaction against extending protection to political groups in other countries, particularly those in which the political process is very violent (as argued by the Venezuelan delegate)." Kuper, *Genocide*, 30.

7. Kuper, *Genocide*; Dower, *War without Mercy*.

8. "I do not doubt that there were and are memories from those nights of destruction; I simply do not trust the form—including the literary form—in which they are expressed, and I do not believe they were a significant factor in the public consciousness of the new Federal Republic in any sense except as encouraging the will to reconstruction." Sebald, *On the Natural History of Destruction*, 81.

9. Kuper, *Genocide*, 46.

10. Nolan, "Air Wars, Memory Wars."

11. Ibid., 8.

12. Calhoun, "We Are Good and They Are Evil," 237.

13. Zelizer, *Remembering to Forget*, 33.

14. Vogel, *Film as a Subversive Art*, 200.

15. Dutch international lawyer and Tokyo Trial Justice B. V. A. Röling had this to say about the experience of viewing *The Beginning or the End*: "I saw the film in Tokyo. Three times it stressed—and each time it was a huge lie—that the population of the Japanese cities

had been warned beforehand. If I remember correctly, the Stimson diaries deal with this question of whether the cities should have been warned. According to those diaries a warning was not possible because it was so uncertain that the bombs would really explode. Anyway, the lies have been solemnly hidden in a lead case, to deceive posterity for half a millennium away about the atrocious behavior of America." Röling and Cassese, *Tokyo Trial and Beyond*, 112.

16. Ibid., 6.

17. According to Röling and Cassese, there were widespread claims that the Tokyo Trial, characterized by one chief prosecutor (from the United States), as opposed to the Nuremberg Trials, which had four (from the United States, the United Kingdom, the Soviet Union, and France), "was either a vehicle for America's taking revenge for the treacherous attack on Pearl Harbor, or a means of assuaging American national guilt over the use of Atomic weapons in Japan." Röling and Cassese, *Tokyo Trial and Beyond*, 5.

18. Röling adds that MacArthur had general misgivings about the trial. In particular, according his aide, General Courtney Whitney, he disagreed with the principle of holding political leaders of the vanquished responsible for war crimes. See Röling and Cassese, *Tokyo Trial and Beyond*, 84–85.

19. Lee, "Arendt's Lesson," 129.

20. Ibid.

21. Donovan, Kimball, and Smith, "Fog of War."

22. Shapiro, *Cinematic Geopolitics*, 66.

23. Ibid., 78.

24. "In international warfare, technological change facilitates genocidal massacre, as in the bombings of Hiroshima and Nagasaki." Kuper, *Genocide*, 17.

25. Laurie Calhoun compares McNamara to Eichmann, suggesting that "like so many others throughout history involved in mass murder, [he] was a functionary, and his leader, like most throughout history, did not ask anyone to murder other people. Rather, Hitler justified his war by appeal to the usual moral rhetoric, most notably in terms of defense." Calhoun, "Death and Contradiction," 6.

26. Donovan, Kimball, and Smith, "Fog of War," 4–5.

27. McNamara, "Apocalypse Soon," 32. McNamara frames the nuclear bombing of Nagasaki and Hiroshima as an unfortunate case of "co-location" in one context in his essay. Elsewhere in the piece, especially when the global threat of nuclear bombs is addressed, he refers to it as the looming threat of nuclear holocaust.

28. See Cornford, *The Republic of Plato*.

29. Shapiro points out that this is one of the few moments in the film in which McNamara's face occupies the center of the frame. He suggests that there is a correlation between McNamara admitting responsibility for his actions and the camera's focus. Shapiro, *Cinematic Geopolitics*, 81.

9

GIs Documenting Genocide

Amateur Films of World War II Concentration Camps

MARSHA ORGERON

It is clear that the time is upon us for the screen to be intently utilized in bringing home to all people a comprehension of the scope of Nazi crimes . . . And the public—or that element of it which might feel its sensibilities abused—must realize that informational pictures, no matter how shocking, are for the general good. . . . The suffering of others must be felt by all of us in some sense if we are to have a comprehension of what has happened in the world in these black years.

BOSLEY CROWTHER, "The Solemn Facts"

I saw and photographed the piles of naked, lifeless bodies, the human skeletons in furnaces, the living skeletons who would die the next day because they had had to wait too long for deliverance. . . . Using the camera was almost a relief. It interposed a slight barrier between myself and the horror in front of me.

MARGARET BOURKE-WHITE, *Portrait of Myself*

I want to use these ideas—one voiced by a popular movie critic writing from the American home front in the spring of

1945, the other by a photographer writing retrospectively (in 1963) about her first-hand experiences of the Nazi concentration camps—as a jumping-off point and a frame for this exploration of the all-but-forgotten amateur cinematographic record of concentration camps at the close of World War II. Crowther advocates for using cinematic evidence of the camps as part of a public mission of education and empathy building. This philosophy regards seeing as the first step to believing the unfathomable. Although "comprehending" may be a bit of an overstatement, the sense that "the public," as Crowther puts it, needed to be exposed to visual evidence of Nazi atrocities was widespread, if equally controversial.[1] Bourke-White, one of the first photographers to document postliberation Buchenwald, speaks from the other side of the camera, articulating the power of the photographic instrument precisely as a means—and perhaps a justification—of psychological distance between the photographer and her horrific subjects. Images of the camps raised—and still raise—the most serious of ethical questions, which were and are confronted by an array of spectators, each with vastly different stakes, at their respective moments of confrontation with these images.

The concentration camps were, almost immediately following their liberation, treated as memorials and as educational displays. American soldiers, the international media, and the local citizenry were encouraged to tour the camps, and German prisoners of war (POWs) were ordered to witness the genocidal traces that remained within camp gates. The 16mm footage shot by Dick Ham at Buchenwald in April 1945 for broadcaster Lowell Thomas (the footage was never used), for example, depicts the postliberation camp already endowed with museum-like qualities.[2] Makeshift exhibits representing Nazi crimes against humanity were on display as part of the emerging project of documenting the genocidal acts that transpired at the camp prior to liberation, with survivors on hand, in this case, as witnesses testifying to their experiences. General Dwight D. Eisenhower, who visited Ohrdruf (a Buchenwald subcamp) on April 12, 1945, strongly encouraged Allied troops to see for themselves the conditions at these newly liberated camps, while Army Signal Corps and journalistic photographers were called in on an explicitly evidentiary mission to shoot both still and moving images.[3] As Jeffrey Shandler argues, Eisenhower "was at the forefront of establishing the act of witnessing the conditions of recently liberated camps as a morally transformative experience."[4] Seeing the camps in person was, according to this logic, ideal; but seeing representations—photographs and films—was an acceptable alternative. This culture of documentation and witnessing was being established in official capacities and policies, but soldiers who entered the camps often created more personal records of what they encountered.

There exists an extensive literature on the official photographic and moving image record of the camps at the close of the war. The unofficial, amateur movie footage shot by enlisted men has been virtually ignored. As Susan Carruthers has put it, "The visual register of genocide continues to be shaped by footage shot by the U.S. Army Signal Corps and Soviet camera crews on entering the camps in 1945."[5] Indeed, our cultural memory of the Holocaust and especially of the concentration camps as the most concrete manifestation of the Nazi's plans for European Jews consists almost entirely of official still and moving images, military as well as journalistic. Both Barbie Zelizer and Janina Struk, in their respective books about photographing and filming the Holocaust, discuss amateur *still* photography—which was widespread at the close of the European segment of the war. However, they entirely ignore the subject of amateur films.[6]

This conspicuous critical neglect is, no doubt, partly due to the difficulty researchers have had in trying to access such films, at least until recently. As 8mm and 16mm collections continue to enter archives, and—equally importantly—as archives recognize the historical value of amateur cinematography and of providing access to these collections, historians and scholars are offered an opportunity to think about new perspectives on the concentration camps as the most coherent symbol of genocide at the close of the war. These films offer us a glimpse into the close of the European segment of the war through the eyes of the soldiers who felt compelled to capture some aspect of it on motion picture film. Their cinematic records are an important alternative source of knowledge about the camps and can be considered a unique type of home movie as well as a horrific visual souvenir of the war.[7]

Home Movies at War

Despite rules against enlisted men shooting personal films during the war, small gauge filmmakers did not all abandon their cinematographic hobbies during World War II. Some were called on to work for the official documentary units of the Signal Corps, during which time they also managed to shoot footage for their personal collections (George Stevens is a well-known example of this). Still others managed to bring with them or to procure 8mm and 16mm cameras while overseas. Much of the amateur footage taken of the camps at the close of the war has been kept in private hands, shown, if at all, to family and friends. In recent years, however, these films have begun to make their way into archives such as the United States Holocaust Memorial Museum (USHMM), the Library of Congress (LOC), the Academy of Motion Picture Arts and Sciences (AMPAS), and Emory University. Collecting institutions have begun the diligent work of preserving and making access copies of these materials, which cannot readily be shown to researchers in their original 8mm and 16mm formats. Some archives have made these films even more widely accessible, not only to scholars but also to the general public, by putting them online. The USHMM has been most active in facilitating access to the moving image holdings in their Steven Spielberg Film and Video Archive, and visitors to their website can search their easily navigable database using such terms as "concentration camps," "liberation," or "Dachau."[8]

Almost all the amateur film that I have encountered from World War II depicts innocuous images of "downtime": shots of clowning around, smoking, and reading, the local landscape and citizenry. Most of this footage was shot by men in the army while they were in Europe. Retired Major Norman Hatch, who was on active duty as a cameraman for the U.S. Marine Corps from 1941 to 1946, explained that marines would have had been hard pressed to shoot their own movies during World War II, likely more so than men in the army or air force.[9] Because of the close quarters kept by marines onboard a ship, hobbyist activities such as filming would likely not have taken place without catching the eye of a ship's skipper, who could confiscate and, if necessary, destroy any unofficial photographic equipment. Soldiers in the army appear to have had different cinematographic fortunes, despite the fact that amateur filming overseas was officially restricted for very logical reasons: the film an enlisted man might shoot could reveal secrets, positions, and so on if captured by the enemy. As retired cameraman Hatch clarified, "You're on duty 24–7; you're never a civilian part time, especially during a war."[10] Despite this, I have tracked down dozens of 8mm and 16mm amateur films shot by soldiers of the camps following their liberation. I am certain that there are other such films to be found in archives, libraries, and historical societies, much as I am sure that similar films exist in private hands as well as in many a landfill.

In October 1944, *Home Movies* magazine published an article by Private First Class Gene Fernette titled "G.I. Movie Makers." It begins: "Not every G.I. Joe succumbed to the feverish impulse to dispose of his worldly goods, including his cine equipment, immediately after receiving that special 'greeting' from Uncle Sam. Many brought their cameras along with them to training camp and found opportunity to carry on with their hobby of making movies. . . . Of course, not every cinefilming G.I. found taking his camera along easy. Certain branches of the services made this impractical or impossible."[11] Despite the range of prohibitions against filming that existed in all of the military branches, Fernette acknowledges that "many have been fortunate to have cine cameras along with them overseas and have succeeded in obtaining some rare pictures in spite of the dearth of film, most of which must be supplied to them from here."[12] In J. H. Schoen's February 1945 *Home Movies* article about the Army Signal Corps, cameraman Corporal Roy

Advertisement for the Universal Camera Corporation. *Home Movies* magazine, March 1944.

Creveling openly discusses "making his own 16mm. movies at every opportunity" when he was not shooting official footage.[13] Although "Combat Cameraman's Communique . . ." is ostensibly about the ways that amateur cinematographers were trained by and integrated into the Army Signal Corps, it is notable that Creveling's hobbyist pursuits are discussed so openly. Personal moviemaking during the war was clearly no secret.

The stateside amateur cinematography trade press took for granted that this kind of filming was taking place during the war, as even an ongoing Universal Camera Corporation campaign made clear. In Universal Camera's March 1944 *Home Movies* advertisement, a GI writes a letter home to accompany the film footage he's shot, which he hopes his family will get a "kick out of."[14] Although his is not European front footage, nor is it imagery that resonates with the idea of war in any way, the advertisement anticipates a continuity of amateur cinematography once the soldier returns home and has more conventional "home movies" to make. It also acknowledges that at least some soldiers were making movies overseas and shipping their film back home for domestic consumption, which appears to have been the most practical method of getting film developed. The fact that a major American magazine promoting home moviemaking frequently represented and discussed the enlisted amateur cinematographer supports considering not only how these films might be understood as a unique kind of home movie but also how they might test the limits of this conceptualization.

Home movies are traditionally associated with leisure, pleasure, and family, taking birthdays, holidays, and other aspects of domestic life as their most frequently recurring subjects. But they also often depict travel (both for work and for recreation), foreign people, and places, filmed primarily with home exhibition in mind. The specific films under discussion here by and large represent traumatic images, but they are still personal mementos and were, based on surviving oral histories, used almost exclusively in home-viewing contexts. Struk has observed that American soldiers, who were encouraged to make still photographs of the atrocities they discovered at the camps, often "kept their photographs hidden" instead of sharing them on their return.[15] Amateur films of the war, then, might be conceived of as the rarest kinds of home movies inasmuch as they typically depict obviously unpleasant but, perhaps, equally necessary memories. They are also uniquely authored films, tied to specific individuals who both shot the footage and, in many cases, thanks in part to the hard work of the collecting institutions themselves, narrate the images in recorded interviews conducted at the time the materials were deposited.[16]

"I Wish All the People Back Home Could Walk through This Place"

I want to begin my exploration of a sampling of these GI movies with Joseph Bernard Kushlis's 8mm film of Ohrdruf, shot at the same Buchenwald subcamp that inspired Eisenhower's commands to witness and record. Kushlis's film is part of the Fred R. Crawford Witness to the Holocaust Project at Emory University and is available online.[17] In a 1979 oral history, Kushlis reports being at the camp April 12 and 13, the same time as Generals Bradley, Patton, and Eisenhower's well-known visit, during which time Ohrdruf became a kind of ground zero for the call to document and report the atrocities encountered by the liberators.[18]

Kushlis, a sergeant in the Third Army at the time, described arriving and filming at Ohrdruf:

> I went over there promptly with several of my buddies and I had a small 8mm movie camera with me, which I was permitted to take with me since I had joined the outfit late in the game as a replacement. Of course, cameras earlier in the war were banned—the use of them was banned at least by the average enlisted personnel. But, I had my camera with me and I have taken these pictures of Ohrdruf—the very emaciated, starved—obviously starved—bodies lying around, most of them shot through the forehead as the Germans retreated and left them. . . . While I was there filming our officers in charge, of course, had already started civilians, picked up on the downtown streets and brought to the Camp, to perform the burial of these bodies. . . . And to bury such a large number at one time—of course, coffins were not available. . . . So, as near as I could make out, they were all being put in linen bags. My movies do show these German civilians digging the long trenches for common graves into which these bodies were then put.[19]

Kushlis's retrospective memory of his footage reminds us of the complexities not only of witnessing but also of capturing these images as a personal record of the genocidal acts that transpired in the camps. Kushlis clearly uses his own film as a conduit to memory—he says "my movies do show" instead of "I remember"—indicating the importance and the limitations of such records. By this I mean to suggest both that the images contained in such films offer a certain portrait of the treatment of those interred in the camps, and that they provide only a partial glimpse of what was witnessed, requiring personal memory and narration to offer even the most rudimentary explanation of what they depict. Clearly the film functions partly as a companion to his memory of the camp; the two might even be considered indistinguishable.

In his footage, Kushlis employs a marked aesthetic sensibility: he appears to be especially interested in making portraits of the dead, focusing on a single body or two in a fashion that tends to them as individuals instead of just shooting scenes of mass death.[20] His film depicts a series of close-up portraits followed by wider shots that convey the scale of death at the camp, alternating between more intimate images and what we might call establishing shots. As Carol Zemel has demonstrated in her discussion of Holocaust liberation photographs, military film most "often took a longer or broader view, showing camp grounds strewn with bodies as liberating armies discharged their work."[21] Kushlis's brief record suggests an interest in individually recognizing the dead, however incomplete (for practical reasons) this representational schema is. From all appearances Kushlis filmed on his own accord, and his images suggest a desire to acknowledge the individual, human consequences of genocide as well as its scale at this camp.

It is also worth noting that Kushlis does not photograph any survivors. In his oral history, Kushlis specifically addresses the ethics of his decision to film what he encountered in the camp: "I viewed the scene in utter disbelief. It did occur to me that there was probably a question of morality or decency in even photographing these unfortunate people, but I quickly resolved the question to my own satisfaction in realizing that here was history that should be recorded."[22] Perhaps this explains his decision not to train his lens on the living?

Although we can only speculate about his representational decisions, similar versions of this justification for filming recur in oral histories of other GIs who filmed the camps. Interviewees repeatedly narrate a transition from incredulity and traumatization to a sense of historical motivation to capture these images, however obscene. As Patricia Zimmermann writes in her introduction to *Mining the Home Movie*, "Amateur films and home movies negotiate between private memories and social histories. . . . Consonant with explanatory models of history from below, the history of amateur film discourses and visual practices are always situated in context with . . . more visible forms of cultural practices."[23] Zimmermann's ideas are especially relevant to understanding this unusual kind of home movie as a private version of the official and widely circulating documentation provided by the military and journalistic sources. These films exist at the shadowy interstices of personal memory and official history, and recuperating them from obscurity is the first step in moving them out of the merely personal realm.

The compulsion to capture such traumatic images—things that should be remembered even if they are not desired or fond memories—reminds us of Bourke-White's explanation of the role the camera played in her ability to witness the scenes at Buchenwald. As she elaborated, "I have to work with a veil over my mind. In photographing the murder camps, the protective veil was so tightly drawn that I hardly knew what I had taken until I saw prints of my own photographs. It was as though I was seeing those horrors for the first time."[24] The distancing effect Bourke-White refers to, a kind of dissociation from the present and a return to it at the moment of witnessing images instead of reality, returns us to the idea of motivation for the enlisted cinematographers under discussion here. Where Bourke-White was doing her job by photographing the camps, we might ask what motivated these soldiers to record history, especially when that history would not be seen by others.

Unlike many other amateur cinematographers who filmed scenes at the camps, Kushlis did not keep these movies to himself. He sent his exposed reels back to the United States to be processed and did not view the footage until he returned home to edit it.[25] After the war ended, he was invited to clubs, such as the YMCA, and to other groups where he would show his movies as often as three times a week. Barbie Zelizer has discussed the experiential power of journalistic representations of the camps: "One did not need to be at the camps; the power of the image made everyone who saw the photos into a witness."[26] Kushlis narrates a similar trust in photographic/cinematic veracity when he explains that audiences who saw his films felt convinced of German atrocities for particular reasons: "They were all interested in seeing firsthand what they had read about. . . . Here was something taken by a strict amateur photographer in which there could be no doctoring of scenes and no faking of film. What I took was there. It was fact."[27]

While the fundamental spirit of Zelizer's and Kushlis's assertions is difficult to argue against, their faith in photographic indexicality and their notion that the viewing of what for them are indisputable images amounted to a sort of firsthand experience is problematic. In this case, Kushlis is—like the government—using moving images as proof of what happened in the camps, so his film might be considered as functioning along the same lines as official footage. But the perception of the amateur as functioning autonomously—we might even say outside of ideology—seems to append a magical quality of truth that is also tied to the maker's own firsthand witnessing, his own status as rememberer. Both film and memory, however, are subject to questioning. As documentarian Errol Morris has put it, "The brain is not a Reality-Recorder."[28] And while film can record the real, it too is subject to any number of (mis)interpretations or (mis)understandings.

This is not, in any way, intended as a questioning of Kushlis's film. Rather, Kushlis's framing here reminds us of the important perception of the amateur cinematographer's implicit relationship to the idea of truth. Indeed, there was a considerable degree of skepticism in the spring of 1945 regarding the reality of the images circulating in newsreels and journalistic photography; many thought that such atrocities were beyond belief. The value of Kushlis's footage resided, in part, in the fact that it was not official and therefore presumably not politically motivated or manipulated. His images were taken as "fact" not only because what they captured was, as he explains it, "there," but also because he acted as a personal eyewitness and narrator when he screened the film. This was also the case with official documentary footage, as Carruthers has explained: "Commentary accompanying both still and moving images needed to acknowledge possible doubts in order to refute them, a task often assigned to the figure of the formerly-cynical GI, a prominent protagonist in documentary, newsreel and press accounts of the camps' liberation."[29] Of course, the scale of newsreel or documentary distribution with prerecorded narration cannot compare to one man showing his home movies to a community group and answering their questions in person. But the intention—the function of the film and person as witness—is difficult to differentiate between. Kushlis's decision to share his films in this public fashion suggests that his "historical" motivation at the moment of filming evolved into a need to disseminate these images, presumably in an attempt to widen—a few audience members at a time—the net of virtual eyewitnesses.

The films of Colonel Alexander Zabin are deposited at the U.S. Holocaust Memorial Museum and are available online, including a reel depicting scenes at postliberation Dachau.[30] A doctor with General Patton's Third Army and the Fourth Auxiliary Surgical Group, Zabin landed on Normandy Beach on June 7, 1944, the day after D-Day, later treated survivors at Dachau, and managed to shoot *several hours* of 16mm footage over the course of the war, in black and white as well as in color. According to a conversation with his son, Steve Zabin, the colonel had no experience making movies prior to the war, so this was not a case of the prewar hobbyist clinging to peacetime pursuits. Steve Zabin believes that his father sent the exposed film home to his family to have it developed stateside. It is quite possible that the 16mm camera he filmed with was procured in Europe; Zabin, in fact, returned home with many souvenirs of the war, including a yellow cloth star (presumably from Dachau) and thirty reels of German-made films that he found in a warehouse (including footage of Hitler).[31]

In spite of his inexperience, Zabin shot truly extraordinary films. According to his son, the colonel would often show these films to his immediate family, his kids, and other relatives after the war, but he did not show the Dachau footage to his friends or anyone else. Steve Zabin remembers that his father would not talk much about the Dachau footage when he did show it to his family beyond saying, in a rather unemotional way (think of Bourke-White's articulation of her emotional distancing), that it was horrendous and that his encounters at the camp justified the whole war. Zabin's own notes (contained in the original film can) indicate that the footage on the Dachau reel is "well spliced." This is somewhat unusual for the films I have encountered, most of which were edited in camera. An inspection of Zabin's film by archivist Lindsay Zarwell at USHMM reveals that the Dachau footage is spliced together in ten different places from at least two reels (one black and white, and one Kodachrome color). It would be fascinating to know if any footage taken by Zabin at Dachau was excluded from the finished reel, but we have no record of Zabin's methods of filming or editing.

Zabin's images of Dachau are careful, providing a brief but comprehensive portrait of the camp as he encountered it. The Dachau sequence begins with shots of the gas chambers (with some American soldiers occasionally in the frame), including a bathhouse label over a door, followed by images of stacked wooden coffins. These shots of inanimate camp details set the stage for what follows, but not in a fashion that prepares the viewer for what is to come. Zabin cuts to a series of shots depicting stacks of emaciated corpses, dead bodies intertwined in various stages of dress. These images are shocking for their graphic and uncensored representation. Although they logically follow from what precedes them, the move from inanimate buildings and structures to inanimate human beings in such an inhumane state is jarring. This is, however, Zabin's cinematic story of Dachau, and the shots of buildings and coffins ground the viewer in the structural realities of the camp prior to introducing the degraded human element.

From the inanimate and the dead, Zabin next includes several underexposed interior shots of the bunkers occupied by surviving prisoners, and then cuts to a sick ward where injured patients stare into the camera as it pans across them. The next cut ventures outside to a group of liberated men wearing striped uniforms. Zabin pans left and then right across the group as they listen to instructions; they, too, directly stare into the camera with blank expressions on their faces. A quick shot of a dead body in the water (perhaps a German soldier, but it is hard to tell) is followed by a series of shots taken outside the camp's gates, including a number of clothed, dead bodies. Zabin alternates between scenes of the prisoners and wider shots of the camp, including some striking high-angle shots that give a sense of the camp's geography and size. The final Dachau images are of a train, presumably at the camp station, where a series of shots reveal dead bodies on a number of the cars. The film then moves on to images of U.S. soldiers at roll call in a field and then, most jarringly, to colorful images of a young girl at a Czech folk festival. The film, much like Zabin's life, goes on.

A month after the liberation of Dachau, Zabin wrote a letter to his hometown newspaper, the *Malverne Herald*. In this letter dated May 31, 1945, he narrates visiting the camp in a fashion that resonates with the many other descriptions that issued from soldiers who entered the camps around the same time, lingering on the sensory shock and indelibility of the experience. Zabin wrote, "I can still smell the stench of the dead, decayed and burned flesh, and the horrible sights will never leave my memory. I think you know me well enough to believe what I say is nothing but the cold, ugly truth, untainted by personal feeling. I had never before been able to believe all the atrocity stories and evil deeds attributed to the Germans." Directly countering the claims that were circulating regarding the impossibility of what was being reported about the camps, Zabin goes on to describe the conditions of slave labor he witnessed, the gas chambers at Dachau, the crematoria, the prisoner barracks, and the stacks of dead bodies. Zabin concludes his letter: "Men broken in body and mind were walking skeletons, red-eyed and bewildered, with empty, helpless expressions. It is all a horrible memory, a nightmare I can never hope to forget. I wish that all the people back home could walk through this place. Then they would realize that any sacrifice they have made—even the loss of their loved ones—was not made in vain. To liberate this camp alone was sufficient reason for our war with Germany."

It is worth considering this letter as a virtual narration of Zabin's footage and of the process of conveying the factuality of the camps to civilians back home, another version of what Kushlis does with his cinematic lectures. It is, in some ways, a brief but explicit "walk through this place" as well as a reminder of how difficult it would have been to possess such devastating images, perhaps especially given Zabin's decision *not* to share them with anyone beyond his inner circle. The indelible nature of what he saw was ensured by his possession of movies that documented his experiences at Dachau and that could function as containers, or sorts, for those "horrible sights." Writing a letter narrating the horrors of the camps is one thing; sharing such explicit and painful images is clearly another.

Documenting Genocide?

As Struk, Shandler, and Zelizer all affirm in their respective research on liberation photographs, American soldiers were encouraged to shoot their own 35mm photographs of the postliberation concentration camps in part to support official reports and allay suspicions that things could not be as bad as they seemed. Amateur cinematographers no doubt were allowed—and on occasion were encouraged—to make movies of the camps for the same reason. While this chapter is framed in the context of "GIs documenting genocide," it is necessary to pause here to reflect on the fact that none of the amateur or official images can live up to that ambitious concept. Although each reel of film captures hints of what transpired in the camps, the films are more opaque than they are revelatory, more reliant on human memory (itself spotty and interestingly reliant on the photographic) than on the sheer explanatory abilities of their own images, and they are always representations of acts that transpired in the past. As many have argued, there is no adequate way to depict what actually happened in any of the camps under discussion in this chapter. I do not believe that this is just a function of the scale and degree of trauma associated with the Holocaust (although this certainly presents representational challenges of its own), but is rather inherent in the nature of documentary images, which are also subjective and partial. What these amateur cinematographers offer, however, is intriguing and valuable precisely because it is so clearly subjective and partial. Each one, in their own way, captures a "walk through" the camp at a particular moment in its postliberation lifeline. These amateur cinematographers' choices—to film the dead, to film the living, not to film the dead, not to film the living—remind us of the deeply personal nature of these men's experiences and of their decisions about what to remember, and what, perhaps, to try to forget. They are also a concrete indicator of the intimate relationship between memory and photography.

In conclusion, I want to consider two differently authored films that occupy divergent ends of the representational spectrum. William Fedeli, who eventually became a lieutenant colonel but was a supply officer with the Quartermaster group when he first went overseas, shot fourteen reels of 8mm footage, mostly in color, which now reside at the Library of Congress. As he reported in an oral history, he started shooting movies while training in Iowa and brought his camera with him overseas, where he reported having it with him all the time. At the end of the war he was in Weimar and made his way to Buchenwald after it was liberated. The notes on this canister of film, which is not available online, read: "1945: Concentration camp in Nordhausen Germany, Ike, Frankfurt, Air trip to England, Cambridge." Fedeli's footage depicts Nordhausen (originally a subcamp of Buchenwald that eventually became a camp with subcamps of its own), which was largely devoted to producing weapons, hence the military detritus seen throughout the footage.[32]

As Fedeli reported in his oral history, "What I saw is what everybody knows; I saw some of the bones that were baked into the oven. I didn't see them being gassed or anything, but I saw how they lived in these bunks four high and so on . . . walking bones." Fedeli narrates his memories of what he witnessed at the camps in a fashion that evokes precisely the kinds of images we see in both Kushlis's and Zabin's footage. His description evokes what have become the iconographic images of the Holocaust: the bones, the ovens, the living skeletons. But Fedeli's footage is notable because it does *not* show us these instantly recognizable, graphic images of deprivation and death that we are accustomed to—and expect—in liberation footage, amateur or otherwise, and which Fedeli claims to have witnessed firsthand. Whether this was an intentional avoidance on Fedeli's part or it reflects the reality of the day on which he shot the film is unknowable, as this is not a subject broached in his oral history. It is worth noting that Fedeli also includes what he *did not see* in his oral history by invoking the genocidal tool of the gas chambers as part of his experience of the camp. While acknowledging that he did not see the gassing for himself, Fedeli witnessed the traces of that process; his knowledge of what happened in the camp clearly went well beyond the parameters of what he witnessed at the specific moment he arrived.

When asked about the pragmatics of shooting during the war, Fedeli reported: "I wasn't supposed to do that but they never said anything to me." Despite prohibitions about filming, Fedeli shot, suggesting a personal motivation that outweighed the risk of potential disciplinary action. But we are left wondering, then, why

Fedeli might have excluded the sights that so traumatized and motivated other amateur cinematographers. In his films, we may be witnessing a version of selective memory enacted on 8mm, something much more in line with our traditional conceptualization of appropriate home movie content. Fedeli may also have censored his own final product, editing out footage that he considered too traumatic or graphic. The footage might also have been underexposed or even lost. Whatever the reason, his film is striking because of what it does not represent.

We encounter the opposite kind of representation in future Hollywood filmmaker Sam Fuller's concentration camp footage. At the close of the war, Fuller was with the First Infantry Division as they liberated Falkenau concentration camp in the former Czechoslovakia. At the request of his commanding officer, Fuller shot his footage with a 16mm Bell & Howell camera his mother sent him while he was overseas. Like many other GIs, it is likely that Fuller sent his exposed film home to be developed; a note to his brother, while likely not the one accompanying this particular footage, indicates that sending film home was part of Fuller's routine.[33] I have written extensively about the Falkenau footage and Fuller's Hollywood World War II films elsewhere, but in the larger context of this discussion there are a few things that make Fuller's film unique and an exemplary instance of a GI attempting to document what happened in the camps.[34] First, Fuller's is the only amateur footage of the camps that I have encountered that is so extensively and carefully edited, and so long in duration that it might reasonably be understood as a narrative film, as opposed to a home movie. The Falkenau footage has about seventy splices in it, almost certainly done after Fuller returned stateside, and runs roughly twenty-two minutes in length, far exceeding any of the other footage under discussion in this chapter.

Fuller later returned to the site of Falkenau camp with documentarian Emil Weiss, whose film *Falkenau, the Impossible* (released in 1988 in France) includes footage of Fuller narrating the film he shot in 1945, which he called "his first movie."[35] Fuller's Falkenau footage shows the removal of dead bodies from a shed; the dressing of corpses by local townspeople; close-ups of the corpses that testify to the abuses they endured; shots of survivors observing the scene; and an extended burial ritual that included parading the dead bodies through town, pushed by the townspeople who denied any knowledge of what had transpired in the camps. Where Fedeli's footage might be viewed without being sure that it was shot in a concentration camp, there is no mistaking what Fuller's camera is witnessing.

Historian Sybil Milton has criticized the use of still photographs documenting the Holocaust without identifying "the origin or purpose of the photograph; whether the photographer was Nazi or Jewish; and whether the image was exploitative, reportorial, or memorial in nature."[36] We know that the films under discussion in this chapter were made by liberators, and that what these men filmed was not intended for or used in any official capacity. These are imagistic souvenirs, memorials of the dead and dying, potential antidotes to disbelief, and supplements to the fragility of both human memory and comprehension. This overview of amateur film records of the camps begins to explore what Patricia Zimmermann describes as "the practical problematic of home movies as artifacts that require mining, excavation, exhumation, reprocessing and reconsideration . . . moving them out of the realm of inert evidence into a more dynamic relationship to provide historical explanation."[37]

Increasing availability of these films in archives and online begins to move these private renderings of the camps into the public sphere. These images can only, as Zimmermann implies, "provide historical explanation" with diligent contextual and historical work, which has only just begun in this chapter. These are not counternarratives to the official records of the camps, but rather supplemental portraits inspired by the very human urge to document. They do not depict genocide per se, but they capture what remained of and in the camps at a crucial moment in their history. Unlike the official records of the camps, which were explicitly evidentiary in nature, these films are striking as equally experiential: their makers were documenting what they saw, but also their own experience with the war and its aftermath. Bourke-White may have used her camera to justify looking at the unbearable sights she encountered, but these men were not explicitly doing their jobs by filming images of the camps. Their films are more than just "informational pictures," to return to Crowther's terminology with which this chapter began, although they are that as well. They are also home movies that affirm the role these men played as "eyewitness to that great agony," to borrow words from then-amateur cinematographer Sam Fuller.[38] Indeed, I think it is fair to say that these men were, in some ways, validating their own work as soldiers or doctors or quartermasters, making films that proved, at least to them, the justifiable nature of the war as a whole.

NOTES

I am grateful for a North Carolina State University College of Humanities and Social Sciences Scholarly Project Award, which facilitated the archival research for this project. A version of this chapter was presented as "Orphans of the War: Amateur Films of Concentration Camps" at the Sixth Orphan Film Symposium at New York University, March 26–29, 2008. I would like to acknowledge the generous archival assistance I received on this project, especially from Lindsay Zarwell and Bruce Levy at the United States Holocaust Memorial Museum; Rosemary Hanes, Mike Mashon, and Alexa Potter at the Library of Congress;

Snowden Becker at the Academy of Motion Pictures; and Nancy Watkins at Emory University. Norm Hatch, Polly Petit, and Steve Zabin all took the time to discuss aspects of this research with me, and my thinking on this subject has been greatly enriched through my conversations with them.

1. For more on the use of film as evidence of Nazi atrocities, see Caven, "Horror in Our Time"; Douglas, "Film as Witness"; Carruthers, "Compulsory Viewing"; Struk, *Photographing the Holocaust*; Losson, "Notes on the Images of the Camps"; and Huppauf, "Emptying the Gaze."

2. Ham's footage of Buchenwald is available at the United States Holocaust Memorial Museum and is viewable online at http://resources.ushmm.org/film/display/detail.php?file_num=1054.

3. Abzug's *Inside the Vicious Heart* discusses the visit made by Eisenhower, who was accompanied by Generals George Patton and Omar Bradley, and the resulting sense of urgency felt by all to encourage both widespread eyewitnessing and documentation of the atrocities they encountered at the camps. See especially pages 20–30 and 132–35.

4. Shandler, *While America Watches*, 3.

5. Carruthers, "Compulsory Viewing," 733–59.

6. Bernd Huppauf references 8mm footage in the context of German soldiers who filmed during the war, but he does not discuss anything beyond still photography in any detail in "Emptying the Gaze," 5.

7. A point about terminology: while I use the term "amateur film" most frequently here, most of the films I am discussing were made by nonprofessional filmmakers for personal use and home viewing, which justifies using the term "home movies" to describe them. However, while many home movies were shot abroad during vacations and business travel, the term "amateur" often seems most appropriate here given the nature of the films' subject matter, which defies most working definitions of the representational parameters of the "home movie." For more on home movie taxonomies, see the report produced for "The Center for Home Movies 2010 Digitization & Access Summit," http://www.centerforhome movies.org/Home_Movie_Summit_Final_Report.pdf.

8. See http://resources.ushmm.org/film/search/index.php.

9. Interview with Major Norman Hatch (U.S. Marine Core Reserve) by the author on November 15, 2007. A complete version of this interview was published as Orgeron, "Filming the Marines in the Pacific."

10. Ibid., 153.

11. Fernett, "G.I. Movie Makers," 409.

12. Ibid., 442.

13. Schoen, "Combat Cameraman's Communique . . . ," 81.

14. Universal Camera Corporation, 1944 advertisement, *Home Movies*.

15. Struk, *Photographing the Holocaust*, 31.

16. For more on the "unsigned" nature of official footage of the camps, see Losson, "Notes on the Images of the Camps," 26.

17. See http://sage.library.emory.edu/collection-0608.html.

18. Kushlis, transcript of interview with Dana Kline.

19. Ibid., 1–2.

20. Ibid., 6.

21. Zemel, "Emblems of Atrocity," 205.

22. Kushlis, transcript of interview with Dana Kline, 5.

23. Zimmermann, "The Home Movie Movement," 4.

24. Bourke-White, *Portrait of Myself*, 259.

25. Kushlis, transcript of interview with Dana Kline, 6.

26. Zelizer, *Remembering to Forget*, 14.

27. Kushlis, transcript of interview with Dana Kline, 5–6.

28. Errol Morris has published a blog at the *New York Times* website with interesting threads on photography, filming, and reality. The quote is taken from the April 30, 2008, posting: http://morris.blogs.nytimes.com/2008/04/03/play-it-again-sam-re-enactments-part-one.

29. Carruthers, "Compulsory Viewing," 739.

30. See http://resources.ushmm.org/film/display/detail.php?file_num=3841.

31. Colonel Zabin's son, Steve Zabin, provided the information about his father and interviewed surviving family members about the colonel's history both during a phone interview with the author and in a fax dated May 16, 2007. He also provided me with a copy of his father's letter to the *Malverne Herald*, dated May 31, 1945, which is quoted as the title of this section and is also in Colonel Zabin's file at USHMM. There is some confusion about when Alexander Zabin arrived at Dachau, as there is conflicting information in his USHMM file.

32. E-mail from Polly Petit, who recorded an oral history with William Fedeli that is available at LOC, to Marsha Orgeron, May 14, 2007. See also http://www.ushmm.org/wlc/article.php?lang=en&ModuleId=10005322. Fedeli's oral history is available on cassette tape in the Veterans History Project at LOC.

33. This letter is in the personal collection of Christa Lang Fuller.

34. See Orgeron, "Liberating Images?" and "The Most Profound Shock."

35. Fuller calls the footage this in Weiss's documentary *Falkenau*.

36. Milton, "The Camera as Weapon," 60.

37. Zimmerman, "The Home Movie Movement," 5.

38. Fuller, *A Third Face*, 374.

10   # Through the Open Society Archives to *The Portraitist*

Film's Impulse toward Death and Witness

STEPHEN COOPER

Before flying to Warsaw early in the summer of 2008 to interview Polish documentary director Irek Dobrowolski, I spent a week in Budapest's Open Society Archives (OSA) grounding myself in the field of film and genocide. For five straight days I took in nonfiction film after video after still photograph, all documenting human behavior at its worst. I had come from Los Angeles with my head full of theories about film and photography in the expectation of "applying" them to what I saw. To be specific, I intended to discover a way of connecting the deathward inclination of some of the most important of those theories to filmed depictions of the murderous megadeath that is genocide. Certainly I had an embarrassment of theoretical riches to work with: André Bazin's ontological conjunction of object and image in the death-defying medium of film; Siegfried Kracauer's insistence on cinema's redemptive capacity for revealing such otherwise overwhelming phenomena as "atrocities of war, acts of violence and terror, sexual debauchery, and death;" and Roland Barthes' rhapsodic embrace of the "return of the dead" contained in the idea of photography itself, including the documentary film.[1]

I now recognize the rashness of my assumptions. Because of what I saw in the OSA's well-appointed research room, I did not accomplish what I set out to do. Several weeks later and after countless false starts, I have no hermeneutic breakthrough to report, no new theoretical approach; and so I begin this chapter with a confession of failure. What I saw in that room crushed any thought of remaining theoretically insulated, if not aloof, from the depicted realities. When it comes to the evil of genocide, as OSA Director Dr. István Rév writes, archival documentation "should not be viewed as being concerned with texts, but rather with access to evidence."[2] This caveat applies first and foremost to the details of documentation—all "the non-intentionally produced records of incidents of the past" that fill any archive—but also, with discretion, to the interpretive tools consciously wrought from those details, the articles, books, films, and videos that attempt to make sense of the proliferating archival trove.[3] When it comes to genocide, in other words, everything must be seen as being concerned with evidence.

There was also the problem of the writing, the then-and-now split of the first-person perspective. In short, I knew then less than I am still coming to know now about the difficulties of processing such a flood of information and images without yielding to the risk of projection. The twin enormities giving rise to this risk have been identified as "either imagined horror or the fear of intellectual defeat," a diagnosis with which I must agree—though I would change the *either-or* construction to *both-and*, even as I admit that, in the present circumstance, I find it impossible *not* to project.[4] I make this admission, moreover, aware of the charge that in today's West, succumbing to the archival-documentary impulse risks being merely a self-interested "'way of writing one's own subjectivity into the historical process.'"[5] To which I can only respond: if not there, then where?

For in today's West (or East or North or South, I should think), it's understandable to be tempted to feel as the alter-ego narrator of Kurt Vonnegut's *Slaughterhouse-Five* feels about his own stumbling efforts to write about the horrors of mass murder, namely, that "there is nothing intelligent to say about a massacre."[6] In the end, I don't believe that, any more than Vonnegut himself could have believed it, or we would not have the proof of his "jumbled and jangled" masterpiece, which goes on to imagine a war film made entirely in reverse, with the bombs falling back up into the bombers and all the "massacre machinery" reverting to its component parts and peaceful, even Edenic purposes.[7] In fact, in the OSA holdings, among all the recorded killing and death, I found just such a film, Jan-Gabriel Périot's artful short film, "Undo"; but as Aristotle reminds us, art is what could happen, history is what did, and if what I saw in the archives has had a fragmenting effect on my ability to produce a conventionally coherent chapter, perhaps that is the way it should be.

A point of disclosure: the day before yesterday—as I write it is late July 2008—the arrest of Radovan Karadzic was reported. Under indictment for his leadership in Serbia's genocidal war on ethnic non-Serbs during the Bosnian conflicts of the 1990s, Karadzic was the subject of a 1998 PBS *Frontline* documentary, "The

World's Most Wanted Man," produced by Pippa Scott. On the basis of a screenplay adaptation that I had written some time earlier of *The Portage to San Cristobal of A. H.*, George Steiner's novel of ideas about the discovery of an ancient Adolf Hitler surviving deep in the Amazon rain forest, Pippa Scott hired me to adapt *Her First American*, a novel by Lore Segal about a young woman's arrival in the United States after surviving the Holocaust. Neither script has been filmed, but I mention this background because it was Pippa Scott who first encouraged me to visit the OSA, where, as founder of the International Monitor Institute, she had donated some 5,000 feet of videotaped documentation of war crimes, crimes against humanity, and acts of genocide.[8] I want to acknowledge her for this, as well as for pointing me toward the vast online catalog of OSA's holdings. Before leaving for Budapest, I had perused this catalog, pausing among the Records of the International Human Rights Law Institute Relating to the Conflict in the Former Yugoslavia (IHRLI). There, among thousands of otherwise neutral descriptions, I had come upon a phrase that arrested my attention: "very moving scenes of injured and dead children."[9] So that by the time I first arrived at OSA's modern, airy quarters at 32 Arany Janos Street, I had in addition to some general theoretical notions one specific question: How could this overtly emotional phrase have found its way into such an enormous field of otherwise objective, even dispassionate descriptions?

In an effort to answer my question, then-senior audiovisual archivist Zsuzsa Zádori showed me the guidelines for workers, often graduate student interns, who do the data entry at this stage of the archiving process. She pointed out the rule stipulating that entries are meant to be kept "neutral" and that "subjective remarks [are] to be avoided."[10] That being the case, she surmised, the phrase might have been written by someone who, at the end of an especially trying day, was temporarily overcome by the nature of the work and felt compelled to insert a note of human feeling into the otherwise muted descriptions of atrocity. Zádori excused herself for a moment; and when she returned, she handed me a cassette labeled HU OSA 304-0-16 so that I could view the footage for myself.

That was the first film I sat down to watch.

The OSA at Central European University was established in 1995 as an arm of the George Soros Foundation's Open Society Institute, an international network of locally based agencies committed to the free flow of information and the opening up of societies in the wake of the collapse of the Soviet Union. Since then, the OSA has become one of the world's most important repositories for audiovisual documentation relating to all aspects of human rights issues.[11] As such, the OSA does more than merely collect and store materials for educational and scholarly purposes related to human rights violations. Recognizing the importance of "the archival imperative" in relation to the question of accountability, both state-based and individual, OSA actively assists international courts, truth and reconciliation commissions, and other organizations that base their work on primary evidence and well-kept, readily available documentation. Additionally, "in order to enhance awareness, documentation and education about ethnic conflicts, war crimes [and] genocide . . . OSA works in close cooperation with various human rights organizations, NGOs and individuals to identify and acquire collections whose preservation is of the utmost importance."[12]

Navigating through the OSA's voluminous records is made possible by a meticulously compiled online thematic search tool. Together with the assistance of OSA staff members, both before I left Los Angeles and once I was in Budapest, this tool enabled me to sift through vast quantities of information in the search for materials best suited to my purposes.[13] Aiming to gain some grasp of the global nature of my subject, I assembled a list of titles that included produced feature documentaries and television programs, as well as raw, often amateur footage from recent or ongoing genocides in the Balkans, the Middle East, Rwanda, Chechnya, India, Burma, and Cambodia, with more historically dated film from Nazi Germany, the Eastern Front, and Hiroshima. And for five straight mornings, I came to work all day in the OSA research room.

I started each day by watching a feature-length documentary film. Thus, in *Final Solution*, I learned about the Muslim point of view regarding "the politics of hate" as played out by right-wing Hindu nationalists in the northern Indian state of Gujarat, where in 2002, as many as 2,000 people were killed and 150,000 displaced during a series of anti-Muslim riots following the deaths of 58 Hindu men, women, and children set ablaze in a railroad car.[14] In *Coca: The Dove from Chechnya—Europe in Denial of a War*, I followed human rights crusader Zainap Gachaïeva in her campaign to videotape the consequences and bring to light the causes of Russia's long war with Chechen separatists, a war that, according to conservative estimates, has cost the lives of tens if not hundreds of thousands.[15] In *Rwanda: Through Us, Humanity*, I saw the post-traumatic effects still lingering a decade after the explosive genocide that erupted in 1994, when rampaging militiamen of the Hutu majority butchered as many as one million people, mostly members of the Tutsi minority but including moderate Hutus as well.[16] *A Secret Genocide* took me deep into the jungles of southeast Burma with guerillas of the Karen National Liberation Army in their lopsided fight against the Burmese military and the ruling junta's brutal policy of eradication against the minority Karen people.[17] And in *The Anatomy of Evil*, subtitled "A Film Essay," I followed Danish director Ove Nyholm to Kosovo, where during the Bosnian civil war of the 1990s, ethnic cleansing aimed at removing the Muslim ethnic Albanian population was conducted with ruthless efficiency by members of Orthodox Serbian paramilitary groups.[18]

The Anatomy of Evil opens on a long hand-held panning shot of scores of corpses heaped in a lush green field. Without a caption to explain the basic facts—Who were these people? Who killed them? Where in the world are we?—we are immediately thrust into a questioning frame of mind. The view changes to a man standing on a ship's deck at night staring into the dark waters ahead. "I have decided to face heartlessness," begins Nyholm's voiceover commentary as the director embarks on his journey. "Heartlessness itself. Face to face." There follows a series of interviews with former Serb paramilitaries, faces silhouetted in shadow. Nor is *heartlessness* too strong a word to denote the general lack of remorse, much less the relish and even pride, openly shown by several in describing genocidal atrocities often committed under the influence of "cocaine, ecstasy, everything": the burning of homes, the rape of female victims, the machine-gunning of entire families, the toying with a twelve-year old boy before murdering him.

Nyholm's anatomy gains darker depth when, pulling historical focus through the use of black-and-white archival films and photographs, he takes us from such relatively recent abominations to those of the *Einsatzgruppen*, the Nazi mobile killing units that swept eastward through German-occupied territories into the Soviet Union. Fomenting pogroms and committing massacres as they went, these operational squads would eventually take credit for death tolls amounting to some 1.25 million Jews and several hundred thousand Soviet nationals. So that when a former *Einsatzgruppe* commander, now a genial retired schoolteacher and doting family man, is confronted on-camera with a photograph of himself giving the signal for his troops to open fire on a group of Jews huddling in a ravine, among them a woman with an infant clutched to her breast, his response—little more than a defiant shrug and a cold stare—would seem to justify the *Evil* of Nyholm's title. But perhaps most troubling is Nyholm's unsparing look within at the conclusion of his film. Having identified evil as "an independent entity that can be freely chosen, a normal part of reality," he says, "I let the murderers' darkness point into myself." But when he follows up by asking, "Could I have acted like them?" the best he can answer is, "Uncertainty. From certainty to 'maybe' is a profound loss. That is the condition I live in."

Spanning the gamut from the qualified communal hope of *Rwanda: Through Us, Humanity* to the radical self-questioning of *The Anatomy of Evil*: these were the produced feature documentaries that I watched in Budapest, along with many network and independent television programs and news reports gathered from around the world. Regardless of their respective political-historical-personal perspectives, such films can be said to take part in the rhetoric of analysis and denunciation and are thus based in the cause-and-effect techniques of exposition, narration, and argument. As such, they appeal to the mind's need for logic and understanding when faced with the unfathomable facts of genocide.

When I turned to samples of the raw footage that makes up as much of 80 percent of OSA's audiovisual holdings in the area of human rights, however, I fast realized that in the absence of such formal structuring elements, the viewing became far more visceral. Captured often clandestinely or on the run in trembling hand-held images, these videos present the murderous event unanchored to any context: a long unblinking zoom shot of Hutu *génocidaires* hacking to death their pleading victims at the side of a nondescript road; panicked citizens in the streets of Sarajevo being shot at and missed and shot at again until they are hit by patient Serb snipers, who keep firing; and a public stoning in Iran, the living victim bound and buried up to his hips in red dirt, the better to present a standing target to the mob. "Let the atrocious images haunt us," Susan Sontag exhorts, while of such imagery acclaimed war photographer James Nachtwey likewise insists, "We must look at it. We are required to look at it. . . . If we don't, who will?"[19] But from the visceral to the spiritual in one dizzying vault? For a moment, Barthes's idea comes to mind of the viewer's complex interaction with the photographic image, an interaction that takes one simultaneously out of one's own shifting subjectivity into the lost otherness of the depicted world and further inward toward the most existential, even religious of questions: "[W]hy is it that I am alive *here and now*?"[20]

By the time I got to these unedited materials, my week of archival research was drawing to a close. Perhaps my demeanor betrayed the effects, for two sympathetic OSA staff members approached separately to offer DVDs featuring very different treatments of much the same subject matter, works by the respectively French and Hungarian film artists Jean-Gabriel Périot ("Undo," previously mentioned, and "200,000 Phantoms," about the atomic bombing of Hiroshima) and Péter Forgács.[21] Although very different in approach and style from Claude Lanzmann's epic nine-hour *Shoah*, Forgács's epic fifty-two-minute *Danube Exodus* proves, like *Shoah*, that genocide can be addressed on film effectively, even sublimely, without resorting to graphic images of violence. Working with found footage originally shot in 1939, Forgács pieces together the story of how on the eve of the Holocaust, with increasingly repressive laws restricting the movement of Jews in eastern Europe, cruise-ship captain and home-movie enthusiast Nándor Andrásovits ferried a group of Slovakian Jewish refugees hundreds of miles along the Danube to the Black Sea and ultimate safety in Palestine.[22] Eschewing stock images of cattle cars, electrified fences, and smoking chimneys, much less any charnel-house shock-value photos, Forgács' film nonetheless succeeds in bringing the off-screen tragedy of the Holocaust powerfully to bear, and never more so for me than during a brief scene showing the boat's passengers dancing on the afterdeck, the simple human joy in their faces emphasizing the undepicted horrors these people were fleeing *and about which I now knew more than they did as they danced.*

At a serendipitous dinner with Forgács on my last night in Budapest, I asked about all that he had left out of his film.[23] He replied that his goal as an artist was to enlist the viewer's imagination in filling as many gaps as possible. In this regard, Forgács might be thought of as going Lanzmann one better, for while Lanzmann is careful to omit all shocking pictures from his film, he presses his on-camera interview subjects to speak directly of terrible Holocaust experiences, the accounts of which inevitably shock.[24] Forgács, by contrast, simply shows us smiling Jewish couples waltzing on the Danube in 1939, and our associational imagination does the rest. I can think of no better way to underline the difference between the indispensable documentary detail to which OSA devotes itself—all that raw, often distressing evidentiary footage—and the broad range of uses to which such details can be put. Still, after a week in the genocide archives, my mind was reeling with the sheer volume and magnitude of all that I had taken in, and I felt myself verging on what Reneé Green has called in her comments about archive overload "the canceling-out effect which is possible when confronted with more than is comprehensible."[25] Strangely enough, as saturated as I was with archival excess, I also felt ready for more. But after the grim gallop of the last week, I now longed to zero in and go deep. It was time to fly to Warsaw to meet with Irek Dobrowolski and talk about his film *The Portraitist.*

Witnessing

The Portraitist tells the remarkable story of Wilhelm Brasse, a man who was almost forgotten by history.[26] More than sixty years after the events of that story, Irek Dobrowolski's film corrects a significant historical blind spot by enabling us to see anew Brasse's long-anonymous images of the Holocaust, and in seeing them to bear witness to times past, present, and future.[27]

In 1940, Wilhelm Brasse was a twenty-two-year-old Polish patriot, a devout Catholic and professional portraitist, when he was arrested by the invading German army and condemned to Auschwitz for refusing to be conscripted. Had his photographic skills not come to the attention of his Nazi captors, Brasse would surely have been worked to death or otherwise liquidated like thousands of other political prisoners who in the initial phases of the war made up most of the camp's population. Instead, he was assigned to the *Erkennungsdienst*, the camp identification center, where over the next four years he would be responsible for producing tens

Wilhelm Brasse (*left*) and Irek Dobrowolski. Photo by Stephen Cooper. Poland, 2008.

of thousands of prisoner identity photographs, as well as some of the most widely known and definitive images of the Holocaust.

Dobrowolski's film begins in darkness, accompanied by a wordless chorus of ethereal female voices. Over the singing an elderly male voice speaks: "First, one shall have a good look at the man." Switching on the bright lights of a photographic studio, the stooped, gray-haired figure of Wilhelm Brasse appears, moving around the imposing period box camera at the studio's center. As Brasse continues to expound on the technical aspects of professional portraiture ("The model being photographed shall behave naturally. The face shall be relaxed, no artificial smile. The quality of a photo depends on disposing the model and lighting. This is how one can make a good portrait"), he goes behind the wooden box, peers into the viewfinder, raises the shutter trip, and lifts his eyes as if directly into ours—about to take, it would seem, our portrait. Instead, the screen trembles and goes gray, filling with the film's title and countless miniaturized photos of prisoners in tell-tale striped canvas, each staring into Brasse's camera more than half a century earlier, and beyond that into the unknowable future.

From the film's opening moment, Dobrowolski focuses on not only the portraitist of the title but also the interlocking relationships among photographer, subject, image, and viewer. Even as we learn the biographical and historical facts of Brasse's early life and times via a combination of voiceover narration, still photographs, and archival footage—born to an Austrian father and a Polish mother, apprenticed young to a master photographer in the darkening years of the Third Reich's ascendancy—we are repeatedly brought back to the scene of the photographic studio where the aged Brasse now sits and speaks. These returns enable Dobrowolski to explore the tripoded camera standing in for the Zeiss 18 x 24mm that Brasse used at Auschwitz. Circling, drawing closer, inspecting, wondering, this reflexive probing of the apparatus leads us to understand that the film we are watching is as much about the uses and abuses of the photographic medium, and the long-range consequences thereof, as it is about the portraitist Wilhelm Brasse and his portraits, scores of which appear throughout the film. Perhaps chief among the questions raised by this camera-on-camera exploration is: whose photographs are we seeing?

This question would seem to be complicated by Brasse's position during his years at Auschwitz. As a prisoner forced under penalty of death to apply his skills toward the smooth operation of history's most productive extermination factory, Brasse was doing the Nazis' bidding. But as *The Portraitist* shows, he had only sympathy for the legions of doomed fellow prisoners whom he photographed, and in an impossible situation he did his best to ameliorate their suffering, smuggling them food, cigarettes, and medicine when possible, intervening when he could to prevent the extra cruelties that were often heaped on the queue outside the *Erkennungsdienst*'s atelier by sadistic kapos and *Schutzstaffel* (SS) guards. However, Brasse's highjacked intentionality must remain a moot point, for in following the orders of his commanders, he was producing what they intended: namely, the photographic expression of a Nazi worldview, a world where might is all and where what the camera faithfully records of each prisoner's existence is abject humiliation in the face of absolute power. But that is not the end of the story.

In his trenchant analysis of Dariusz Jablonski's *Fotoamator*, Ulrich Baer corrects historicist misconceptions about the Nazi gaze as it was perpetrated both in official photographic propaganda and in amateur snapshots taken by the head accountant of the Łódź Ghetto.[28] Although such representations were meant to be seen as originating from a place of unquestionable power, thus rendering the human victims captured by the camera as helplessly dehumanized, Baer contends that in neither case do these images constrain us to seeing only "seamless illustrations of Nazi ideology."[29] Baer founds his contention on the radical temporal split that dwells in every photograph, the split between an unchangeable past and its "possibilities for redemption."[30] As long as we are willing to "re-see" the images "from positions that break with the photographer's perspective of mastery"—that is, as active, even creative witnesses—we can see through the purported ideological hegemony of such photographs to the people depicted therein and the way they continue looking into our present for a response.[31]

Dobrowolski helps accomplish this forward-looking act of retrospective resistance by reading Brasse's photos through multiple, overlapping perspectives. For one thing, the technically informed portraitist who took the photos so long ago returns now as the critically and historically informed viewer of his own works. Holding glossy black-and-white prints of his portraits in age-spotted hands, Brasse comments on the composition, the lighting, the disposition of his subjects, all the while riveting us with illuminating background stories that give life to the still, posed pictures. While Dobrowolski was preparing to conduct the ten days of on-camera interviews around which his fifty-two-minute film is fashioned, he pored through hundreds of Brasse's photographs at the Auschwitz-Birkenau Museum archive, searching in each for some small but arresting element to help focus his questions. It is in this regard that Barthes speaks of searching out the photograph's "punctum," the easily overlooked detail that, once discovered, stings or "pricks" the viewer like a cut, leading thereby to a heightened level of receptivity.[32] So that when Brasse is asked about a literal cut—the spot of blood on the lip of a young girl in one compelling photograph—he recalls how a female SS guard, enraged by the girl's inability to understand commands barked in German, fell to whipping the young prisoner about the head and face immediately prior to her portrait session. Displayed in a slow inward zoom until the girl's face and eyes fill the screen, the portrait is thus wrested from monolithic Nazi intention. That intention—to enshrine in each prisoner's official photo the triumph of Aryan superiority over such subhuman specimens as this anonymous girl (now known to us as Czesława Kwoka, a fourteen-year-old Polish Catholic)—*that* intention could never have included the photo's use as testimonial evidence against the genocidal ideology that led to the photo's production. But in the hands of the portraitist as he is filmed telling the story of the spot of blood, the photo is turned from triumphalist propaganda into searing exposé.

At certain points during other stories, Dobrowolski's pensive exploration of the vintage photographic instrument captures in the camera's lens the distorted reflection of Brasse speaking. This reflexive distortion signals Dobrowolski's willingness to risk coming at his subject on terms that defy received notions of documentary realism, not least the bias against tampering with photographic evidence. Such tampering is often the all-too-obvious sign of false historical revisionism, from the youthful blush painted onto the cheek of this or that decrepit glorious leader to the crudely excised figures of the formerly favored but lately disappeared. By contrast, Dobrowolski wants to make us see not only what lies before our eyes but also the realities behind it and potentially beyond. Accordingly, he deploys subtle computer animation effects to alter certain of Brasse's originals, and photos by others as well, in order to defamiliarize them. Working with Adobe Photoshop and Adobe After Effects, Dobrowolski and his animators made a variety of changes. In some cases, they removed key parts of certain photographs and replaced them on different planes, a procedure that instills affected images with a strangely kinetic sense of depth amounting, at times, to virtual movement and thus a heightened, hyperrealistic visibility.[33]

This and other computer-generated effects occur strategically throughout the film. So, for example, the portrait that Brasse was ordered to make of a particularly sadistic *Obersturmführer* becomes, with the aid of almost subliminal animation, a grinning death's head. An unexpected wedding portrait of a kapo and his Spanish bride with her cherubic baby son seated between them, all dressed in their civilian best, shifts apart into shadowed disconnection as Brasse recounts the kapo's subsequent escape attempt and execution by hanging. An innocently tinted shot of a bunch of pansies taken by Brasse as a reminder that beauty might still exist seems to shudder as if recoiling from the fact that the image was appropriated, mass-reproduced, and sold as a postcard in the SS canteen for soldiers to send home from Auschwitz, with love. And time and again, by ones and twos and dozens and scores, prisoners' faces float or lunge toward us from out of the dark, cascading galleries of expressiveness that again calls Barthes to mind, his observation that "photography is subversive . . . when it thinks."[34]

These formative interventions provoke closer, more thoughtful attention to all the photographs featured in *The Portraitist*, whether or not they are computer animated. While most, in fact, are not, the photograph that Dobrowolski considers most central to his story comes to us uniquely. Unlike every other photo focused on in the film, this one is introduced through the viewfinder of Brasse's camera, upside-down at first, then rotating slowly closer, as if to pull the viewer directly into the photographer's work of seeing. "I recognize this photograph," Brasse says, our perspective now over his shoulder and thus almost identical to his as he holds the print in his hands. "Dr. Mengele ordered me to take it." Again the ethereal chorus rises; Brasse blinks back tears. "When I see this, all the horrific past comes back again, the past I have been trying to forget." And slowly we pan across the photo in extreme close-up, moving from right to left, the shaven head and staring eyes of one adolescent girl giving way to a second, then a third, all gazing across the chasm of time into the moment where we live. When we get to the eyes of the fourth girl, we see that they remain cast down and averted as if at our dawning awareness that this is a photograph we have seen a hundred times before, and perhaps looked away from every time: the iconic grouping of four emaciated girls, their

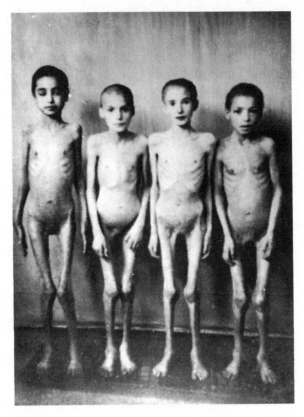

Auschwitz photo taken by Wilhelm Brasse. Courtesy of the Auschwitz-Birkenau State Museum, www.auschwitz.org.pl.

fleshless ribs, pelvises, and knees reiterating the awful nakedness in which they are made to stand before the all-seeing camera. But there is no looking away now from Brasse's story: "They were thirteen, fourteen years old, so they felt ashamed, very much. They did not speak, but their eyes were full of terror. They looked at me and . . . I tried with the nurses to make them feel comfortable, that nothing would happen to them, nobody would hit or frighten them. . . . They were completely helpless, forced to be photographed."

We alternate between Brasse's testimonial narrative and the incriminating photograph. In one of the film's most powerful moments, Dobrowolski's camera moves almost imperceptibly—or is it the girls themselves who seem to be moving?—as if to take us behind the flat white screen behind them into some darker depth of focus; the reflection of Brasse reappears in the lens of the antique Zeiss; and then to an extreme close-up of Brasse's eyes as he continues, faltering: "Everybody wants to have a child. This is a normal feeling, paternal or even more, the maternal feeling. When I saw how . . . horrible was their fate, I pitied them very much. I knew perfectly well that those poor children would be killed after they were exploited. I cursed God—and I cursed my mother—that she had given birth to me."

Brasse weeps. After Auschwitz, we are told in several published accounts, he was unable to resume his profession as a portraitist, for every time he put his eye to the viewfinder, he saw the four girls.[35] He went on to make another life, and for some sixty years he kept his story inside, making as little as possible of his experiences during the Holocaust, including the deed for which he deserves most to be thanked. Near the end of the war, with the Nazis in a panic to escape the advancing Red Army, all photographs were ordered to be burned. Defying the order, Brasse managed with a colleague to save as many as 40,000 images for use as documentary evidence.[36] Still, until Dobrowolski identified Brasse as the man who made the photograph of the four girls, the image was reprinted for more than half a century in countless publications around the world, and more recently on many Internet websites, without being credited to anyone. And even as the photograph gained ever more exposure, Brasse lived in anonymity, with his nightmares.

To be sure, the fact that we now know something human about the origins of this infamous image and the circumstances of its production does nothing to change the fate of those four young girls, nor will the knowledge ever enable us to fathom the abyss of their suffering. At these gravest of limitations, we must stand in awed respect even as we recognize our new affective understanding—"what assails the self from within"[37]—as a call to continue fulfilling the role of witness that Mr. Brasse bravely accepted in answering Dobrowolski's invitation to show the world his pictures and tell his stories. In this respect, *The Portraitist* is also an act of witness, the practical results of which continue to ripple outward. As I write, for example, a one-week seminar for young Polish, German, and Israeli photographers has just concluded at Auschwitz. Centering on guest instructor Wilhelm Brasse and his work, the seminar aimed to give students the chance to visualize personal reflections on this remarkable man in terms of the ongoing histories of Auschwitz and the larger world.[38] Given that aim, we should be as grateful to acknowledge *The Portraitist*'s practical fulfillment of theoretical notions—about film's redemptive capacities, for one, and the unknowable futures conjured up by certain photographs—as we are eager to extend the results.

I am the reference of every photograph," Barthes announces in *Camera Lucida*.[39] Animated by the past's "lacerating" emanations, swept up in "the love stirred by the Photograph" and "gone mad for pity's sake," he rhapsodizes

Stephen Cooper (*left*) and Irek Dobrowolski. Photo by Wilhelm Brasse. Poland, 2008.

about passing "beyond the unreality of the thing represented [and entering] crazily . . . into the image, taking into my arms what is dead, what is going to die."[40]

Before leaving Los Angeles, I had noted these passages and taken them with me to Budapest, where in my anxiety to stake out the field of film and genocide I encountered almost more than I knew what to do with. Halfway through my week-long dialogue with Irek Dobrowolski in Warsaw, however, a certain point of concentration began to crystallize, so that when he offered to take me to meet Wilhelm Brasse, I gladly accepted. In one day, we drove almost six-hundred miles in order to share dinner with Mr. Brasse in the southern Polish town of Żywiec, where he has lived since the war. We talked for nearly three hours, Mr. Brasse assuring me from the outset that I should feel free to ask him anything and that he would try his best to answer. Irek translated for Mr. Brasse while I recorded the conversation, and when it was over I asked if he would allow me to take his picture. Of course, he said, and we stepped outside to the restaurant's entrance, where I centered both men in the digital screen and snapped. Then, indicating Irek and myself, I asked Mr. Brasse one more question: Would he please take our picture?

Into what future will we be looking?

NOTES

I am grateful to the College of Liberal Arts at California State University, Long Beach, and Dean Gerry Riposa for supporting this project, and to Misako Miyagawa, a student in my Theory of Fiction and Film class, for first putting me in touch with Irek Dobrowolski.

1. For Bazin, photography, like cinema, "embalms time, rescuing it from its proper corruption" (Bazin, *What Is Cinema?* 1:14); Kracauer, *Theory of Film,* 57; Barthes, *Camera Lucida,* 9.

2. Rév, "The Document," 4.

3. Rév, "Documentary and Archive," 4.

4. Baer, *Spectral Evidence,* 126.

5. Anthony Spira, quoted in Cummings and Lewandowska, "From Enthusiasm to Creative Commons," 149.

6. Vonnegut, *Slaughterhouse-Five,* 19.

7. Ibid.

8. See Mithers, "From 'Knot's Landing' to Pandora's Box."

9. Item 212 in the IHRLI container list, a videocassette titled "Suffering of Civilians and Children."

10. "AV Description: Step by Step Instructions."

11. Other main areas of OSA's holdings include the history of communism and the cold war and the activities of the Soros Foundation network. OSA also houses the complete archive of the International Helsinki Federation for Human Rights (1982–2007) and preserves its website for posterity. It will soon manage online the Public Digital Archive of the High Representative in Bosnia and Herzegovina.

12. "Research Information Paper 9: Human Rights." Among the many educational activities and events sponsored by OSA is the week-long Annual Verzió Human Rights International Documentary Film Festival, held every November or December.

13. In addition to OSA Director István Rév, I would like to thank especially staff members Csaba Szilagyi, Aniko Kovecsi, Robert Parnica, and intern J. P. Ditkowsky.

14. *Final Solution,* directed by Rakesh Sharma (India, 2004).

15. *Coca: The Dove from Chechnya—Europe in Denial of a War/Die Taub aus Tschetschenien,* directed by Eric Bergkrant (Switzerland, 2005).

16. *Rwanda: Through Us, Humanity,* directed by Marie-France Collard (Belgium-Rwanda, 2006).

17. *A Secret Genocide/Une génocide à huis clos,* directed by Alexandre Dereims (France, 2006).

18. *The Anatomy of Evil/Ondskabens anatomi,* directed by Ove Nyholm (Denmark, 2005).

19. Sontag, *Regarding the Pain of Others,* 115; James Nachtwey, in *War Photographer,* directed by Christian Frei (USA, 2001).

20. Barthes, *Camera Lucida,* 84. This catechetical question arises from what

Barthes calls the enduring "astonishment" of photography, which "reaches down into the religious substance out of which I am molded." Barthes, *Camera Lucida*, 82.

21. "Undo," directed by Jan-Gabriel Périot (France, 2005); "Nijuman no borei" (200,000 Phantoms), directed by Jan-Gabriel Périot (France, 2007).

22. *Danube Exodus*, directed by Péter Forgács (Hungary, 1998). A marvel of structural and ironic symmetries, the film traces not one exodus but two: the escape of the Slovakian Jews from the reach of the Nazis and, one year later, the parallel "reverse" exodus that occurred when ethnic Germans fleeing the Soviet annexation of Bessarabia were ferried on Andrásovits's boat back into the Third Reich. For the extensive Péter Forgács Collection of Home Movies of the Private Photo and Film Foundation, see the container lists of HU OSA 320-1-1, 320-1-2, 320-1-3, and 320-1-4.

23. The serendipity was facilitated by OSA Director István Rév, who (without my asking) put me in touch with Forgács.

24. For an assessment of Lanzmann's technique of "pressured interrogation," see Hartman, *The Longest Shadow*, 86.

25. Green, "Survival," 49.

26. *The Portraitist/Portrecista*, directed by Irek Dobrowolski (Poland, 2005).

27. For a persuasive explanation of this blind spot to matters pertaining to the Holocaust, see Gross, *Fear*.

28. Baer, *Spectral Evidence*, 127–78.

29. Ibid., 22.

30. Ibid., 23.

31. Ibid., 22.

32. Barthes, *Camera Lucida*, 27.

33. Dobrowolski's artful use of technology demonstrates and reinforces what has been called "photography's oscillating status between document and aesthetics." Liss, *Trespassing through Shadows*, xviii. I wish to thank photographer Ryszard Horowitz, himself a survivor of Auschwitz, for generously corresponding with me via e-mail about this aspect of *The Portraitist*.

34. Barthes, *Camera Lucida*, 38.

35. For example, see Struk, "'I Will Never Forget These Scenes'"; and Lucas, "Auschwitz Photographer Haunted by Memories."

36. For an account of the work done by various camp photographers, including Brasse's part in saving these photographs, see Struk, *Photographing the Holocaust*, 102–16.

37. Baer, *Spectral Evidence*, 12.

38. For a description of this seminar, go to "german-israeli-polish photo seminar" at http://schimaere.wordpress.com/2008/05/.

39. Barthes, *Camera Lucida*, 84.

40. Ibid., 96, 117, 117.

Part IV

Interviews

11   Greg Barker, Director of *Ghosts of Rwanda* (2004)

Interviewed by RICHARD O'CONNELL

Tell us a little bit about the movie to start us off.

The idea was to look not so much at the cause of the genocide, but actually the way in which the international system responded to the genocide, which for me was the deeper question that I wanted to get into. I'm fascinated by the nature of evil and how each one of us reacts when confronted by evil. I didn't necessarily believe in evil when I started this film, but I ended up believing in it afterward. I think Rwanda is one of these challenges that come from nowhere, both for individuals and also for the international system. I wanted to see how individuals, and through them, how the international system—basically the United Nations (UN) and its key member states and members of the Security Council—responded or didn't respond. The idea being that we could then learn from those mistakes, so that hopefully this might not happen again in the future.

Notwithstanding your interests, what in your life brought you to this movie?

I knew nothing about Rwanda. When it happened I was traveling on a sailboat in the South Pacific, I really was not tuned in at all to what was going on, I just remember hearing it on the news on an island, Manawatu, and thinking, "oh that's weird and terrible," but I wasn't really engaged with it. Then a couple years afterward, I ended up making a film about Idi Amin. And as it happened, my key fixer was Ugandan, and his mother was a Tutsi refugee. She, as it turned out, was not a refugee from the genocide but from the years of violence in the fifties, when a lot of Rwandan Tutsis moved to Uganda. She was one of them. I got talking to him while we were making this other film and became interested in Rwanda more deeply. Then I just went there on my own, I guess in '97 with my friend. Just to kind of learn something about what happened there. I was literally on break between other films, decided to take several weeks and just go. I turned up there and just started talking to people and actually then met some of the people who ended up in the film. I still thought all of the UN and all of the NGOs had left, and I realized that, in fact, some of the people stayed behind, and I became really interested in their stories. And that was the beginning of the film; I just didn't know what it was going to be at the time. I didn't imagine it was going to be a *Frontline* piece. I didn't know what it was going to be. I just knew I had some characters that fascinated me, and while I was there, I got to know people in the Rwandan government very well. Philip Gourevitch's book hadn't come out yet, and there really wasn't a lot of interest in the genocide at that time. Not a lot of journalists were digging into what was going on. So it was actually an easy place to cover, because they felt like their story was being forgotten, but people did want to talk. That was the beginning of it. And over the period of years, it just deepened and deepened. Eventually I got *Frontline* interested and the film evolved, but I found it was a personal journey of mine.

During this interim period, how did you start to build a framework where you could actually undertake the film? And how did you think about how you might frame the piece?

It was actually over a period of a few years, I would go back to Rwanda whenever I could. I began reading whatever was written about both the genocide, not much, and history books, just trying to learn more about the culture, as much as I could. But I would go back, probably a few times a year, just on my own, or passing through on other projects I would find a way to get to Kigali and deepen contacts. And I began tracking people down who had been there during the genocide, you know foreigners, the UN, peacekeepers, whatever, they had since scattered around the world, and I began tracking them down. It just slowly developed in my mind. At the time I was also doing work for *Frontline* on other projects, and I told them what I was doing, and we talked back and forth, they had actually done some other stuff on Rwanda, and the film, in my mind, wasn't ready to go anyway, and it just became a passion of mine. I was thinking about whether to turn it into a feature film, whatever, I knew I had a couple of key stories that had not been told before. Eventually, with the tenth anniversary coming up, I was having a conversation with a couple of execs at *Frontline* and we decided it was actually a good time to pursue a bigger project. Because what had happened was, some of the key players on a higher political level, like Tony Lake, had begun speaking about Rwanda for the first time. He talked to Samantha Power for what became her book, but she first published an article in *The Atlantic*, and I read Samantha's piece in 2000, and I knew that there was a higher political story that hadn't really been told on television yet, and some of these people I talked with were expressing regret. I also knew through contacts that Kofi Annan had deep, deep regrets about what had happened on a private level and had talked about it. It struck me that one could tell a story that began on the ground and went all the way up, sort of through the food chain of the international system, all the way to the very top, sort of take a slice of that and get a picture of what actually went on. The contrast between the heroes on the ground who actually stayed when everybody else who left, who I knew, whose stories had never been told, and I don't just mean General Dallaire, we can get into that at some point, but I mean others; there are contrasts with them and what actually happened. What was going on in the halls of power and the Security Council was just mind-boggling. When it was clear there was probably a way in, then that's when finally we decided to go in and do this big project.

What documentaries were out there in the media about the topic? And how did that affect the way you moved forward?

The way I work is that I tend not to look at anything else that has ever been done on any subject that I'm working on, unless I have to. There have been documentaries done about Rwanda; I generally didn't watch them. I had to look at some news footage and all that. I just knew that there was a vacuum. On a practical level, *Frontline* and the BBC had done some great work on Rwanda, and I saw the films later. So they had laid down the baseline. And I knew the execs there obviously didn't want to make the same kind of film over again, but we knew we were in a much deeper territory and that we could do something that really hadn't been done before. On a personal level, I don't find it helpful to look at what else has been done. You could see with the success of Gourevitch's book, for instance, and Samantha Power's article and later her book, we went ahead even before she won the Pulitzer. The book had come out in 2002, and it was clear that there was some growing interest and a hunger to understand what had happened in Rwanda. I also just had a hunch that with the tenth anniversary coming up, it would be an opportunity to give people who hadn't talked before at a higher level to go on camera, like Madeleine Albright and Kofi Annan. And I also knew, just from talking to the people that I knew who had been through it, that this experience, not just for Rwandans but for anyone who was involved in any way, had a deep, searing impact on their own psyche, and I had a feeling that it was probably the same way for people at a higher political level as well. Those people, after a time, just wanted to talk. And I had a feeling that people would want to talk and there would be stuff out there that you could get people to reveal—their own sense of regret—in a way that they possibly hadn't done before.

So just during this interim period, what did you think the major challenges with this film were going to be?

I knew the major challenge would be to get people at the top level to talk. Because on one level, there is absolutely no reason for them to talk about Rwanda. Why would Kofi Annan, why would Madeline Albright, why would Tony Lake actually want to go on camera and talk about it, because there was nothing that they . . . you could look at it at one level, and they are going to come across as being part of a policy failure that cost all those lives. So I knew that that would always be a challenge. I just had a gut feeling that we could overcome that. That was probably the biggest challenge in my head, could we actually deliver that part of the story that I felt I wanted to really, really get. Until then, people in the earlier films that *Frontline* had done in conjunction with the BBC were actually the other way around. They had some people from the U.S. government and the British government, but they weren't really decision makers, they were low-level aides. So that was the biggest challenge in my mind, to deliver that part of it. The rest of it I knew would be difficult, and it was difficult to get people to talk about what became of the most dramatic moments of their lives, and it would be hard for me to make on a lot of levels, but I just had a confidence that it would work out. That one angle was a big question mark; it was kind of a roll of the dice that I just decided to take.

Once you had gotten that far, what were the next steps?

There was a question with some of the bigger interviews developing trust. It took about a year to convince General Dallaire to do it, and yet I interviewed him four times. Kofi Annan took a year, and that was through intermediaries, his top aides really. That took a long, long time. And Albright took basically about a year. Tony Lake had talked to Samantha Power and was a little more eager to talk. Once we got the green light from *Frontline*, which would have been January 2003, 16 months before the 10th anniversary, the idea always was we'd broadcast the film right before the 10th anniversary. I just started off with what I knew would be the hardest, getting those people, and then going to Rwanda. In a way I sort of knew Rwanda fairly well at that point, and I knew a lot about the genocide there, and the run-up to it. That has its own challenges. But I actually knew a lot of the players there. I knew of course the president, I knew they wanted to tell their stories,

Romeo Dallaire in *Ghosts of Rwanda*, 2004. Directed by Greg Barker.

and I knew they knew it had never been told this way before. So it was a question of putting some of these old contacts back into play and saying, okay now we're actually moving forward. I think they were relieved, I'd been going there for a long time saying, I'm working on a big project, and finally I was.

In terms of your approach to getting these bigger interviews, were you appealing to them in a certain way? You said earlier that you had sensed a willingness. Was that part of your approach in terms of building the relationship around the trust, giving people the opportunity to talk about something that you know a lot of the world had an issue with?

Well, each one was different. I think often with a public figure like that, who knows they are going to be part of a project in which they might not come off particularly well, at least that policy of theirs might not come off well, they just want to know they are getting a fair shake. They felt, I think, that some of the earlier films had been too much like got-you-journalism, trying to point the blame, like how could you evil people have stood aside and done nothing? And I remember saying the purpose of this film is not to point a finger, not to cast blame, because there is plenty of blame to go around. The purpose of this film was to describe what actually happened. And how you had a situation where lots of people with the best intentions made what they considered at the time to be the most rational, best decisions, that were in both the U.S. national interest and the British national interest, and also sort of serve the wider interest of the region in the best possible way. What astounded me and what really hit home—I remember saying to Tony Lake and some other people—is that if I put myself in your shoes, I may very well have, I probably would have, made the same decisions they had. And I wanted to convey that sense. That these were not bad people, that it was a product of the system, of the way decisions are made at that level, and a product of the time, as well. It is always about context.

In terms of the audience and the construction of the film, you're talking ultimately about interviewing a lot of politicians. What were you thinking about the audience at that early stage? Who were you making the film for?

I just tried to make an interesting film. I'm trying to make a film that's interesting, probably to me. I guess I thought about somebody who is educated and interested in how the world actually works, but I also tried to make a film that fundamentally just tells a story. I don't like just policy-driven films, I try to make something that works as a piece of film, that draws people in, conveys fundamental human emotions and dilemmas, and touches people on an emotional level. That transcends any particular story or any particular set of policy questions. Those are the kinds of films that I like, and I'm trying to delve into that kind of area. But honestly, I'm not really thinking about an audience as I go about doing it. Because if you ask them, people don't particularly want to see films about genocide. So I always find, when working with difficult subjects, I just generally try to make the best film and try to tell the best story, and I try to keep it connected to basic human emotions and tell a good narrative and hope that the audience is going to come along.

In terms of finding the narrative on the ground in Rwanda, tell us a little about how you built that story. And how did you think about depicting that story, given the fact that it is so violent?

The actual depiction of the genocide itself was a very difficult question in the process of making of the film, because how much do you show, and when do you cross the line where you are turning the audience off? In the editing of the film, we didn't use any footage for months, any stills or any footage, because it was all so horrible. I often work that way, where I don't use a lot of footage, I just try to get it to work, put in the interviews, and add the footage to it later. But in this case we took it to the extreme, my editor and I, because it was just awful. We knew once we crossed that line, there was no going back, and we would just have to immerse ourselves in it. It was an issue we talked about a lot, especially among ourselves and *Frontline*, how much to put in. But in the end, we decided you have to actually feel the trauma and see a fair amount of it to feel like you were there, or else it just felt too detached. There are a lot of very, very horrible gruesome images in the film, and I hope it doesn't cross the line. It's awful, you're seeing people who are dying, or are being killed, or have just been killed. I find those kinds of images are often used in a very exploitative way. When an image becomes part of a media product. In fact, you are dealing with a very intimate moment in someone's life—the end of it. What right does any of us have to show that, be a part of it, and actually witness that? It was a struggle throughout the whole process.

There are obviously multiple layers to the film that required multiple approaches. In terms of approaching locals, talk a little bit about how you got access to their lives and the trauma they'd been through.

Respect. Treating people with respect and dignity and being interested in their story. That's fundamental. And try your best to understand the culture and not romanticize it. Frankly, I have no time for people who go to Rwanda and want to talk about how amazing it is that the country has recovered from this trauma. Because I think: (a) it's probably not true, and (b) they go off into putting ideas of their own on how the world should be, how human nature should be to another country, and that patronizes it. My approach really is to go in with as open a mind, as clean a slate, as possible. In any situation in another culture, particularly when I'm trying to tell a story about another country that has been through some kind of trauma, I try to be very humble, both in the way I act and in the requests that I make. So that's what I did. I had been there long enough, and I had Rwandan friends. In the end it became, I wouldn't say easy, but it became possible, to tell the story. And too, I wouldn't say convince, but people became convinced that this was a project they wanted to be a part of. I don't recall any pushback or any problem with it. It's a delicate situation. Some people have watched this film and have said that it doesn't have enough about Rwanda and what happened to the Rwandans. That it's too much about foreigners; which is what I set out to do. I actually don't feel qualified to make a film about the Rwandans. The Rwandans know what happened to them. They know who did it, and they know why. So they don't actually need us to tell these stories to them. They've already got it covered. They don't need *Hotel Rwanda*; they don't need my film or any other documentaries or other feature films. If I was to be honest about this, we're actually making films for us. The audience for these sorts of films is generally a Western, developed-world audience. At the same time, I felt like I wanted to get at the universality of their experience. Because although Rwandans did this to themselves and this was ultimately their responsibility—and there are lots of layers to that—on a deeper level, this is the kind of thing that happens in society; it's part of human nature— the dark side of human nature, or evil, or whatever you want to call it—that comes out in different moments in history in different societies. There are lots of reasons that are particular to that society, but there is something universal about it. So I wanted to get at that universality. And I tried to talk to people on that level, tried to get a human emotion that we can all relate to. And that's generally my approach with any other country that I don't particularly know very well or don't pretend to know very well. I did this with the language; I just try to learn as best I can and keep an open mind. I try to be as honest as possible to their experiences and emotions.

You did. If there is something that you learned from the film, personally, or something you were able to take away from it, or equally, and maybe there's both; or if there was a profound moment for you in the film personally, in terms of your career, or in terms of making this piece, where something struck you, about the film, about your work, and how all this would come out and how important that is?

Making this film, for me, was one of the most difficult and rewarding experiences of my life, just on a personal level. It was a very, very hard film to make. That sounds self-indulgent, because it was nothing like going through the genocide, but it was a very taxing film to make and doing these interviews for the film, which were very hard. I remember in the very last interview, it was with Fergal Keane, which we did at the very end near the end of the edit. We had just begun, and suddenly I felt I would rather be anywhere than in the room when the camera started rolling once I started an interview. I just thought, I don't want to be here, I don't want to hear this story again, and I just want to leave. That was a very profound feeling that lasted through the interview. I thought, I can't be doing this anymore. It's just horrible to be doing this again. It's horrible to know the stories. I found that when people tell stories about traumatic events in their lives, you can't just ask them about that moment or that day. They want to tell their whole story, or wherever it begins for them. For some people, it begins when they were a child. For the U.S. Ambassador at the time, he [Rawson] had grown up in Rwanda, so his story begins back there. And you have to actually go all the way back there, to where the story begins for that individual character. So they were long and epic interviews. So on a personal level, I'll never forget those interviews and what I learned, and the privilege of listening to those interviews, and what I learned about myself and humanity just from being in a room with those people who were amazing. I think in the film, when I felt like there was something I was proud of, that moment was right before we broadcast the film. We had a big screening at the Holocaust Museum in Washington; they were very supportive of the project. They have a big wonderful theater, it seats 600 to 700 people or more, and we invited people from the government and the media, and there were senior administration officials there. I remember at the end of it, we showed an hour, the last hour, and at the end of it there was this absolute, total silence for several minutes. People didn't know what to say. People were just really profound. That's when I realized we were doing something with real impact. Because these people, who are usually full of words, were totally speechless. And it was right at the beginning of the wider awareness of Darfur. People came up to me afterward and said, I can't believe you got people like Tony Lake; government officials came up to me and said, I can't believe you did this. It was actually instructive for me because they realized smart, good people did these things for all these reasons, and that's a warning sign. What struck me is that Rwanda, at the time for senior policymakers, wasn't actually what was going on, it was a blip, it was in the news, but they had much more important things going on, or so they thought at the time, like Bosnia. If you had told them at the time, that ten years later they'd be sitting watching a film about Rwanda, which would be a defining moment in their legacy, they would never have believed it. And so it was a warning sign to people in the government now, and hopefully in the future, that these little things that don't seem important, or seem impossible to solve at the time, actually nag away at you and at your legacy, and they come back. Anyway, it was at that particular moment that I really thought we have something that people are going to find powerful.

Thank you. I want to go up a level. How important are documentary films, and what kind of impact can they have?

I have no idea. I think, whenever I start out making a film like this, well, we'll change the world. But you're not, obviously. I actually have no idea how important they are, honestly, because I think it's impossible to quantify. I think a film like this—PBS has shown it once, maybe twice, it does very well on Netflix, it's at all these colleges, it has been shown elsewhere in the world, and it's in schools. What kind of impact does it really have? I don't know. Hopefully some. For me it's enough, not enough, but it's satisfying to know some people in some positions of power may have seen it—and they have—and may think twice when another situation comes up. But look, [Rwanda] happens, and one of the points we make in the film is that nobody called it genocide in the U.S. government. They went to great lengths to not call it genocide. Okay, so Darfur happens, and the U.S. government calls it genocide. And still nothing happens.

Documenting something as important as this, and it being a historical document, among other historical documents, do you have an opinion on that? What type of burden gets put on a filmmaker?

Documenting something as important as genocide?

Yes, or in your case Rwanda.

It never felt like a burden. It still doesn't. For me, and I think for a lot of filmmakers, you start with personal questions. It's really not about documenting genocide; it is inherently so boring, on a filmic level, to document something. You actually have to tell a story or answer a question that is going on in your head. For me, the question became what happens to any of us when confronted with evil? I came to that in the course of making it, and of course it started with a question. And I'm still curious about that. So the film was really a way of exploring my own curiosity on that, following my own intellectual journey. I'm just privileged enough to actually be able to do that, and get access to people, and make a film. So there's no burden, because it's actually something that I—enjoy is the wrong word—but find intellectually satisfying to do, and I'm very privileged to do it. I think on a wider level, you want to reach as many people as possible.

You're touching on the idea of finding the narrative, finding the story but also trying to maintain the balance between the story and the reality and depicting both at the very same time.

Well, the challenge is that the facts get in the way of the story; that's the big challenge. You know the fleet saying about the fact that's too good to check. That's the problem; you sort of buy into a story or a version of events and maybe find out later that actually it wasn't quite that way and maybe you're telling the wrong story. That's the problem. I think that I felt very comfortable with my knowledge of Rwanda, and particularly of the international response to the genocide, and some very, very specific things, like what actually happened at the Hotel des Mille Collines, what actually happened with the UN forces, what was really going on with the Rwandan Patriotic Front and with Dallaire's team, and what was actually happening on the ground with those who stayed behind. I really felt like I knew that story inside and out, as best as I could without having been there. I felt very confident of that, so I knew I was unlikely to go down a path that I would later discover was the wrong path. I just felt comfortable with the material. When I make films, I don't normally have that level of knowledge as sort of a requirement to making a film. But this had been years in the making so I just knew it. I knew of the story that became *Hotel Rwanda*, and chose not to tell that in the film, in a film where I was looking for heroes. Because I knew, and through people I talked to over there, had a different understanding of what actually happened. I knew flat out that the evacuation of that hotel was led by one of the guys that became a hero in my documentary, Captain Mbaye Diagne of Senegal, because I had footage of it, not the manager of the hotel, not that he wasn't important. Now the fact is that that footage we discovered through days and days of trolling through archives, which hadn't been disseminated, which hadn't been written about. So it's easy to go and fictionalize an account and not actually be that accurate. Hollywood does it all the time, and that's fine. But I felt very, very confident that I was choosing the right stories to tell and that they would stand the test of time.

As an outsider, one of the challenges we face, working at ITVS [Independent Television Service], is that a lot of films are being made by people outside of their community. What did you face, and I know you've touched on it a little bit and your film has a different perspective, and as you were making it for a Western audience and you had a good relationship with these people, but you were still an outsider. Number one, how did you feel about that, and second, how do you negotiate that? How do you negotiate the challenges around being an outsider and telling the story of a very different people, and obviously one of the biggest stories in their history? How do you negotiate the challenge of that for you as an individual?

Humbly and with dignity, and not presuming to know everything. I also knew the Rwandans were interested in this story. Like I said before, they know what happened to them. They're not particularly interested in what they often consider naïve Westerners coming to make stories about why they did this to each other or how they are learning about the goodness of humanity through their reconciliation process. As worthy as those sums may be, Rwandans don't care about them; they find them frankly insulting, in my experience. What they were interested in is how the hell did this happen internationally? How the hell did the international community drop the ball on this? And they really wanted that story told. So I knew that I was telling a story that they felt passionately about and that they were interested in. That's a story they felt they didn't know, and they wanted to know about it, so I felt that I was making it for a Western audience, purely on a numbers level, but the Rwandans who saw this, and it was shown on Rwandan television, were really interested in it. I would dare to say more so than they would have been just in the story of what happened in their own country, because they know that. They felt this wider story hadn't been told properly, and they didn't know it either.

But again, there's lots of stuff that I wanted to make, the whole relationship between the Rwandan Patriotic Front and its role at the beginning of the genocide; all of that stuff was very interesting, and a minefield.

What's been the overall feedback to you on the film from lay people?

It's been overwhelming. I got tons of e-mails after the film went out. *Frontline* itself got a lot of e-mails. I think people were really affected by it. I remember having one screening—we showed it in a theater in London—and somebody stood up at the end and said, "You're just taking me through this emotional journey, what do I do with this, what do you want me to do with these emotions that you've stirred up? I don't know what to do." Which was amazing. I remember hearing from this high school senior in New York who had seen it in her class; her teacher had shown it to her for a social studies class or something. And she tracked me down; she was making a film about the impact of *Ghosts of Rwanda* on people in her class. Because she said for her and her friends, it sparked this much deeper awareness of the wider world and the importance of individuals to be conscious of the decisions they are making and how they impact on humanity. So she was really, really affected by it, and she made this film about her class and how they were all affected by it, which was amazing. And it became this story about how they started agitating about Darfur and wanting to do something to effect change in the world, which was great. I heard from a professor in the United Kingdom who used it in his class; he was teaching human rights policy or something like that at one of the universities, and a student of his who had gone into law instead of pursuing NGO work saw the film and gave up law because she realized she should be doing this humanitarian work instead. So I've had lots of anecdotes, and they still come in from people who saw the film and feel like somehow it's touched them or changed them, and that's really gratifying. Less so now than a couple of years on; from the first couple of years, it would be at least once a week I'd be hearing stories along those lines.

12　Nick Hughes, Director of *100 Days* (2001)

Interviewed by P I O T R A. C I E P L A K

Introduction

Imagery related to the 1994 Rwandan genocide mostly consists of photographs and videos of the aftermath of violence. Dead, mutilated, and often decomposing bodies scattered around the streets of Kigali and other Rwandan towns as well as recorded testimonies of survivors and perpetrators dominate the aggregate of available images. The footage of actual killings is rarely accessible and seen. However, at the trial before the International Criminal Tribunal for Rwanda of one of the genocide's organizers and most prolific supporters, Georges Rutaganda, a film clip showing a cruel murder of two women was presented as evidence. It was labeled Exhibit 467. The footage was accompanied by a testimony from Nick Hughes, a reporter responsible for its recording.

Hughes was in Rwanda in April 1994 working as a cameraman. The harrowing film clip of the two women's undignified death in the street of Kigali, which he managed to record from the roof of the French school in the capital's center, has become one of the only known pieces of footage representing the actual genocidal killing. When describing his experience of witnessing the violence, Hughes states that there were times when his camera had to remain turned off: "The blood ran down the side of the road and collected in the gutter. The gutters actually flowed with blood. Between the frenzied roadblocks, the bodies and the small shops, some residents went about seemingly normal business, some walking slowly in conversation. I couldn't use my camera during that ride. I did not have the courage. I know that what I saw was human evil in majesty" (Hughes, "Exhibit 467," 234).

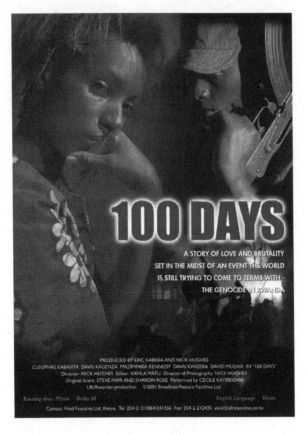

Poster for *100 Days*, 2001. Directed by Nick Hughes.

In the interview presented in this volume, Hughes discusses the reality of being a reporter in Rwanda in 1994, but he primarily focuses on the analysis of his film about the genocide, *100 Days*. It was shot shortly after the event in the Eastern region of Kibuye and produced by Hughes's Rwandan colleague Eric Kabera. The film tells a story of two Rwandan families and focuses on the relationship of two young people — Baptiste (Eric Bridges Twahirwa) and Josette (Cleophas Kabasita) — whose love and lives are shattered by the genocide. Josette and her family flee the Interahamwe militias and seek shelter in a church, supposedly protected by the UN, where Josette is repeatedly raped by the head priest. Baptiste's parents and siblings are slaughtered in their own house, while he manages to escape and hide in fields and forests until he is picked up by the Rwandan Patriotic Front, a rebel army that liberated the country from the genocidal regime.

Hughes's film is exceptional in numerous ways. Unlike many other fictionalized filmic narratives about the genocide, it does not use a Western/white protagonist as a tool of identification for external audiences. Instead it focuses on ordinary Rwandans and conveys the horror of their experience without artificial mediation. Hughes's direct knowledge of the event as well as the fact that the majority of the actors and crew had been part of the tragedy reinforces the eerily realistic and accurate nature of *100 Days*. The film has been widely circulated at festivals around the world and met with critical acclaim. It has been praised for its intimate focus on the individual, human experience of the genocide, which is so often lacking from the big budget productions made about Rwanda for popular consumption.

In this interview Hughes speaks about the film as a text, but he also describes the circumstances surrounding its production: about the way artistic expression is often reined in by pragmatic considerations. He also contextualizes the genocide by discussing the roles of different institutions in its execution. Having set the action of *100 Days* in a church, Hughes tackles the difficult issue of the Catholic Church's involvement in the slaughter, which despite being proven remains unacknowledged by the institution itself. Finally, Hughes discusses the issue of oversimplification and compromise, which need to be performed in order to make a film about the Rwandan genocide accessible to audiences outside the country. This leads to a contemplation of the more general trend of representing Africa, and especially African conflict and suffering, in the West.

You were in Rwanda when the genocide unfolded. As a journalist and filmmaker, what do you think about the boundary between observational and participational approaches to reporting and recording such events?

First and foremost, you are a reporter of an event. You are meeting and talking to the people who are going through their experience. It's about them. You are there to act as a medium and a mouthpiece for your audience. I think the boundaries should be reasonably well kept. As a journalist or a cameraman, you shouldn't get too involved because you lose your objectivity. You very quickly get sucked into it and become a part of the story.

But Rwanda was different. Genocide is different, because the crime and its extent are so enormous. This was no longer an African story of a small country. This was one of the most horrific incidents ever. The problem was that we had very little knowledge of it before it happened. And we had to realize what was going on before we could understand its nature. At first, we didn't know it was genocide. The killings of the people, which were played out in front of us, seemed to have been just a part of the war. They weren't, but it took time to work out it was genocide. Your movement was restricted, particularly in Kigali, where the fighting took place. But most of the country was perfectly peaceful; there was *just* genocide. The Western governments had knowledge of this; they had been told by the UN [United Nations]. They had much more knowledge than journalists on the ground. It's usually the other way round.

We should have behaved differently. This was an event when you had to put your profession to one side and act as a human being. It was not something just to be reported on. Almost nobody did that. There were one or two nonjournalists who realized that this was different. We just reported it as another story.

Africa is often portrayed as the exotic, "other" place. Could you comment on the way in which Africa, and especially African conflict, is represented in the West?

There is no reason why Europe shouldn't use Africa as a backdrop for its story-telling, as long as those stories don't pretend to be representations of the African experience, and to many people they end up being such. I think the failure occurs—this goes across documentary, news, and politics—when we only understand what is going on in Africa through an intermediary, through somebody who is not African. We should have heard from Rwandans themselves, but people in the West will not listen to Rwandans when they talk about what happened. The difference with Rwanda was the nature of the event. And I feel justified in having a very strong view against experiencing the genocide through the eyes of outsiders, because the crime was so enormous. Its meaning gets lost.

Do you believe in the idea of collective memory and would you agree that a film can turn this concept into collective stipulation by choosing what to show and what to conceal?

I believe in both. It is a problem in Rwanda; there is no film or television industry to bring that up. There is an extraordinary history of ethnic killing and collective memory there. It was because of collective memory that the genocide was able to happen. Rwandan people were retracting their own history, which the government used in order to fulfill its genocidal aims. Rwanda is overflowing with deep collective memory. It's trapped in its own history and it does not have the means of describing its past and taking control over it through film and TV. My friend and colleague, Eric Kabera, is trying to change this. The one thing that *100 Days* did achieve was that it began the process of creating film and TV industry in Rwanda. Eric Kabera has set up the Rwandan Cinema Centre, which is training students to make films about their country and experience, not just about the genocide. You can't just say Rwandans should go out and make a film, because they don't know how to make a film. They need to set up an industry and gain an enormous amount of experience. On the set of *100 Days*, none of the crew and cast had ever worked on a film and hardly any had been to a cinema before.

What is the boundary between strong images, which are designed to disturb and provoke reactions, and sensationalism?

Filmmaking is a practical art. There are many ways of showing and storytelling, but you cannot describe, you cannot show the true horror of genocide. It's impossible, because you are dealing with masses and masses, hundreds of thousands of silent, individual deaths, and that's extremely hard to describe or even imagine.

Making films about the genocide in Rwanda is particularly difficult, because it is so immediate. You are not dealing with a distant memory. The genocide was still going on when we were filming *100 Days*. So I think you could have a more immediate attempt at showing it through linear storytelling.

As to sensationalism, as long as it works, as long as it tells the story, I don't have a strong opinion. As long as the film is as miserable, as true to life as the genocide was. Because there is nothing good about genocide. Some filmmakers look for something that can end on a note of hope, a note of progression, a note of humanity. In the real story of the genocide, there is no hope. This needs to be established before you can move beyond it. Before you start looking for *Schindler's List*, you need to establish what happened in Auschwitz. The problem with the Rwandan genocide is that everybody started making human films about the humanity of the people and the possibility of hope surviving the genocide. You shouldn't do that before you establish that there is no hope and nothing good can come out of this particular event.

Is a filmmaker a witness?

I was a witness, because I was a cameraman in Rwanda during the second war and then during the genocide. I was the first cameraman to go in while Paul Kagame's war was underway. So, in that sense, I was in a unique position. This doesn't mean that I know Rwanda better than people who have studied it. But I do have this unique position of being able to say: "I was a witness, I can tell you what it was like on the ground to see the genocide and film it." I've made *100 Days* because I was a witness and because I felt my own failure. But I don't think you have to be a direct witness to make a good film about the Rwandan genocide.

100 Days is set in the western region of Kibuye. Was it important for you to place the story outside Kigali?

You have to be pragmatic about filmmaking. Shooting a film in Kigali would have cost a lot more money and would have been much more difficult to manage.

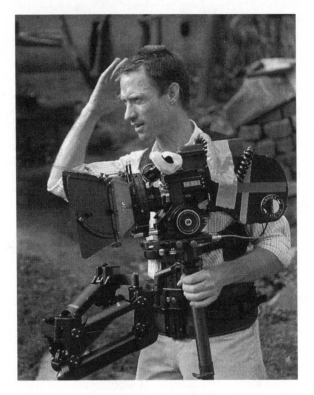

Nick Hughes on the set of *100 Days*. Courtesy of Nick Hughes.

We were first-time feature filmmakers. So we did it where we thought would be manageable.

The film tells several stories and deals with many issues. It's very broad in trying to describe many of the players in the genocide. The reason we picked Kibuye was that it was accessible. The landscape added enormously to the film. I really wanted to set it somewhere where we would be filming right in the shadow of what had happened, and Kibuye was the epicenter of the killings.

What budget did you work with and how long did the production process take?

I don't know the exact budget for *100 Days*, because we got most of our resources as we went along. We were independent filmmakers, and we heavily relied on

222

borrowing things. We started the film without the means to finish it. It was Eric Kabera's idea. I wanted to get much more in place and he said: "No, let's just start, because people will only believe that we *will* make this film when we are actually making it." So we borrowed trucks, we borrowed catering, we borrowed houses, we borrowed locations, we borrowed the resources from the government, from the locals, and we sometimes even grabbed a couple of UN trucks when they weren't even supposed to be working with us. Just anything to make the film. We had to pay the actors, and we paid them well by local standards. It all took about a year: three months postproduction, three months training the actors, two months solid shooting, and another month recording extra material and then editing.

Did you have a target audience in mind and do you think that the film would be fundamentally different if you used professional actors rather than amateurs?

We wanted the people in the West to watch the film. It wasn't really made for Rwandans. Eric and I thought Rwandans wouldn't watch it anyway. So we shot it originally in English, and then we added a track in Kinyarwanda. We weren't going for the popcorn crowd. We hoped an intelligent, educated cinemagoer would watch it. And in the end, they did. They watched it all over the world at film festivals.

It would have been a different film if I had used professional actors. I absolutely did not want a Western lead. This might have been a mistake; perhaps in that way, we would have been able to reach a wider audience. It's not really a black-and-white issue. There are ways of doing it. I think that the filmmakers who came afterward saw that and that's what they did in their films.

But I was not unhappy at all with the acting in *100 Days*. Another thing was that there were no professional Rwandan actors, and I wanted it to be performed by Rwandans. So the issue was not whether I wanted professionals, but whether I was prepared to do it with non-Rwandan actors, and I wasn't.

Some of the actors were genocide survivors. Could you comment on the process of working with them?

They all knew that it was something that nobody from outside could understand. They didn't have to be told what was going on. There was no production design for the killings, for the roadblocks, or the attacks on houses. Everybody in the film knew what had happened and how it had happened. I do believe that they just reenacted what they had seen. Marching past us every single day were members of the Interahamwe in their pink clothes, collecting wood for the prison, and they would make crass comments as to what was going on. They shouted that we should let them act so they could show us how it was done. But all the actors knew what had happened in the genocide and how everybody reacted, from the victims all the way through to the killers.

In the casting we didn't separate people into ethnic groups, and we had Hutus playing Tutsis and Tutsis playing Hutus. Over 90 percent of the cast were either Hutu or Tutsi. So in *100 Days*, the most evil man in the film, the prefect, who actually organizes the killings, is a Tutsi. But he knew how to act as a Hutu prefect. We had survivors from the church with us. Right at the beginning, we took a group of women survivors and we sat in the church. It stank of dead bodies. There was blood on the floor. You could smell the cadavers that had been in there. And they sat in the dark and talked to the actors about the actual killing in that church. That was very powerful. I think the actors took that on board. If we had outsiders, they would have all brought their cultural identity with them.

100 Days focuses on nature and the link between the people and the land. Do you think this relationship is particularly strong in Rwanda?

The connection between the Rwandan people and the landscape goes all the way. The Tutsis lived on the top of the hill; Hutus cultivated the valley. The whole issue was about lack of communication. You can't see what's happening on the other side of the valley. It's the gossip and the fact that it is easy to hide things in Rwanda, in the hills, the forests, and the fields. This is especially significant in northern Rwanda; it's called the land of a thousand hills. Rwandans are tied to and affected by their landscape. I think it's a mistake to make a film that doesn't bring the two together.

In representing the genocide, what do you think should be the balance between collective and personal suffering?

You need to identify with someone. That's what I really wanted. People saw Rwanda as a country full of backward, illiterate people. I'm sure Rwandans weren't perceived as people like "us." The Tutsis who were killed and the Hutus who killed were not people who had hopes and fears and families and history and friends whom they loved, like "we" do.

Rwanda is a very civilized country. People live in very close proximity to each other in a civil society. Because of the population density, the control of the state goes down to the smallest hamlet. The genocide wasn't an explosion of mindless, tribal killing. It was a national, state-organized campaign. And the people who died had feelings and aspirations just like anybody else. They wanted their kids to go school. That's why I chose a middle-class family, because it is in middle-class

families that the kids go to school, they have jobs, and they were very much iden-
tifiable with any middle-class family in the world.

**One of the most striking scenes in the film is the burning
of the Tutsi schoolboys. Could you comment on it?**

The scene tells a real story of the burning of Tutsi school kids, but it didn't
happen in Rwanda. It happened in Burundi, eight months before, when the country
exploded into ethnic violence. I saw the aftermath of that as well as the gas station that they had used. There were many events from Rwanda that I could have
used to portray the horror of the genocide. One that we looked at was the priest
employing bulldozers to bring down his own church as his congregation hid inside.
He stood outside with his pistol shooting them as they tried to escape the building.
With our budget we couldn't do that. The reason I chose the burning was that the
event involved the same ethnic groups and they were Tutsi kids. I felt completely
justified in using it and it was something we could do.

**One of the protagonists of the film, Baptiste, escapes the
genocidaires and is absent from the story for a long time, until his return
with the RPF [Rwandan Patriotic Front] in the end. Did you think that
following his journey would take the focus away from the church?**

It's a historical truth. The ones who went into hiding just hid. They starved
and suffered before they were picked up. This emerged in the editing rather than
in the filming. Yes, we were worried that people wouldn't remember where we left
the characters as the genocide took place. But it was a conscious storytelling decision.

**Can the ending of *100 Days* be considered in the categories
of positive and negative?**

When Josette leaves her child behind, it is a sign of despair. But the boy-
soldier who picks the baby up represents the next generation. One who is orphaned
and rejected by his mother because he is the product of the genocide, and the
other one who has become a soldier. They are both the next generation. It's not a
comment on reconciliation. It's just a comment on the fact that it doesn't end
here. Neither hope nor despair.

**Can you comment on the representation of white journal-
ists in the film?**

This little cameo expressed my relationship to the genocide: I turn up and ask
incomprehensible questions to people who actually are living through genocide.
That's what journalists do. It was an incomprehensible meeting between people. I

feel that as a cameraman, you just turn up in a moment of hectic rushing around, you film something, take it away, and then you disappear. That's what journalists do. I don't condemn that; otherwise I wouldn't do it. I think that what we do in relation to the people we meet in our job must seem pretty incomprehensible sometimes.

What were the most important factors governing the portrayal of the Catholic Church, France, and the UN in the film?

None of them were to be seen in a positive light. At the same time, I hoped that people would gain the idea that they were big part players. The Catholic Church added their part to the disaster. To make a film about the UN or anybody in the organization would be to exaggerate their role. All you can say is that they didn't do anything and that they didn't play a part that was in anyway positive. Just the fact that they had the opportunity is a point of condemnation. There were individual UN officers who were heroes. They have not been spoken of. The UN strand in the film refers to the Belgians in Kigali when they left the technical school that was under their protection. This isn't an exact representation because it doesn't take place in the capital. This is just to show the audience: this is what the UN did. They were there with guns, they were protecting people, and they left. They left because they were ordered to do so, and that's a condemnation of the UN as an organization.

The French were the ones who had all the various relationships with the really evil men. They controlled parts of the country, protected them, and gave them the means and logistics to carry out the genocide, as well as the training and the moral support. There were individual French officers who tried to do a good and honorable job, but they were exceptions. And there were very evil French officers. The quote in the film, "Next time I come back not so many dead bodies," is not my imagination. It's an actual quote from a French officer whom I filmed in that part of the country. He was addressing the Interahamwe. So that's an exact re-creation. The Interahamwe laughed when he said it. He was having a good joke with them.

The Catholic Church was a Rwandan institution and played a significant part in the genocide. It's a very good story. My worry is that people will think that this is how the Catholic Church behaves in Rwanda in general. And I wouldn't want them to think that. Just like I wouldn't want them to think that all members of the Catholic Church took part in the genocide. There were those who did their best not to. But this was the world institution of the Catholic Church, all the way from the Vatican. This was how it was behaving in Rwanda. This is not, and I really hope it doesn't seem like that, just a comment on Rwanda. This is a condemnation of the whole institution, which allowed that to happen.

Many films about the Rwandan genocide are framed by captions and written commentary. Do you think this is a simple stylistic choice or is there a more significant motivation behind it?

100 Days starts with a written commentary, but it doesn't end with one. I don't think there is anything you can really say. We didn't even mean to have any written commentary at the beginning. But I talked to people and we decided that was the best way for the film to be the least confusing.

That's the problem with making a film about Rwanda; people don't understand what's going on. But I don't think there is anything you can say at the end. To write something is to suggest that it has come to a conclusion, and that's just not true. I think it would be a mistake to try to summarize what had happened in Rwanda. It's impossible to summarize the politics and the social history in a caption. It's also a question of learning. When you look at a European film about World War II you learn a great deal. You learn about the history of the time. But I think in a lot of African films, the Western films about Africa, even if they include the story of the African spirit, you only learn about the character, that particular character's experience, not about the history of the time.

13   Irek Dobrowolski, Director of *The Portraitist* (2005)

Interviewed by S T E P H E N C O O P E R

What **motivated you to make** *The Portraitist?*
The question of my motivation is very simple. If I am a filmmaker, making documentaries, and I meet such a person as Mr. Brasse, the situation is absolutely obvious. I must do everything I can possibly do to make a movie about such a character. He had an extraordinary story. He was, and is, a very special person. And his story had never been recorded on film.

So you considered it an obligation.

Exactly. It was a very strong obligation for me as a documentarian to tell his story for the future. That's my basic understanding of the documentary. The documentary film is saving, in an artistic way, important stories for the future. And this person, and his story, were absolutely perfect examples.

How did you first hear about Mr. Brasse?

A friend of mine told me, some time ago. He had coproduced an Israeli documentary about the contemporary results of medical experiments. You must know that a lot of medical solutions used today came from Nazi medical experiments. So they made a documentary about those experiments and the results. And one of the people interviewed in this documentary was Mr. Brasse. He was talking about Dr. Mengele, about how he had met him and photographed his victims. And my friend told me that Mr. Brasse's story was much bigger than what they had used in this documentary. And I decided at once to go to Żywiec to meet Mr.

Brasse and talk with him. We met the first time in a restaurant. He had his own private table, where he was meeting with friends, talking about politics. I told him who I was and we started talking. This first conversation was very normal and social. So when I told him I was interested in his story, he said, "What for?" He said there were hundreds of books about this story, and better and cleverer men had told it.

The story of Auschwitz.

The story of Auschwitz. But I told him that he was special because as a photographer at Auschwitz, he had a completely different point of view. And I was interested in what he remembered, what pictures he remembered from those days.

What was his response?

"I don't know," "I'm not good at that," "I'm not sure I can talk to the camera." And we started from the Israeli documentary. He told that story again, and I listened. And from this, we made a first step. Because he found me as a man who was not dangerous, who was not looking for sensation.

There was simpatico.

Yes, simpatico. And we agreed that we would meet again to talk about details. After some days, I called him by phone, and again he tried to avoid everything. "It's already been done. You can read a book or watch a film." I said, "Mr. Brasse, I am sure you are the right person to make this movie." I tried to force him a little bit in this conversation. And he agreed to meet with me again. In our next meeting, the conversation was easier.

He was starting to tell his stories.

Yes. Stories, anecdotes. And he agreed. "Okay, we can try but you shouldn't expect miracles." After that, I wrote a proposal for Polish television. It was 1997. To the documentary department of Channel One. In those days, they were the only producer and broadcaster of documentaries. The first reaction was polite, like Okay, this sounds interesting and nice, but then we were waiting six months to hear something more. And after six months we got a letter signed by the head of this department, a famous Polish documentary filmmaker, with just one sentence: "Thank you very much but we are not interested in this subject."

That was the whole letter?

Yes. "Thank you very much but we are not interested in this subject." Signed by this famous filmmaker. What could we do? The situation was not easy because in Poland in those days there was not any other possibility to sell documentaries than to Channel One of Polish television. So because I had a friend in London, I wrote a bigger proposal and sent it to the documentary department of BBC, producers of high-quality documentaries, etcetera. And the initial response was, Oh wow, what a character, what a story, perfect. After three months came the official answer. They told my friend, "It is not moral for us to produce this documentary because this man was part of the Holocaust machinery." I am not kidding.

Even though you had explained to them that Mr. Brasse was a prisoner?
Yeah. For them he had collaborated, like a kapo.

So this was what, 1998?
1998. I was sending the proposal to everyone I knew. I spent a lot of time on this. Finally in 2001, I decided that I had no other choice. I had to start shooting by myself. Otherwise the story would disappear.

During these three or four years you stayed in contact with Mr. Brasse?
That was very important. Our relationship was so strong that he told me, "Okay, we can wait. If somebody else comes to me I'll say no." Because we had a gentleman's agreement.

You had not yet begun to film anything?
Before this BBC episode, I went to Mr. Brasse with a digital video camera and we traveled to Auschwitz with my cameraman. And we recorded four or five hours of conversation, in the car and in the museum. And in the museum, he told this story about his Jewish friends who were killed in Auschwitz, and he broke down. He had an emotional breakdown, telling this story. So I understood that this story was so important to him.

Up to this point he had been what, detached? Objective?
Yes. Objective. Professional. Cool. But this story was so powerful to him. Because he asked, using his position in the camp, he asked this kapo from the kill bloc, the death bloc, to kill them . . .

. . . with mercy.
Yeah, with mercy.

My God. And you heard that story the first time in Auschwitz.

In Auschwitz, yeah. But it was still not enough to start the production because my general question was how to find the form, the formal level for the sub-story. How to do it. It was crucial. But in 2001, when I decided it was my last chance to record this story, I made the decision to keep the filming as simple as possible. The man was the most important, and the form—it's a complicated question. But the most important thing was to record the story. And having so many facts from our other meetings, and from reading books about Auschwitz, and from talking about Mr. Brasse with employees of the museum archive, I knew there were some very important stories for the main narrative, and that I had to collect these stories on film as soon as possible.

So for example, he had already mentioned perhaps the German woman who worked for the SS, the one who came to have her portrait taken and bared her breast and then committed suicide?

Yes. But my duty during this proper shooting was to change perspective from objective to subjective. Mr. Brasse tried of course to tell everything objectively, to protect his emotions, not to let me come in. And for me, it was very important to find the key to every story, to make him speak subjectively and emotionally. So I was asking him sometimes three, four times, the same question in different ways, in order to drive him to the right point. That was my most important job. That was my directing. Asking little questions, leading him to remember colors, the temperature of the air, and the sound of a voice. I tried to place his senses in the moment.

Tell me about your use of Mr. Brasse's photographs in the film. For example, the scene where he is holding the photograph of the four girls.

This picture was the most important icon of the Holocaust for me for all my life. When I was very young, a little boy, my father had a book about the Nazis, *If Hitler Had Won* [*Gdyby Hitler zwyciężył*, by Tadeusz Kułakowski, 1959]. And when I found this photograph, it horrified me. It horrified me my whole life. So when I learned that Mr. Brasse was the author of this photograph, I knew that it would be the most important story of the film.

You were accessing not only Mr. Brasse's attachment to the story but your own as well.

Of course. I knew this photograph was one of the most iconic images of Auschwitz, printed in books and encyclopedias around the world. And yet its author was unknown.

Describe the moment when you discovered that Mr. Brasse had taken this picture.

He told me that he was the only photographer working for Dr. Mengele. And when I found this photo in the Auschwitz Museum I asked, "Who made this photo?" And Mr. Brasse said, "Who? Me. I made this photo for Dr. Mengele." So I understood that this would be the most important part of the film. How he made this photo. What it was about. What it was for. And what he felt about it. What is also very important is, because of this particular photo, he was not able to continue with his profession after the war, because when he looked into the camera he always saw those girls.

So at this point you were making the film completely on your own, you and your cameraman and soundman, without institutional support or any promise of distribution.

Yes. So we edited a short demo. It started with Mr. Brasse holding the photo of the four girls and telling the camera, "This is my work. I made it for Dr. Mengele." We put in graphics and music and I sent it to some independent producers. And to Polish state television, the same department as before, because the authorities of this department had changed. And the answer came very fast: the demo was brilliant and we must absolutely do it. And we finished the film in December 2005.

The other day we were talking about the film's subtle use of computer animation. Can you talk about your decision to do that?

I knew that we had to present those photographs in a special way. We had to find a technique to make those very well-known icons come alive.

To defamiliarize them?

Yes.

People had seen these photos countless times, and when you see things too frequently you stop seeing them.

So I knew that I had to find in each photograph some detail I could ask Mr. Brasse about. A good example is the young Polish girl with blood on her mouth. No one had cared about this photo before. It was just another picture. But when I asked Mr. Brasse what had happened to her, he told me this amazing story, that she was beaten before her portrait session because she didn't understand German. It's such a strong and moving story. And we decided to present this photograph as a view from the camera, using animation to make like those half-seconds when the photographer is looking at this object through the camera and taking the photo. A very small, very short moment. Of course it was also a big danger because some conservative and orthodox guards of history could have crucified us.

Have you had such responses?

No. *No*. That was the big surprise. No one has ever said, How could you do this?

Can you say which of the photographs you use this technique on?

The one of the girl with the bloody lip. The photograph of the four girls. The famous one with the dead bodies on the cart. There are others.

To put it in simple terms, your animator separates parts of the image and replaces them on different planes.

Yes.

And each time you apply this technique, is there one effect that you are trying to produce? Or does it depend on—

The image.

And the viewer?

Yes. Sometimes the light changes. Sometimes there is movement. Sometimes both. What was most important is not the animation, but helping the viewer to look at the photo carefully and in the right way. There is a famous picture of several Jewish women after the Hungarian transport, sitting on grass. Old ladies, young ladies, a small girl. If you're looking at the whole picture, this girl is not important. She's not in the center. She's not the subject of this photograph. But if we focus very, very close on this photo and start from the old woman, then another old woman, then a young woman, sitting, eating, talking, and we are finishing this movement on the young girl, we are telling the sensitive viewer that all of them are going to the gas chamber.

It's a way of making a still photograph tell a story.

The animation is always connected to the story and the dramaturgical effect.

Did you have a plan for the use of this effect?
It was a question of working and experimenting. Everything had to be fitted to the story. The music, the rhythm of each sequence. So the graphics people, four guys including the main animator, my friend Robert Manowski, they spent fifteen hours on each photo. Sometimes more, sometimes less. But approximately fifteen hours on each photo to create the effect. Because they had to work frame by frame. There was no special program. They had to do it using two programs, Adobe Photoshop and Adobe After Effects, frame by frame.

Tell about screening your film at the Auschwitz museum and the response of the audience. Who was there?
It was a very special audience, the scientific board of the Auschwitz Museum. Professors, people who are responsible for everything going out about Auschwitz. Of course, I was afraid, especially about the animation. I hadn't consulted with them about it. I was sure I had done it well, but it was impossible to know how they would take it. So I decided I would show them the effect and then we could talk.

Show just the effect or the entire film?
I screened the entire film. And after the screening, there was a silence. They were very moved. And Professor Piper, who is chairman of this board, said, It's a piece of art, like sculpture, like a painting about the Holocaust. Not a documentary like the hundreds they have seen before, different productions from around the world. This was not only a documentary. I asked them what they thought about the animation, because I was still a little afraid, and they said that because the story and the truths were so strong and so important, everything was acceptable. And they liked this animation because it made the film fresh and new.

This morning I was reading Janina Struk's book, *Photographing the Holocaust*, where she mentions Claude Lanzmann's *Shoah*. Evidently, Lanzmann rejects the term documentary. He says his film is not a documentary, that every decision he made was an aesthetic decision. And in this respect, I find *The Portraitist* doubly compelling. It's a documentary, no question, because it's teaching us history. And it is also art.
I knew that if I was the one who was going to protect this story—

Protect?

Yes, protect. I must do it better than my best.

After meeting Mr. Brasse yesterday, I would say your film does honor to both his spirit and his art. He may not have been a pure artist. He was an artisan, a professional portrait artist. But in the opening of your film, the way he is speaking about his approach to portraiture. He's speaking from an artist's perspective.

Not only the artistic perspective but also from cool professionalism.

Which is not a contradiction.

Yes. Working on the construction of this film, I wanted the viewer to understand Mr. Brasse, but not from the very beginning. That's why I start from the cool professional position. He's talking about skills. Also when he is talking about taking pictures in Auschwitz, he's talking about where was the light, how he was preparing the object, how he was working with the camera, etcetera. And only at the end am I opening up Mr. Brasse as the man who went through the Holocaust burned alive. And who defied the Nazis when they ordered his photos to be burned by saving thousands and thousands, for evidence.

Which is the furthest thing from a collaborator, a kapo.

It's easy to judge, easy to judge. I wanted to show that it's easy to judge, and then . . .

Was there anything that you would like to have put into the film but weren't able to?

Of course, there are absolutely brilliant stories that I couldn't put into the film because of the running time. I have extraordinary material, ten hours of interviews with Mr. Brasse, two hundred pages of transcripts. But the film had to be fifty-two minutes. And that helped me make decisions. I decided to avoid all the other perfect stories and tell only the story of a professional photographer who is photographing hell.

Is there anything you would change?

Maybe some corrections in the editing, some rhythms in some sequences. But I know that this film is now a living being, and it lives on its own.

And what about the afterlife of *The Portraitist*?

After this film, Mr. Brasse became one of the main witnesses of Auschwitz. A man whose photographs have been famous for so long and yet he was unknown until this film. Now he is invited to special programs to tell his story directly to people, to young people, from Israel, from Germany. And that is very important. There is a policy in Auschwitz to trust no one because they hear a lot of stories that are not true. But because of this film and our scientific consultant, Professor Piper, every word of Mr. Brasse was double- or triple-checked. So now he is trusted and he is telling his stories, such important stories, as one of the main witnesses of this history. And this is very important for him, and for history.

Filmography

The Anatomy of Evil/Ondskabens anatomi, 2005. Directed by Ove Nyholm.

Ararat, 2002. Directed by Atom Egoyan.

The Beginning or the End, 1947. Directed by Norman Taurog.

Blood Diamond, 2006. Directed by Edward Zwick.

Broken Arrow, 1950. Director by Delmer Daves.

Calendar, 1993. Directed by Atom Egoyan.

Calle Santa Fe, 2008. Directed by Carmen Castillo.

Casino Royale, 2006. Directed by Martin Campbell.

Catch-22, 1970. Directed by Mike Nichols.

Chile: La memoria obstinada, 1997. Directed by Patricio Guzmán.

Citizen Kane, 1941. Directed by Orson Welles.

Coca: The Dove from Chechnya—Europe in Denial of a War/ Die Taub aus Tschetschenien, 2005. Directed by Eric Bergkrant.

Compañero presidente, 1971. Directed by Miguel Littín.

Confessions of a Nazi Spy, 1939. Directed by Anatole Litvak.

The Constant Gardener, 2005. Directed by Fernando Meirelles.

Dances with Wolves, 1990. Directed by Kevin Costner.

Danube Exodus, 1998. Directed by Péter Forgács.

The Diary of Immaculée, 2006. Directed by Peter LeDonne.

Two Down and One to Go, 1945. Directed by Frank Capra.

Falkenau: The Impossible, 1988. Directed by Emil Weiss.

Family Viewing, 1987. Directed by Atom Egoyan.

Final Solution, 2004. Directed by Rakesh Sharma.

The Fog of War: Eleven Lessons from the Life of Robert S. McNamara, 2003. Directed by Errol Morris.

Fury, 1936. Directed by Fritz Lang.

Ghosts of Rwanda, 2004. Directed by Greg Barker.

The Great Dictator, 1940. Directed by Charles Chaplin.

Hangmen Also Die!, 1943. Directed by Fritz Lang.

Hiroshima, 1970. Directed by Motoo Ogasawara. and Yasuo Matsukawa.

Hiroshima, mon amour, 1959. Directed by Alain Resnais.

Hotel Rwanda, 2004. Directed by Terry George.

Imaginary Witness: Hollywood and the Holocaust, 2004 (released 2007). Directed by Daniel Anker.

In Rwanda We Say . . . The Family That Does Not Speak Dies, 2004. Directed by Anne Aghion.

In the Tall Grass: Inside Gacaca, 2006. Directed by John Metcalfe.

Is Paris Burning?, 1948. Directed by René Clément.

Ivan's Childhood, 1962. Directed by Andrei Tarkovsky.

Ivan the Terrible Part One, 1941. Directed by Sergei Eisenstein.

Judgment at Nuremberg, 1961. Directed by Stanley Kramer.

Keepers of Memory, 2004. Directed by Eric Kabera.

Killers, 2004. Directed by Fergal Keane.

A Killer's Homecoming (TV special, BBC2), February 22, 2004. Directed by Daniela Volker.

Know Your Enemy: Japan, 1945. Directed by Frank Capra and Joris Ivens.

La batalla de Chile: La lucha de un pueblo sin armas (parts I, II, and III), 1975, 1977, 1979, respectively. Directed by Patricio Guzmán.

The Last King of Scotland, 2006. Directed by Kevin Macdonald.

Let There Be Light, 1946. Directed by John Huston.

Life Is Beautiful, 1997. Directed by Roberto Benigni.

Little Big Man, 1970. Directed by Arthur Penn.

Machuca, 2004. Directed by Andrés Wood.

M*A*S*H, 1970. Directed by Robert Altman.

Mothers Courage, Thriving Survivors, 2005. Directed by Léo Kalinda.

Nazi Concentration Camps, 1945. Directed by George Stevens.

The Nazis Strike, 1945. Directed by Frank Capra and Anatole Litvak.

Next of Kin, 1984. Directed by Atom Egoyan.

Niemandsland [No Man's Land], 1931. Directed by Victor Trivas.

Night and Fog, 1955. Directed by Alain Resnais.

"Nijuman no borei" [200,000 Phantoms], 2007. Directed by Jan-Gabriel Périot.

Notorious, 1946. Directed by Alfred Hitchcock.

100 Days, 2001. Directed by Nick Hughes.

Open House, 1982. Directed by Atom Egoyan.

The Portraitist/Portrecista, 2005. Directed by Irek Dobrowolski.

A Portrait of Arshile, 1995. Directed by Atom Egoyan.

Rabbit-Proof Fence, 2002. Directed by Phillip Noyce.

Rwanda: Do Scars Ever Fade?, 2005. Directed by Paul Freedman.

Rwanda: Living Forgiveness, 2003. Directed by Ralf Springhorn.

Rwanda: Through Us, Humanity, 2006. Directed by Marie-France Collard.

Ryan's Daughter, 2006. Directed by David Lean.

Sabotage, 1936. Directed by Alfred Hitchcock.

Salvador Allende, 2004. Directed by Patricio Guzmán.

Schindler's List, 1993. Directed by Stephen Spielberg.

The Searchers, 1956. Directed by John Ford.

A Secret Genocide/Une géocide à huis clos, 2006. Directed by Alexandre Dereims.

Shadow of a Doubt, 1943. Directed by Alfred Hitchcock.

Shake Hands with the Devil: The Journey of Roméo Dallaire, 2004. Directed by Peter Raymont.

Shake Hands with the Devil, 2007. Directed by Roger Spottiswoode.

Shoah, 1985. Directed by Claude Lanzmann.

Shooting Dogs/Beyond the Gates, 2005. Directed by Michael Caton-Jones.

The Shop on Mainstreet, 1965. Directed by Ján Kadár.

Soldier Blue, 1970. Directed by Ralph Nelson.

Sometimes in April, 2005. Directed by Raoul Peck.

The Sorrow and the Pity, 1969. Directed by Marcel Ophüls.

The Stranger, 1946. Directed by Orson Welles.

A Sunday in Kigali, 2006. Directed by Robert Favreau.

The Sweet Hereafter, 1997. Directed by Atom Egoyan.

Through My Eyes: A Film about Rwandan Youth, 2004. Directed by Eric Kabera.

The Triumph of Evil, 1999. Directed by Mike Robinson.

The Triumph of the Will, 1935. Directed by Leni Riefenstahl.

Two Down and One to Go, 1945. Directed by Frank Capra.

Un dimanche à la piscine à Kigali [A Sunday at the Pool in Kigali], 2000. Directed by Gil Courtemanche.

"Undo," 2005. Directed by Jan-Gabriel Périot.

Vertigo, 1958. Directed by Alfred Hitchcock.

War Comes to America, 1945. Directed by Frank Capra and Anatole Litvak.

War Photographer, 2001. Directed by Christian Frei.

Bibliography

Abzug, Robert. *Inside the Vicious Heart: Americans and the Liberation of Nazi Concentration Camps*. New York: Oxford, 1985.

Aguilar, Gonzalo. *Otros mundos: Un ensayo sobre el nuevo cine argentino*. Santiago: Arcos, 2006.

Aleiss, Angela. *Making the White Man's Indian: Native Americans and Hollywood Movies*. Westport, CT: Praeger, 2005.

Amado, Ana. "Ficciones críticas de la memoria." *Pensamiento en los confines* 13 (December 2003): 54–63.

Anderegg, Michael A. *Orson Welles, Shakespeare, and Popular Culture*. New York: Columbia University Press, 1999.

Arlen, Michael J. *Passage to Ararat*. New York: Farrar, Straus and Giroux, 1975.

"AV Description: Step by Step Instructions." Budapest: Open Society Archives, n.d.

Avisar, Ilan. *Screening the Holocaust: Cinema's Images of the Unimaginable*. Bloomington: Indiana University Press, 1988.

Baer, Ulrich. *Spectral Evidence: The Photography of Trauma*. Cambridge, MA: MIT Press, 2002.

Barnouw, Erik. *Documentary: A History of the Non-Fiction Film*. Oxford: Oxford University Press, 1983.

Baron, Lawrence. *Projecting the Holocaust into the Present: The Changing Focus of Contemporary Holocaust Cinema*. Lanham, MD: Rowman and Littlefield, 2005.

Baronian, Marie-Aude. "Archiving the (Secret) Family in Egoyan's *Family Viewing*." In *Shooting the Family: Transnational Media and Intercultural Values*, edited by Patricia Pisters and Wim Staat, 147–62. Amsterdam: Amsterdam University Press, 2005.

———. "History and Memory, Repetition and Epistolarity." In *Image and Territory: Essays on Atom Egoyan*, edited by Jennifer Burwell and Monique Tschofen, 157–76. Waterloo, ON: Wilfrid Laurier University Press 2006.

Barthes, Roland. *Camera Lucida: Reflections on Photography*. Translated by Richard Howard. New York: Hill and Wang, 1981.

Bartov, Omer. *Murder in Our Midst: The Holocaust, Industrial Killing, and Representation*. Oxford: Oxford University Press, 1988.

———. "Spielberg's Oskar: Hollywood Tries Evil." In *Spielberg's Holocaust: Critical Perspectives on Schindler's List*, edited by Yosefa Loshitzky, 41–60. Bloomington: Indiana University Press, 1997.

Bartrop, Paul R. "The Holocaust, the Aborigines, and the Bureaucracy of Destruction: An Australian Dimension of Genocide." *Journal of Genocide Research* 3, no. 1 (2001): 75–87.

Basinger, Jeanine. *The World War II Combat Film: Anatomy of a Genre.* Middletown, CT: Wesleyan University Press, 2003.

Bauman, Zygmunt. *Postmodern Ethics.* Oxford: Blackwell, 1993.

Bazin, André. *What Is Cinema?* Vol. 1. Translated by Hugh Gray. Berkeley: University of California Press, 1967.

Bazin, André, Charles Bitsch, and Jean Domarchi. "Interview with Orson Welles (II)." In *Orson Welles: Interviews,* edited by Mark W. Estrin, 48–76. Jackson: University of Mississippi Press, 2002.

Beattie, Keith. *Documentary Screens: Non-fiction Film and Television.* New York: Palgrave Macmillan, 2004.

Benigni, Roberto, and Cerami, Vincenzo. *Life Is Beautiful: Screenplay.* New York: Faber and Faber, 1999.

Berkhofer, Robert F. *The White Man's Indian: Images of the American Indian from Columbus to the Present.* New York: Vintage, 1979.

Beverley, John. "The Neoconservative Turn in Latin America Literary and Cultural Criticism." *Journal of Latin American Studies* 17, no. 1 (March 2008): 65–83.

———. "Rethinking the Armed Struggle in Latin America." *Boundary 2* 36, no. 1 (2009): 47–59.

Bogdanovich, Peter. *The Cinema of Orson Welles.* New York: Doubleday, 1961.

Bogdanovich, Peter, and Jonathan Rosenbaum. *This Is Orson Welles.* New York: Da Capo Press, 1998.

Bonaldi, Pablo Daniel. "Hijos de desaparecidos: Entre la construcción de la política y la construcción de la memoria." In *El pasado en el futuro: Los movimientos juveniles,* edited by Elizabeth Jelin and Diego Sempol, 143–84. Madrid: Siglo XXI Editores, 2006.

Bourke-White, Margaret. *Portrait of Myself.* New York: Simon and Schuster, 1963.

Boutros-Ghali, Boutros. *Unvanquished: A U.S.– U.N. Saga.* New York: Random House, 1999.

Boym, Svetlana. *The Future of Nostalgia.* New York: Basic Books, 2001.

Brady, Frank. *Orson Welles.* London: Hodder Stoughton, 1990.

Brown, Wendy. *States of Injury: Power and Freedom in Late Modernity.* Princeton, NJ: Princeton University Press, 1995.

Brunton, Ron. "Genocide, the 'Stolen Generations,' and the 'Unconceived Generations.'" *Quadrant* 5, no. 42 (1998): 19–24.

Bruzzi, Stella. *New Documentary: A Critical Introduction.* New York: Routledge, 2000.

Burgin, Victor. *Thinking Photography.* London: Macmillan, 1982.

Burwell, Jennifer, and Monique Tschofen. "Mobile Subjectivity and Micro-Territories: Placing the Diaspora." In *Image and Territory: Essays on Atom Egoyan,* edited by Jennifer Burwell and Monique Tschofen, 125–32. Waterloo, ON: Wilfrid Laurier University Press, 2006.

Calhoun, Dave. "White Guides, Black Pain." *Sight and Sound: International Film Quarterly* 17, no. 2 (2007): 32–36.

Calhoun, Laurie. "Death and Contradiction: Errol Morris' Tragic View of Technokillers." *Jump Cut: A Review of Contemporary Media*, no. 47 (2005). http://www.ejumpcut.org/archive/jc47.2005/technokillersMorris/text.html.

———. "We Are Good and They Are Evil." *Peace Review* 19, no. 2 (2007): 237–45.

Callow, Simon. *Orson Welles*. Vol. 2, *Hello Americans*. New York: Viking, 2006.

Calveiro, Pilar. *Política y/o violencia: Una aproximación a la guerrilla de los años 70*. Buenos Aires: Grupo Editorial Norma, 2005.

Carruthers, Susan. "Compulsory Viewing: Concentration Camp Film and German Re-education." *Millenium* 30, no. 3 (2001): 733–59.

Caruth, Cathy. "Recapturing the Past: Introduction." In *Trauma: Explorations in Memory*, edited by Cathy Caruth, 151–57. Baltimore, MD: Johns Hopkins University Press, 1995.

———, ed. *Trauma: Explorations in Memory*. Baltimore, MD: Johns Hopkins University Press, 1995.

Castillo, Carmen. *Un día de octubre en Santiago*. Santiago: LOM, 1999.

Castillo, Carmen, and Mónica Echeverría Yáñez. *Santiago-París: El vuelo de la memoria*. Santiago: LOM, 2002.

Caven, Hannah. "Horror in Our Time: Images of the Concentration Camps in the British Media, 1945." *Historical Journal of Film, Radio and Television* 21, no. 3 (2001): 205–53.

Chalk, Frank, and Kurt Jonassohn. *The History and Sociology of Genocide: Analyses and Case Studies*. New Haven, CT: Yale University Press, 1990.

Chamberlain, Mary, and Paul Thomas, eds. *Narrative and Genre*. New York: Routledge, 1998.

Charlton, Alan. "Racial Essentialism: A Mercurial Concept at the 1937 Canberra Conference of Commonwealth and State Aboriginal Authorities." *Journal of Australian Studies* 75 (2002): 33–45.

Charny, Israel W., ed. *The Encyclopedia of Genocide*. 2 vols. Santa Barbara, CA: ABC-CLIO, 1999.

Cheyette, Brian. "The Holocaust in the Picture-House." *Times Literary Supplement*, no. 4742 (February 1994): 18–19.

Chorbajian, Levon, and George Shirinian, eds. *Studies in Comparative Genocide*. New York: St. Martin's Press, 1999.

Chouliaraki, Lilie. *The Spectatorship of Suffering*. London: Sage, 2006.

Churchill, Ward. *A Little Matter of Genocide: Holocaust and Denial in the Americas, 1492 to the Present*. San Francisco: City Lights, 1997.

Cohen, Stanley. *States of Denial: Knowing about Suffering and Atrocity*. Malden, MA: Polity Press, 2001.

Cole, Tim. *Selling the Holocaust: From Auschwitz to Schindler; How History is Bought, Packaged, and Sold*. New York: Routledge, 2000.

Colombat, Andre Pierre. *The Holocaust in French Film*. Metuchen, NJ: Scarecrow Press, 1993.

Connery, Christopher. "The End of the Sixties." *Boundary 2* 36, no. 1 (2009): 183–210.

Cornford, Francis MacDonald. *The Republic of Plato*. New York: Oxford University Press, 1945.

Cowie, Peter. *The Cinema of Orson Welles*. London: Zwemmer, 1965.

Crowther, Bosley. "The Solemn Facts: Our Screen Faces a Responsibility to Show Newsreels and Similar Films." *New York Times*, April 29, 1945.

———. "The Stranger." *New York Times*, July 11, 1946.

Cummings, Neil, and Marysia Lewandowska. "From Enthusiasm to Creative Commons: Interview with Anthony Spira." In *The Archive: Documents of Contemporary Art*, edited by Charles Merewether, 149–53. Cambridge, MA: MIT Press, 2006.

Davis, Colin. *Levinas: An Introduction*. Notre Dame, IN: University of Notre Dame Press, 1996.

Debo, Angie. *A History of the Indians of the United States*. London: Pimlico, 1995.

Denzin, Norman K. *The Cinematic Society: The Voyeur's Gaze*. London: Sage, 1995.

Dillon, Mathew. "Summertime Blues." *Metro Magazine* 133 (2002): 30–34, 36.

Dinges, John. *The Condor Years: How Pinochet and His Allies Brought Terrorism to Three Continents*. New York: New Press, 2005.

Doneson, Judith E. *The Holocaust in American Film*. New York: Syracuse University Press, 2002.

Donovan, Timothy, A. Samuel Kimball, and Jillian Smith. "Fog of War: What Yet Remains." *Postmodern Culture* 16, no. 1 (2005). http://muse.jhu.edu/journals/postmodern_culture/vo16/16.1donovan.html.

Douglas, Lawrence. "Film as Witness: Screening *Nazi Concentration Camps* before the Nuremberg Tribunal." *Yale Law Journal* 105, no. 2 (1995): 449–81.

Dower, J. W. *War without Mercy: Race and Power in the Pacific War*. New York: Pantheon, 1986.

Egoyan, Atom. *Ararat: The Shooting Script*. New York: Newmarket Press, 2002.

———. "Calendar." Translated by Michel Sineux. *Positif* 406 (1994): 93–94.

———. "In Other Words: Poetic License and the Incarnation of History." *University of Toronto Quarterly* 73, no. 3 (Summer 2004): 886–905.

Egoyan, Atom, and Paul Virilio. "Video Letters." In *Atom Egoyan*, edited by Carole Desbarats, Jacinto Lageira, Danièle Rivière, and Paul Virilio, 105–15. Paris: Dis Voir, 1993.

Eltit, Diamela. *Jamás el fuego nunca*. Santiago: Planeta, 2007.

Erbal, Ayda. Review of *Ararat*. *American Historical Review* 108, no. 3 (June 2003): 957–58.

Erikson, Kai. "Notes on Trauma and Community." In *Trauma: Explorations in Memory*, edited by Cathy Caruth, 183–99. Baltimore, MD: Johns Hopkins University Press, 1995.

Feierstein, Daniel. "Genocidio, delito mal tipificado." *Clarín*, January 5, 2009.

Felman, Shoshana, and Dori Laub. *Testimony: Crisis in Witnessing in Literature, Psychoanalysis and History*. New York: Routledge, 1992.

Fernette, Gene. "G.I. Movie Makers." *Home Movies*, October 1944, 409, 442–43.

Firbas, Paul, and Pedro Meira Monteiro, eds. *Andrés Di Tella: Cine documental y archivo personal; Conversación en Princeton*. Buenos Aires: Siglo XXI Editores. 2006.

Fresco, Nadine. "La Diaspora des cendres." *Nouvelle revue de psychoanalyse* 24 (Fall 1981): 205–20.

Freud, Sigmund. *Moses and Monotheism*. Translated by Katherine Jones. New York: Vintage, 1939.

Fuller, Samuel. *A Third Face*. New York: Alfred A. Knopf, 2002.

Furman, Nelly. "Called to Witness: Viewing *Lanzmann's Shoah*." In *Shaping Losses: Cultural Memory and the Holocaust*, edited by Julia Epstein and Lori Lefkovitz, 55–74. Urbana: University of Illinois Press, 2001.

Gellately, Robert, and Ben Kiernan, eds. *The Specter of Genocide: Mass Murder in Historical Perspective*. Cambridge: Cambridge University Press, 2003.

George, Terry. "Smearing a Hero: Sad Revisionism over 'Hotel Rwanda.'" *Washington Post*, May 10, 2006, A25.

Giller, Earl L., Jr., ed. *Biological Assessment and Treatment of Post-Traumatic Stress Disorder*. Washington, DC: American Psychiatric Press, 1990.

Glover, Jonathan. *Humanity: A Moral History of the Twentieth Century*. New Haven, CT: Yale University Press, 2001.

Goffman, Erving. *Frame Analysis*. New York: Harper Colophon, 1974.

Goldberg, Elizabeth Swanson. *Beyond Terror: Gender, Narrative, Human Rights*. New Brunswick, NJ: Rutgers University Press, 2007.

Green, Reneé. "Survival: Ruminations on Archival Lacunae." In *The Archive: Documents of Contemporary Art*, edited by Charles Merewether, 49–57. Cambridge, MA: MIT Press, 2006.

Greenberg, Mark S., and Bessel A. van der Kolk. "Retrieval and Integration of Traumatic Memories with the 'Painting Cure.'" In *Psychological Trauma*, edited by Bessel A. Van der Kolk, 191–215. Washington, DC: American Psychiatric Press, 1987.

Gross, Jan T. *Fear: Anti-Semitism in Poland after Auschwitz*. New York: Random House, 2006.

Guerin, Frances, and Roger Halles. *The Image and the Witness: Trauma, Memory and Visual Culture*. London: Wallflower Press, 2007.

Hahn, Emily. *China to Me*. New York: Doubleday, Doran, 1944.

Hand, Seán, ed. *The Levinas Reader*. Oxford: Blackwell, 1992.

Hansen, Miriam. "*Schindler's List* Is Not *Shoah*: The Second Commandment, Popular Modernism, and Public Memory." In *The Historical Film: History and Memory in Media*, edited by Marcia Landy, 201–17. New Brunswick, NJ: Rutgers University Press, 2001.

Hartman, Geoffrey H. "The Cinema Animal." In *Spielberg's Holocaust: Critical Perspectives on Schindler's List*, edited by Yosefa Loshitzky, 61–76. Bloomington: Indiana University Press, 1997.

———. *The Longest Shadow: In the Aftermath of the Holocaust*. Bloomington: Indiana University Press, 1996.

Hatzfeld, Jean. *La Stratégie des antilopes*. Paris: Seuil, 2007.

Heylin, Clinton. *Despite the System: Orson Welles versus the Hollywood Studios*. Chicago: Chicago Review Press, 2005.

Higham, Charles. *Films of Orson Welles*. Los Angeles: University of California Press, 1970.

——. *Orson Welles: The Rise and Fall of an American Genius*. New York: St. Martin's Press, 1985.

Hight, Craig, and Jane Roscoe. *Faking It: Mock-Documentary and the Subversion of Factuality*. Manchester, UK: Manchester University Press, 2001.

Hilsum, Lindsey. "Rwanda's Genocide Could Have Been Prevented." *The Guardian*, March 28, 2004.

Hinton, Alexander Laban, and Kevin Lewis O'Neill, eds. *Genocide: Truth, Memory, and Representation*. Durham, NC: Duke University Press, 2009.

Hirsch, Joshua. *Afterimage: Film, Trauma, and the Holocaust*. Philadelphia: Temple University Press, 2004.

Hirsch, Marianne. *Family Frames: Photography, Narrative, and Postmemory*. Cambridge, MA: Harvard University Press, 1997.

Hite, Katherine. *When the Romance Ended: Leaders of the Chilean Left, 1968–1998*. New York: Columbia University Press, 2000.

Hogikyan, Nellie. "Atom Egoyan's Post-Exilic Imaginary: Representing Homeland, Imagining Family." In *Image and Territory: Essays on Atom Egoyan*, edited by Jennifer Burwell and Monique Tschofen, 193–217. Waterloo, ON: Wilfrid Laurier University Press, 2006.

Hopper, Hedda. "Orson Reveals Life Goal: Wants to Be a Teacher." *Los Angeles Times*, November 28, 1945.

Horowitz, Sarah. "But Is It Good for the Jews? Spielberg's Schindler and the Aesthetics of Atrocity." In *Spielberg's Holocaust: Critical Perspectives on* Schindler's List, edited by Yosefa Loshitzky, 119–39. Bloomington: Indiana University Press, 1997.

Hron, Madelaine. *Translating Pain: Immigrant Suffering in Literature and Culture*. Toronto: University of Toronto Press, 2008.

Hughes, Nick. "Exhibit 467: Genocide Through a Camera Lens." In *The Media and the Rwanda Genocide*, edited by Allan Thompson, 231–34. Ottawa: International Development Research Centre, 2007.

Hughes D'aeth, Tony. "Which Rabbit-Proof Fence? Empathy, Assimilation, Hollywood." *Australian Humanities Review* (September–November 2002). http://www.australian humanitiesreview.org/archive/Issue-September-2002/hughesdaeth.html.

Human Rights and Equal Opportunity Commission. *Bringing Them Home: Report of the National Inquiry into the Separation of Aboriginal and Torres Strait Islander Children from Their Families*. Sydney: Human Rights and Equal Opportunity Commission, 1997. http://www.hreoc.gov.au/social_justice/bth_report/report/index.html.

Huppauf, Bernd. "Emptying the Gaze: Framing Violence through the Viewfinder." *New German Critique* 72 (Autumn 1997): 3–44.

Huyssen, Andreas. "Present Pasts: Media, Politics, Amnesia." *Public Culture* 12, no. 1 (2000): 21–38.

——. *Present Pasts: Urban Palimpsests and the Politics of Memory*. Palo Alto, CA: Stanford University Press, 2003.

Ienaga, Saburo. *Pacific War, 1931–1945: A Critical Perspective on Japan's Role in World War II.* New York: Pantheon Books, 1979.

Insdorf, Annette. *Indelible Shadows: Film and the Holocaust.* 2nd ed. Cambridge: Cambridge University Press, 1989.

Jones, Adam, ed. *Evoking Genocide: Scholars and Activists Describe the Works That Shaped Their Lives.* Toronto: Key Publishing Houses, 2009.

———. *Genocide: A Comprehensive Introduction.* New York: Routledge, 2006.

Kaplan, E. Ann. *Trauma Culture: The Politics of Terror and Loss in Media and Literature.* New Brunswick, NJ: Rutgers University Press, 2005.

Kearney, Richard. *Dialogues with Contemporary Continental Thinkers: The Phenomenological Heritage; Paul Ricoeur, Emmanuel Lévinas, Herbert Marcuse, Stanislas Breton, Jacques Derrida.* Manchester, UK: Manchester University Press, 1984.

Kellogg. E. R. "Testimony." In *Nazi Conspiracy and Aggression*, 2:433. Office of the United States Chief of Council for Prosecution of Axis Criminality. Washington, DC: United States Government Printing Office, 1946.

Kielburger, Craig, and Marc Kielburger. "A Vision of Stability in Rwanda." *Toronto Star*, August 7, 2007, AA2.

Klawans, Stuart. "Lest We Remember: Saying 'Never Again' to Holocaust Movies." *Tablet*, December 5, 2008.

Kleinman, Arthur. "The Appeal of Experience; the Dismay of Images: Cultural Appropriations of Suffering in Our Times." In *Social Suffering*, edited by Arthur Kleinman, Veena Das, and Margaret Lock, 1–24. Berkeley: University of California Press, 1997.

Koch, Gertrud. "The Aesthetic Transformation of the Unimaginable: Notes on Claude Lanzmann's *Shoah*." Translated by Jamie Owen Daniel and Miriam Hansen. *October* 48 (1989): 15–24.

Kracauer, Siegfried. *Theory of Film: The Redemption of Physical Reality.* New York: Oxford University Press, 1971.

Krystal, John. "Animal Models for Post-Traumatic Stress Disorder." In *Biological Assessment and Treatment of Post-Traumatic Stress Disorder*, edited by Earl L. Giller Jr., 1–26. Washington, DC: American Psychiatric Press, 1990.

Kuper, Leo. *Genocide: Its Political Use in the Twentieth Century.* New Haven, CT: Yale University Press, 1981.

Kurihara, Sadako. "When We Say 'Hiroshima.'" Translated by Richard H. Minear. In *Atomic Ghosts: Poets Respond to the Nuclear Age*, edited by John Bradley, 202–3. Minneapolis: Coffee House Press, 1995.

Kushlis, Joseph Bernard. Transcript of interview with Dana Kline, Witness to the Holocaust Project at Emory University. March 30, 1979. Box 2, folder 56.

LaCapra, Dominique. *History in Transit: Experience, Identity, Critical Theory.* Ithaca, NY: Cornell University Press, 2004.

Lacey, Marc. "The Rwandan Nightmare through a Lens, Darkly: Ten Years Later; Filming with Survivors in the Cast." *International Herald Tribune*, February 18, 2004.

Lader, Melvin P. *Arshile Gorky.* New York: Abbeville Press, 1985.

Landsberg, Alison. *Prosthetic Memory: The Transformation of American Remembrance in the Age of Mass Culture*. New York: Columbia University Press, 2004.

Lanzmann, Claude. "Le Lieu et la parole." In *Au Sujet de Shoah—Le Film de Claude Lanzmann*, edited by Bernard Cuau et al., 293–305. Paris: Editions Belin, 1990.

———. *Shoah: The Complete Text*. New York: Da Capo Press, 1995.

Laub, Dori. "An Event without a Witness: Truth, Testimony, and Survival." In *Testimony: Crises of Witnessing in Literature, Psychoanalysis, and History*, by Shoshana Felman and Dori Laub, 75–92. New York: Routledge, 1992.

———. "Truth and Testimony: The Process and the Struggle." In *Trauma: Explorations in Memory*, edited by Cathy Caruth, 61–75. Baltimore, MD: Johns Hopkins University Press, 1995.

Lazzara, Michael. "Guzmán's Allende." *Chasqui: Revista de literatura latinoamericana* 38, no. 2 (November 2009): 48–62.

Leaming, Barbara. *Orson Welles: A Biography*. New York: Viking, 1985.

Le Bon, Gustave. *The Crowd: A Study of the Popular Mind*. Atlanta: Cherokee, 1982.

Lee, Christopher Joon-Hai. "Arendt's Lesson: The Challenge and Need for Teaching Empire in the Present." *Radical History Review* 95 (2006): 129–44.

Levene, Mark, and Penny Roberts, eds. *The Massacre in History*. New York: Berghahn Books, 1999.

Levinas, Emmanuel. *Collected Philosophical Papers*. Translated by Alphonso Lingis. Dordrecht, The Netherlands: Kluwer Academic, 1993.

———. *Otherwise than Being or Beyond Essence*. Translated by Alphonso Lingis. 2nd ed. The Hague: Martinus Nijhoff, 1981.

Liss, Andrea. *Trespassing through Shadows: Memory, Photography, and the Holocaust*. Minneapolis: University of Minnesota Press, 1998.

Loshitzky, Yosefa, ed. *Spielberg's Holocaust: Critical Perspectives on Schindler's List*. Bloomington: Indiana University Press, 1997.

Losson, Nicholas. "Notes on the Images of the Camps." Translated by Annette Michelson. *October* 90 (1999): 25–35.

Lucas, Ryan. "Auschwitz Photographer Haunted by Memories." *Los Angeles Times*, March 5, 2006.

Lydon, Jane. "A Strange Time Machine: *The Tracker*, *Black and White*, and *Rabbit-Proof Fence*." *Australian Historical Studies* 35, no. 123 (2004): 137–48.

Maclear, Kyo. *Beclouded Visions: Hiroshima-Nagasaki and the Art of Witness*. Albany: State University of New York Press, 1989.

Mann, Michael. *The Dark Side of Democracy: Explaining Ethnic Cleansing*. Cambridge: Cambridge University Press, 2005.

Manne, Robert. "Aboriginal Child Removal and the Question of Genocide, 1900–1940." In *Genocide and Settler Society: Frontier Violence and Stolen Indigenous Children in Australian History*, edited by A. Dirk Moses, 217–43. New York: Berghahn Books.

Manchel, Frank. "A Reel Witness: Steven Spielberg's Representation of the Holocaust in *Schindler's List*." *Journal of Modern History* 67, no. 1 (March 1995): 83–100.

Margalit, Avishai. *The Ethics of Memory*. Cambridge, MA: Harvard University Press, 2003.

Markovitz, Jonathan. "Ararat and Collective Memories of the Armenian Genocide." *Holocaust and Genocide Studies* 20, no. 2 (Fall 2006): 235–55.

Markusen, Erik, and David Kopf. *The Holocaust and Strategic Bombing: Genocide and Total War in the Twentieth Century*. Boulder, CO: Westview Press, 1995.

Martín-Barbero, Jesús. *Al sur de la modernidad: Comunicación, globalización y multiculturalidad*. Pittsburgh: Instituto Internacional de Literatura Iberoamericana, 2001.

Matossian, Nouritza. *Black Angel: A Life of Arshile Gorky*. London: Chatto and Windus, 1998.

McBride, Joseph. *Orson Welles: Actor and Director*. New York: Harvest/HBJ, 1977.

———. *Whatever Happened to Orson Welles? A Portrait of an Independent Career*. Lexington: University Press of Kentucky, 2006.

McNamara, Robert. S. "Apocalypse Soon." *Foreign Policy*, no. 148 (May/June 2005): 29–35.

McSorley, Tom. "Faraway, So Close: Atom Egoyan Returns Home with Ararat." *Take One* 11, no. 39 (September–November 2002): 8–13.

Megahey, Leslie. "Interview from *The Orson Welles Story*." In *Orson Welles: Interviews*, edited by Mark W. Estrin, 177–209. Jackson: University Press of Mississippi, 2002.

Melson, Robert. *Revolution and Genocide: On the Origins of the Armenian Genocide and the Holocaust*. New Brunswick, NJ: Transaction Books, 1992.

Merewether, Charles, ed. *The Archive: Documents of Contemporary Art*. Cambridge, MA: MIT Press, 2006.

Miller, Donald E. and Lorna Touryan Miller. "Memory and Identity across the Generations: A Case Study of Armenian Survivors and Their Progeny." *Qualitative Sociology* 14, no. 1 (1991): 13–38.

Milmo, Cahal. "Flashback to Terror." *The Independent* (London), March 29, 2006.

Milton, Sybil. "The Camera as Weapon: Documentary Photography and the Holocaust." In *Simon Wiesenthal Center Annual*, 45–68. Chappaqua, NY: Rossel Books, 1984.

Mintz, Alan. *Popular Culture and the Shaping of Holocaust Memory in America*, Seattle: University of Washington Press, 2001.

Mitchell, W. J. T. *Picture Theory: Essays on Verbal and Visual Representation*. Chicago: University of Chicago Press, 1994.

Mithers, Carol Lynn. "From 'Knot's Landing' to Pandora's Box." *Los Angeles Times Magazine*, January 17, 1999.

Moeller, Susan. *Compassion Fatigue: How the Media Sell Disease, Famine, War, and Death*. New York: Routledge, 1999.

Monaco, James. *How to Read a Film*. Oxford: Oxford University Press, 1981.

Naficy, Hamid. *An Accented Cinema: Exilic and Diasporic Filmmaking*. Princeton, NJ: Princeton University Press, 2001.

———. "The Accented Style of the Independent Transnational Cinema: A Conversation with Atom Egoyan." In *Cultural Producers in Perilous States: Editing Events, Documenting Change*, edited by George E. Marcus, 179–231. Chicago: University of Chicago Press, 1997.

Naremore, James. *The Magic World of Orson Welles*. New York: Oxford University Press, 1978.

Neville, A. O. *Australia's Coloured Minority: Its Place in the Community*. Sydney: Currawong, 1947.

Nolan, Mary. "Air Wars, Memory Wars." *Central European History* 38, no. 1 (2008): 7–40.

Novick, Peter. *The Holocaust in American Life*. Boston: Mariner Books, 2000.

Nowell-Smith, Geoffrey, and Steven Ricci, eds. *Hollywood and Europe*. London: British Film Institute, 1998.

Nozick, Robert. *The Examined Life: Philosophical Meditations*. New York: Simon and Schuster, 1989.

Olivera-Williams, María Rosa. "La década del 70 en el Cono Sur: Discursos nostálgicos que recuerdan la revolución y escriben la historia." Unpublished manuscript, 2009.

Olsen, Theodore V. *Arrow in the Sun*. New York: Doubleday, 1969.

Orgeron, Marsha. "Filming the Marines in the Pacific: An Interview with WWII Cinematographer Norman Hatch." *Historical Journal of Film, Radio and Television* 28 (June 2008): 153–73.

———. "Liberating Images? Sam Fuller's Film of Falkenau Concentration Camp." *Film Quarterly* 60, no. 2 (Winter 2006): 38–47.

———. "'The Most Profound Shock': Traces of the Holocaust in Sam Fuller's *Verboten!* and *The Big Red One*." *Historical Journal of Film, Radio and Television* 27 (October 2007): 471–96.

"Orson Welles Plans Anti-Fascism Tour." *Los Angeles Times*, January 6, 1945, 7.

Ouzounian, Richard. "Dealing with the Ghosts of Genocide: Egoyan and Khanjian Tell of Their Passion for Armenia." *Toronto Star*, September 5, 2002.

Parker, Mark. "Something to Declare: History in Atom Egoyan's *Ararat*." *University of Toronto Quarterly* 76, no. 4 (2007): 1040–54.

Perks, Robert, and Alistair Thomson, eds. *The Oral History Reader*. 2nd ed. New York: Routledge, 1998.

Peters, John Durham. "Witnessing." *Media Culture and Society* 23 (2001): 707–23.

Picart, Caroline Joan (Kay) S., and David A. Frank. *Frames of Evil: The Holocaust as Horror in American Film*. Carbondale: Southern Illinois University Press, 2006.

Plantinga, Carl R. *Rhetoric and Representation in Nonfiction Film*. Cambridge: Cambridge University Press, 1997.

Porton, Richard. "The Politics of Denial: An Interview with Atom Egoyan." *Cineaste* 25, no. 1 (December 1999): 39–41.

Power, Samantha. *"A Problem from Hell": America and the Age of Genocide*. New York: Basic Books, 2002.

Prunier, Gérard. *The Rwanda Crisis: History of a Genocide*. New York: Columbia University Press, 1995.

Raczymow, Henri. "Memory Shot through with Holes." Translated by Alan Astro. *Yale French Studies* 85 (1994): 98–105.

Razack, Sherene. *Dark Threats and White Knights: The Somalia Affair, Peacekeeping, and the New Imperialism*. Toronto: University of Toronto Press, 2004.

Read, Peter. *The Stolen Generations: The Removal of Aboriginal Children in New South Wales 1883 to 1969.* Sydney: New South Wales Department of Aboriginal Affairs, Sydney, 1998.

Rebolledo, Loreto. *Memorias del desarraigo: Testimonios de exilio y retorno de hombres y mujeres de Chile.* Santiago: Catalonia, 2006.

Rees, Lauwrence. *Horror in the East: Japan and the Atrocities of World War II.* London: BBC Books, 2001.

Reiter, Andrea. *Narrating the Holocaust.* New York: Continuum, 2004.

The Relief of Belsen, April 1945: Eyewitness Accounts. London: Imperial War Museum, 1995.

Renov, Micheal, ed. *Theorizing Documentary.* New York: Routledge, 1993.

"Research Information Paper 9: Human Rights." Budapest: Open Society Archives, n.d.

Rév, István. "The Document." In *Verzió 2,* edited by Oksana Sarkisova and Zsuzanna Zádori. Budapest: Open Society Archives, 2005.

———. "Documentary and Archive." In *Verzió 4,* edited by Oksana Sarkisova and Erzsébet Bori. Budapest: Open Society Archives, 2007.

Richard, Nelly. "La historia contándose y la historia contada: El contratiempo crítico de la memoria." In *Fracturas de la memoria: Arte y pensamiento crítico,* 197–211. Buenos Aires: Siglo XXI Editores, 2007.

———. *Residuos y metáforas: Ensayos de crítica cultural sobre el Chile de la Transición.* Santiago: Cuarto Propio, 1998.

Roht-Arriaza, Naomi. *The Pinochet Effect: Transnational Justice in the Age of Human Rights.* Philadelphia: University of Pennsylvania Press, 2005.

Röling, B. V. A., and A. Cassese. *Tokyo Trial and Beyond: Reflections of a Peacemonger.* Cambridge: Polity Press, 1993.

Romney, Jonathan. *Atom Egoyan.* London: British Film Institute, 2003.

Rose, Gillian. *Mourning Becomes the Law: Philosophy and Representation.* Cambridge: Cambridge University Press, 1996.

Rosen, Philip. "Document and Documentary: On the Persistence of Historical Concepts." In *Theorizing Documentary,* edited by Michael Renov, 58–89. New York: Routledge, 1993.

Rosenbaum, Jonathan. *Movies as Politics.* Berkeley: University of California Press, 1997.

Rosenfeld, Alvin H. *A Double Dying: Reflections on Holocaust Literature.* Bloomington: Indiana University Press, 1980.

Rusesabagina, Paul. *An Ordinary Man: An Autobiography.* New York: Viking, 2006.

"Rwanda: Anarchy Rules." *Time,* April 25, 1994, 44–46.

Ryan, Tom. "Making History: Errol Morris, Robert McNamara and *The Fog of War.*" *Senses of Cinema* 31 (2004). http://www.sensesofcinema.com/2004/31/errol_morris_interview/.

Saltzman, Lisa. *Anselm Kiefer and Art after Auschwitz.* Cambridge: Cambridge University Press, 2000.

Sarlo, Beatriz. *Tiempo pasado: Cultura de la memoria y giro subjetivo, una discusión.* Buenos Aires: Siglo XXI Editores, 2005.

Schaffer, Kay, and Sidonie Smith, eds. *Human Rights and Narrated Lives: The Ethics of Recognition.* New York: Palgrave Macmillan, 2004.

Scherrer, Christian. *Genocide and Crisis in Central Africa: Conflict Roots, Mass Violence, and Regional War.* Westport, CT: Praeger, 2002.

Scheuer, Philip. "Cinematic Tricks Aid 'Stranger.'" *Los Angeles Times,* July 3, 1946.

Schoen, J. H. "Combat Cameraman's Communique . . ." *Home Movies,* February 1945, 56.

Sebald, W. G. *On the Natural History of Destruction.* Translated by Anthea Bell. New York: Modern Library, 2004.

Semprun, Jorge. *The Cattle Truck.* Translated by Richard Seaver. London: Serif, 1993.

Shandler, Jeffrey. "Films of the Holocaust." In *Encyclopedia of Genocide,* edited by Israel W. Charny, 228–32. Santa Barbara, CA: ABC-CLIO, 1999.

———. *While America Watches: Televising the Holocaust.* New York: Oxford, 1999.

Shapiro, Michael J. *Cinematic Geopolitics.* New York: Routledge, 2009.

———. *For Moral Ambiguity: National Culture and the Politics of the Family.* Minneapolis: University of Minnesota Press, 2001.

Shaw, Martin. *What Is Genocide?* Cambridge: Polity Press, 2007.

Shirinian, Lorne. *The Landscape of Memory: Perspectives on the Armenian Diaspora.* Kingston, ON: Blue Heron Press, 2004.

Siraganian, Lisa. "Telling a Horror Story, Conscientiously: Representing the Armenian Genocide from Open House to Ararat." In *Image Territory: Essays on Atom Egoyan,* edited by Monique Tschofen and Jennifer Burwell, 133–56. Waterloo, ON: Wilfrid Laurier University Press, 2007.

Skloot, Robert, ed. *The Theater of Genocide: Four Plays about Mass Murder in Rwanda, Bosnia, Cambodia, and Armenia.* Madison: University of Wisconsin Press, 2008.

Slaughter, Joseph. *Human Rights, Inc.: The World Novel, Narrative Form, and International Law.* New York: Fordham University Press, 2007.

Smith, Roger. "The Armenian Genocide: Memory, Politics, and the Future." In *The Armenian Genocide: History, Politics, Ethics,* edited by Richard Hovannisian, 1–20. New York: St. Martin's Press, 1992.

Smith, Roger, Eric Markusen, and Robert Jay Lifton. "Professional Ethics and the Denial of the Armenian Genocide." *Holocaust and Genocide Studies* 9, no. 1 (Spring 1995): 1–22.

Sontag, Susan. *On Photography.* New York: Farrar, Straus and Giroux, 2001.

———. *Regarding the Pain of Others.* New York: Farrar, Straus and Giroux, 2003.

Stannard, David E. *American Holocaust: The Conquest of the New World.* New York: Oxford University Press, 1992.

Stein, Stuart. *Web Genocide Documentation Centre.* January 1, 2008. http://www.ess.uwe.ac .uk/genocide/genocide.htm.

"The Stranger." *Hollywood Review,* May 21, 1946, 12.

Struk, Janina. "'I Will Never Forget These Scenes.'" *Guardian,* January 20, 2005.

———. *Photographing the Holocaust: Interpretations of the Evidence.* New York: I. B. Tauris, 2004.

Sturken, Marita. *Tangled Memories: The Vietnam War, the AIDS Epidemic, and the Politics of Remembering.* Berkeley: University of California Press, 1997.

Tatz, Colin. "Confronting Australian Genocide." *Aboriginal History* 25 (2001): 16–36.

———. *Genocide in Australia*. AIATSIS Research Discussion Paper 8. Canberra: Australian Institute of Aboriginal and Torres Strait Islander Studies, 1999. http://www.aiatsis.gov.au/research/docs/dp/DP08.pdf.

———. *With Intent to Destroy: Reflecting on Genocide*. New York: Verso, 2003.

Taylor, Richard. *Film Propaganda: Soviet Russia and Nazi Germany*. New York: I. B. Tauris, 1999.

Tchilingirian, Hratch. "Reinventing Life." *Armenian International Magazine* (April 2000): 42–47.

Thomson, David. *Rosebud: The Story of Orson Welles*. New York: Knopf, 1996.

Totten, Samuel, and Steven Leonard Jacobs. *Pioneers of Genocide Studies*. New Brunswick, NJ: Transaction, 2002.

Truffaut, François. Foreword to *Orson Welles: A Critical View*, by André Bazin, 1–27. New York: Harper and Row, 1978.

Tusa, Ann, and John Tusa. *The Nuremberg Trial*. New York: Skyhorse, 2010.

United Nations Office of the High Commissioner for Human Rights. "Convention on the Prevention and Punishment of the Crime of Genocide." December 9, 1948. http://www2.ohchr.org/english/law/genocide.htm.

Universal Camera Corporation. Advertisement. *Home Movies*, March 1944, 96.

Ussher, Clarence D. *An American Physician in Turkey: A Narrative of Adventures in Peace and in War*. Boston: Houghton Mifflin, 1917.

Utley, Robert M., and Wilcomb E. Washburn. *Indian Wars*. New York: American Heritage Press, 1977.

van Alphen, Ernst. "Second Generation Testimony, Transmission of Trauma, and Postmemory." *Poetics Today* 27, no. 2 (Summer 2006): 473–88.

Vogel, Amos. *Film as a Subversive Art*. New York: Random House, 1974.

Vonnegut, Kurt. *Slaughterhouse-Five, or, The Children's Crusade*. New York: Dell, 1971.

Walker, Janet. *Trauma Cinema: Documenting Incest and the Holocaust*. Berkeley: University of California Press, 2005.

Walsh, David. "Vancouver International Film Festival, 2008—Part 1." October 13, 2008. http://www.wsws.org/articles/2008/oct2008/vff1-o13.shtml.

Wasserman, Steve. "Dialogue with Samantha Power." *Perspectives on Evil and Human Wickedness* 1, no. 3 (2003): 217–22.

Watenpaugh, Keith. "Human Rights in the Classroom." Symposium, University of California–Davis, October 27, 2008.

Welles, Orson. "Orson Welles Today." *New York Post*, May 7, 1945.

———. "Orson Welles Today." *New York Post*, May 8, 1945.

———. "Orson Welles Today." *New York Post*, May 21, 1945.

———. "Orson Welles Today." *New York Post*, May 29, 1945.

———. "To Be Born Free." *Orson Welles Commentaries*. American Broadcasting Company, August 11, 1946.

———. "The Nature of the Enemy." Orson Welles Manuscripts, Lilly Library, Indiana University, box 4, folder 26.

———. *The Stranger*. Orson Welles Manuscripts, Lilly Library, Indiana University, box 21, folder 10.

———. "Survival of Fascism." Speech, Wilshire Ebell Theater, Los Angeles, CA, December 4, 1944. Orson Welles Manuscripts, Lilly Library, Indiana University, box 5, folder 12.

Whitehead, Anne. *Trauma Fiction*. Edinburgh, UK: Edinburgh University Press, 2004.

Wiesel, Elie. "Art and the Holocaust: Trivializing Memory." *New York Times*, June 11, 1989.

———. *Night*. Translated by Stella Rodway. London: Penguin, 1981.

Wildt, Michael. "The Invented and the Real: Historiographical Notes on *Schindler's List*." *History Workshop Journal* 41 (Spring 1996): 240–49.

Wilson, James. *The Earth Shall Weep: A History of Native America*. London: Picador, 1998.

Wollen, Peter. *Signs and Meaning in the Cinema*. London: Secker and Warburg, 1972.

Woods, Tim. "The Ethical Subject: The Philosophy of Emmanuel Levinas." In *Ethics and the Subject*, edited by Karl Simms, 53–60. Critical Studies 8. Amsterdam: Rodopi, 1997.

Young, James. *At Memory's Edge: Alter-Images of the Holocaust in Contemporary Art and Architecture*. New Haven, CT: Yale University Press, 2000.

Zabin, Alexander. Letter to the Editor of the *Malverne Herald*, May 31, 1945. United States Holocaust Memorial Museum Archives.

Zelizer, Barbie. *Remembering to Forget: Holocaust Memory through the Camera's Eye*. Chicago: University of Chicago Press, 1998.

Zemel, Carol. "Emblems of Atrocity: Holocaust Liberation Photographs." In *Image and Remembrance: Representation and the Holocaust*, edited by Shelley Hornstein and Florence Jacobowitz, 201–19. Bloomington: Indiana University Press, 2003.

Zimmerman, Patricia. "The Home Movie Movement: Excavations, Artifacts, Minings." In *Mining the Home Movie*, edited by Patricia Zimmermann and Karen Ishizuka, 1–28. Berkeley: University of California Press, 2008.

———. *States of Emergency: Documentaries, Wars, Democracies*. Minneapolis: University of Minnesota Press, 2000.

Zimmermann, Patricia, and Karen Ishizuka, eds. *Mining the Home Movie*. Berkeley: University of California Press, 2008.

Contributors

GEORGIANA BANITA is an assistant professor of literature and media studies at the University of Bamberg, Germany (currently on leave as postdoctoral fellow at the United States Studies Center, University of Sydney, Australia). She was a doctoral fellow at Yale University, and she is the recipient of several academic prizes and research grants, including a visiting fellowship at the Humanities Research Centre, Australian National University (2011). Banita's work has appeared or is forthcoming in *Peace Review: A Journal of Social Justice, Parallax, Biography: An Interdisciplinary Quarterly, LIT: Literature Interpretation Theory, Critique: Studies in Contemporary Fiction,* and *Textual Practice*, in addition to chapters for several edited volumes, including *John Huston: Essays on a Restless Director* (2010) and *Eco-Trauma Cinema: Technology, Nature, and the End of the World* (forthcoming).

JENNIFER L. BARKER is an assistant professor of English and film at East Tennessee State University, and she is director of the film studies program. She has published articles on film and antifascism in *Literature/Film Quarterly* and *Women in German Yearbook,* and on African American film in *Journal of African American Studies* and *African Americans in Cinema: The First Half Century.* She is coediting a special issue of *Women's Studies: An Interdisciplinary Journal* and revising a book manuscript about the legacies of antifascist filmmaking.

PAUL R. BARTROP is head of the Department of History at Bialik College, Melbourne, Australia. He was an Honorary Fellow in the Faculty of Arts and Education at Deakin University, Melbourne, between 2003 and 2010. He has been a Scholar-in-Residence at the Martin-Springer Institute for Teaching the Holocaust, Tolerance, and Humanitarian Values at Northern Arizona University and a visiting professor at Virginia Commonwealth University. Bartrop's many published works include *Fifty Key Thinkers on the Holocaust and Genocide* (2010); *The Genocide Studies Reader* (2009); *A Dictionary of Genocide* (2 vols.) (2008); *Teaching about the Holocaust: Essays by University and College Educators* (2004); *Bolt from the Blue: Australia, Britain and the Chanak Crisis* (2002); *Surviving the Camps: Unity in Adversity during the Holocaust* (2000); *False Havens: The British Empire and the Holocaust* (1995); *Australia and the Holocaust, 1933–1945* (1994); and *The Dunera Affair: A Documentary Resource Book* (1990). His current projects include *A Biographical Encyclopedia of Modern Genocide: Portraits of Evil and Good* and *Genocide Goes to the Movies: An Annotated Filmography of the Holocaust and Genocide*. He is a member of the International Association of Genocide Scholars; the Australian representative on the International Committee of the Annual Scholars' Conference on the Holocaust; a member of the Editorial Advisory Board of the international journal *Genocide Studies and Prevention*; a member of the Editorial Advisory Board of the journal *Holocaust and Genocide Studies*; and a member of the Advisory Board of the Genocide Education Project, California. Dr. Bartrop is a former president of the Australian Association of Jewish Studies.

PIOTR A. CIEPLAK is a Harper-Wood Scholar in English Poetry and Literature at St John's College, Cambridge. Cieplak completed his doctoral research in the Department of French, University of Cambridge, where he investigated the representation of the Rwandan genocide and its aftermath in photography and documentary film. He has an interest in and has written about cultural memory, commemorative practices, documentary film, photography, African film festivals, Rwandan and East African cinema, and representations of Africa, especially African conflict and its aftermath outside the continent.

STEPHEN COOPER is a professor of English at California State University, Long Beach, where he teaches creative writing, literature, and film. Dr. Cooper is the author of *Full of Life: A Biography of John Fante* and the editor of *The John Fante Reader* and *Perspectives on John Huston*.

TOMÁS F. CROWDER-TARABORRELLI is a visiting professor at Soka University. Dr. Crowder-Taraborrelli was born in Buenos Aires, Argentina, and moved to the United States in 1986. He received a PhD in Spanish and Portuguese from the University of California, Irvine. Dr. Crowder-Taraborrelli was a fellow in the humanities at Stanford University, where he cofounded the Stanford film lab and completed most of the research for this book. He has published articles in *CineAction, Revista Cine Documental*, and *Latin American Perspectives*, is a contributor to *Italian Neorealism and Global Cinema* (2007), and is the coeditor of *Bakhtin and the Nation* (1999). He has taught a variety of subjects at Soka University of America since 2007: Latin American film and human rights, Latin American literature, and a course on documentation of atrocities. He is currently working on a manuscript titled "Documentary Film and the Condor Years." His website is www.tcrowdertaraborrelli.com.

DONNA-LEE FRIEZE is a research fellow and genocide studies scholar in the School of History, Heritage and Society at Deakin University in Melbourne, Australia. Dr. Frieze is working on a joint venture between Deakin University and the Jewish Holocaust Centre in Melbourne on a book titled *A History of the Jewish Holocaust Centre*.

Contributors

MADELAINE HRON is an associate professor in the Department of English and Film at Wilfrid Laurier University in Canada. Dr. Hron specializes in human rights issues, African, postcolonial, and global issues in literature and film. Author of *Translating Pain: Immigrant Suffering in Literature and Culture*, she has also published in such varied journals as *Research in African Literature, Forum for Modern Language Studies, Peace Review, French Literature Studies, Disability Studies Quarterly,* and *Slavonic and East European Review.* She is currently writing a book on the representations of Rwanda in literature and film.

MICHAEL J. LAZZARA is an associate professor of Latin American literature and culture at the University of California, Davis. Dr. Lazzara is the author of *Luz Arce and Pinochet's Chile: Testimony in the Aftermath of State Violence* (2011); *Chile in Transition: The Poetics and Politics of Memory* (2006); *Diamela Eltit: Conversación en Princeton* (2002); *Los años de silencio: Conversaciones con narradores chilenos que escribieron bajo dictadura* (2002), and articles on Latin American literature and culture. He is also coeditor of *Telling Ruins in Latin America* (2009) with Vicky Unruh.

RICHARD O'CONNELL is a filmmaker working in both documentary and fiction film. His most recent film, *Los Maravillistas*, premiered at the Vancouver International Film Festival. He is the director of production at the Independent Television Service (ITVS) in San Francisco, California.

MARSHA ORGERON is an associate professor of film studies at North Carolina State University. Dr. Orgeron is the author of *Hollywood Ambitions: Celebrity in the Movie Age* (2008) and a dozen articles in books and in such journals as *Film Quarterly, The Moving Image, Cinema Journal, Quarterly Review of Film and Video,* and *Historical Journal of Film, Radio and Television.* She is at work on a book about director Sam Fuller's war films, beginning with the 16mm amateur footage he shot of Falkenau concentration camp at the close of World War II. She is coeditor of *Learning with the Lights Off: A Reader in Educational Film* with Devin Orgeron and Dan Streible (2011) as well as coeditor of the journal *The Moving Image.*

KRISTI M. WILSON is an assistant professor of rhetoric and humanities at Soka University of America. Dr. Wilson's research and teaching interests include classics, film studies, and cultural studies and rhetoric. She cofounded the Stanford film lab and taught at Stanford University for nine years before going to Soka University. She is the coeditor of *Italian Neorealism and Global Cinema* (2007) and author of numerous publications in such journals as *Screen, Yearbook of Comparative and General Literature, Signs,* and *Literature/Film Quarterly.* In addition to teaching, she directs the writing program at Soka University and serves on the editorial board of the journal *Latin American Perspectives.* Her website is www.professorkristimwilson.com.

SOPHIA WOOD is a senior lecturer in the Department of Film, Media, and Creative Studies at the University of Portsmouth. Dr. Wood's (formerly Marshman) past publications relate to the moral sociology of Zygmunt Bauman, with specific reference to the Holocaust. Dr. Wood is currently completing *The Holocaust as Spectacle in Visual Culture*. Dr. Wood's other research interests and publications in preparation relate to the mediated representation of Islam following 9/11 and the London bombings of 2005.

Index

Page numbers in italics refer to illustrations.